NEARLY EVERYBODY READ IT

NEARLY EVERYBODY READ IT

SNAPSHOTS OF THE PHILADELPHIA *BULLETIN*

Edited by
PETER BINZEN

Camino Books, Inc.
Philadelphia

Manufactured in the United States of America

1 2 3 4 5 00 99 98

Library of Congress Cataloging-in-Publication Data

Nearly everybody read it : snapshots of The Philadelphia Bulletin / by former
    Bulletin staff members ; edited by Peter Binzen.
            p. cm.
        ISBN 0-940159-40-6 (alk. paper)
        1. Bulletin (Philadelphia, Pa.)   2. Evening bulletin (Philadelphia, Pa.)
I. Binzen, Peter.
PN4899.P5B87   1997
071'.4811—dc21   97-16200

Cover and interior design: Robert LeBrun
Unless otherwise noted, photographs courtesy of the contributors.

For information write:
Camino Books, Inc.
P.O. Box 59026
Philadelphia, PA 19102

CONTENTS

CONTRIBUTORS

PETER BINZEN was born in Montclair, New Jersey, in 1922. He served with the U.S. Army's 10th Mountain Division in World War II, graduated from Yale University in 1947, and was a Nieman Fellow at Harvard University in 1962. After joining the Philadelphia *Bulletin's* staff in 1951, he was, successively, education writer, urban affairs editor, metropolitan editor and business columnist. He now writes a business column for the *Philadelphia Inquirer*. He is the author of *Whitetown USA*, and with Joseph R. Daughen, *The Wreck of the Penn Central* and *The Cop Who Would Be King*.

HENRY R. DARLING was born in New Rochelle, New York, in 1916. After graduating from the University of Pennsylvania in 1938, he worked briefly for the *Philadelphia Inquirer's* advertising and merchandising department. His job was to ask retailers if their sales increased after certain of their products were advertised in the *Inquirer*. In most cases the answer was no. Darling was soon jobless. But he worked for International News Service and then the United Press before joining the U.S. Navy at the outset of World War II. He served four years as a Navy officer. On his discharge in 1945, Darling landed a job with the *Bulletin* that lasted for 36 years before his retirement in December 1981. He was an extraordinary feature writer with a deft touch that never failed to entertain and inform.

JOSEPH R. DAUGHEN, who was born in Philadelphia in 1935, joined the news staff of the *Philadelphia Daily News* after graduating from Temple University in 1956. He moved to the Philadelphia *Bulletin* in 1963, and served as one of its top political writers and general assignment reporters. After the *Bulletin* ceased publication in 1982, Daughen rejoined the staff of the *Philadelphia Daily News*. His books include *The Wreck of the Penn Central* and *The Cop Who Would Be King*, both coauthored with Peter Binzen.

ROSE DEWOLF, a native of Reading, Pennsylvania, and a graduate of Temple University, joined the Philadelphia *Bulletin's* staff in 1969, and wrote a local column for 12 years. She is now a staff writer for the *Philadelphia Daily News* and a panelist on WPVI-TV's Sunday morning public affairs program, *Inside Story*. She is the author of five books: *The Bonds of Acrimony, The Best Defense, How to Raise Your Man, Woulda, Coulda, Shoulda: Overcoming Regrets, Mistakes and Missed Opportunities*, and *The Ten Dumbest Mistakes Smart People Make and How to Avoid Them*. Her writing has also appeared in the *New York Times Magazine*, the *Ladies Home Journal*, and other publications.

PIERRE C. FRALEY was born in Philadelphia in 1916. He joined the *Bulletin* as a copy boy in 1938, after graduating from Harvard University, and became the newspaper's medical and science writer in 1950. He covered all the major science and medical stories in the decade of the 1950s and gained a national reputation in that field of reporting. He won writing awards from

Temple University and the Philadelphia County Medical Society before leaving the paper in 1959 to become executive secretary of the Science Writers Council. That same year he was elected president of the National Association of Science Writers. He later served on the board of the National Science Foundation and was extremely active in Philadelphia's cultural life. He died at 79 in 1995. This essay has been excerpted from his memoirs.

HANS KNIGHT was born in Vienna in 1923. One year after Hitler's troops entered Austria and made it part of the German Reich, Knight escaped to England, where he spent the war years as a factory laborer. He worked as a translator for the U.S. War Department at the Nuremberg trials and came to this country in 1948. After working briefly as a copy boy for the *New York Times*, he reported for small papers and for six years was a feature and editorial writer for the Harrisburg *Patriot-News*. Knight joined the *Bulletin* in 1961, and remained with the paper until its closing. His wide-ranging articles included interviews with Gore Vidal, Linus Pauling, Riccardo Muti, Sophia Loren, Gordie Howe and Frank Rizzo, among other personalities. His freelance articles and book reviews have appeared in the *New York Times*, the *Baltimore Sun*, the *Philadelphia Inquirer*, *Travel Holiday*, *Catholic Digest* and other publications. He lives in the Philadelphia area and plays ice hockey with the Main Line Hockey Club "at the approximate speed of chess."

ADRIAN LEE, JR. was born in 1920 in Lemon City, Florida, and was educated at Spring Hill College, a Jesuit institution in Mobile, Alabama, where he majored in classical Greek. Following World War II service with the U.S. Navy in the South Pacific, he joined the *Bulletin* in 1948, and remained with the paper until its closing in 1982. Following the police reporting described in his essay, he worked as a general assignment reporter, rewriteman, political reporter, editorial writer and columnist. He covered the Cuban missile crisis, the assassination of President John F. Kennedy, Barry Goldwater's campaign for the Presidency and elections in Canada, Panama and Vietnam, among other major events.

CLAUDE LEWIS was born in the Bronx in 1936, and grew up in Harlem. After majoring in English at the City College of New York, he joined the staff of *Newsweek* magazine, where for 10 years he reported on music, sports, education, medicine and other subjects. He worked for the *New York Herald Tribune* for one year and served as a television reporter before returning to print journalism. He spent 15 years with the Philadelphia *Bulletin*, and when the paper closed in 1982, he was a columnist and associate editor. He now writes a column for the *Philadelphia Inquirer* and serves on its editorial board. Lewis has taught journalism at Drexel University in Philadelphia and Columbia University in New York and has served as a visiting professor at Villanova and Temple Universities. He appears regularly on television panel shows and has served four times as a Pulitzer Prize juror. He and his wife, Beverly, a registered nurse, live in New Jersey.

JOHN F. MORRISON was born in Media, Pennsylvania, in 1929. After graduating from Media High School, he enlisted in the U.S. Air Force and got his first taste of journalism working on the service newspaper, the *Skydozer*, at the Francis E. Warren Air Force Base in Cheyenne, Wyoming. He learned how to write the lead of a news story when a staff sergeant there gave him a thick journalism textbook and told him to read the section on leads. As Morrison later recalled, "I experienced enlightenment that was almost spiritual, a revelation that any monk would have given his sandals for." He joined the *Bulletin* in its newly opened Main Line bureau in Wayne on June 1, 1958, and when the paper expired nearly 24 years later, he was its night city editor. His final duty was to write the *Bulletin*'s obit that was published in the paper's last edition on January 28, 1982. He is now the night city editor of the *Philadelphia Daily News*.

JAMES M. PERRY was born in Elmira, New York, in 1927, and grew up in Philadelphia. After graduating from Trinity College in Hartford, Connecticut, he was a reporter for the *Hartford Times* from 1950-1952, for the Philadelphia *Bulletin* from 1952-1962, and for the *National Observer* from 1962-1977. He notes that all three papers are now defunct. Perry covered politics for the *National Observer* and for the *Wall Street Journal*, whose staff he joined in 1977. He attended 18 political conventions before retiring in 1997. His books include *Barry Goldwater: A Biography, The New Politics, Us and Them* and *Arrogant Armies*.

POLLY PLATT was born in Bryn Mawr, Pennsylvania, in 1927, and was graduated from Wellesley College in 1948. She joined the Philadelphia *Bulletin* later that year and worked there until 1951. From 1952 to 1954, she was a staff reporter for the *New York Post*. For the last 30 years, she has lived in Paris, where she conducts very popular cross-cultural seminars for English-speaking executives and their spouses. Her book, *French or Foe?* has been described by the *Chicago Tribune* as "a must for anyone who yearns to understand French behavior and culture." Self-published by her company, Culture Crossings Ltd., the book has sold more than 40,000 copies and is now in its sixth printing. Polly Platt's Serbian husband, Alexander Grchich, is an official with UNESCSO.

REX POLIER was born in 1916 in northwestern Illinois. After graduating from St. Ambrose College in Davenport, Iowa, he began his newspaper career with the *Davenport Times*, whose society editor was Emily Shaw. The two were married and traveled east. Polier landed a job with the Philadelphia *Bulletin* in 1942, and remained with the paper until just before it closed in 1982. His colorful feature writing and his whimsy brightened the *Bulletin*'s pages and he served as its television critic for 18 years. Although he retired in December 1981, Polier returned to write his column, "Around the Dials," for the paper's final edition. An avid traveler, he had visited Russia, Egypt, Turkey, China and Japan and was planning a trip to India when he died on October 13, 1995. This essay is excerpted from his unpublished memoirs.

REM RIEDER, editor and senior vice president of *American Journalism Review*, was born in Philadelphia in 1944. His journalism career began in the summer of 1964 as a police reporter for the *Philadelphia Inquirer*. After graduating from Harvard the following year, he joined the *Inquirer* as a suburban reporter and moved to City Hall to cover the courts in 1966. He defected to the *Bulletin* in 1969 and spent eleven years there as a reporter, Washington correspondent, assistant metro editor and deputy metro editor. Rieder later served as deputy metro editor of the *Washington Post*, assistant managing editor of the *Milwaukee Journal*, national editor and city editor of the *Miami Herald* and managing editor of the *Trenton Times*. He joined *American Journalism Review* in 1991. Rieder, 52, is also an adjunct professor at the University of Maryland College of Journalism. He lives in McLean, Virginia, with his wife, Ellen.

JAMES SMART, who was born in Philadelphia in 1930, spent 25 years at the *Bulletin*, advancing from copy boy to feature columnist. Smart's knowledge of the city's history, culture and rowhouse living made him an invaluable member of the newspaper's staff. His writings included a 50,000-word series on Philadelphia neighborhoods as well as *Sunday Magazine* articles and theater reviews. In 1958, his series on teenage gang wars won the Philadelphia Press Association's award for best news writing. One year later, he became the third writer of the newspaper's "In Our Town" column. In his hands, the column focused on Philadelphians, their lore and often whimsical activities. He left the staff in 1973, but contributed to the paper frequently until its closing. In this essay, he describes his work at the *Bulletin* before winning promotion as a reporter with his first bylined article—an interview with Dinah Shore.

HARRY G. TOLAND was born in Philadelphia in 1922. After graduating from Yale University in 1944, he served as a Marine officer in the South Pacific in World War II and joined the Philadelphia *Bulletin* in 1950. Over the succeeding 32 years, he covered the labor beat and served as an editorial writer, local government editor, regional columnist and deputy metropolitan editor. Among other prizes, he won an American Political Science Association award for distinguished reporting of public affairs and first awards from the Pennsylvania Society of Newspaper Editors and the Associated Press Managing Editors of Pennsylvania.

ROBERT J. WILLIAMS was born in North Philadelphia in 1912. He landed a summer job with the *Bulletin* in 1929, while still in high school, and joined the staff one year later at the age of 17. He started as newsroom receptionist and concluded his career in 1971 as the *Bulletin*'s amusements editor. In the intervening 41 years, he worked as district police reporter, general assignment reporter, assistant city editor, assistant news editor and television critic-columnist. After retiring in 1971, he traveled around the world by ship with his wife, Aline, a portrait painter. They now live in suburban Philadelphia.

INTRODUCTION

By Rem Rieder

Mrs. McKeon's life revolved around the *Evening Bulletin*.

Mrs. McKeon was the total Main Line lady. And every afternoon she'd sit on her front porch in Rosemont, eagerly awaiting the newspaper carrier. When the papers arrived, she was a happy woman.

When it didn't, when there was, say, serious snow, she'd move into action. She'd call my wife (we lived next door) and ask her to make sure that I brought an extra copy when I came home from work. She was always delighted when I dropped it off.

That's the hold the *Bulletin* had on many Philadelphians.

Today there's much moaning about the fact that newspapers have lost touch with the residents of their communities. The buzzword du jour is that papers need to "reconnect" with their audiences.

The *Bulletin* was connected.

In the stories by *Bulletin* veterans that follow, you'll experience firsthand the deep love that many of them still feel for a newspaper that hasn't been published since 1982.

And I'll always be in debt to my boss during those years, Peter Binzen, the prime mover behind this book. Peter was and remains a journalist of impeccable integrity, great wisdom and generous spirit. Did someone say role model?

As always, it's the people who make the difference. And there were lots of *Bulletin* people, in my era as before, who were something special. Classic old-school beat reporters like Harmon Y. Gordon ("the Judge") and Gene Herman (the best labor reporter ever to come out of Wissinoming). Wily, streetwise reporters like Bill Storm, who taught me it was important to always have two kinds of gin: the good stuff for martinis, and lesser brands for fools who might want to mix it with tonic.

Rewritemen like Ray Brecht, a marvelous blend of talent and class. Delightful-to-read sportswriters like George Kiseda and Alan Richman and Sandy Grady (I still have copies of some of Sandy's work from the mid-1960s. I still crack up every time I read his column on the old Phillie, Wes Covington.)

Carole Rich, the education reporter, who attacked her beat with more zeal and joy and commitment than anyone I've ever known. Doris Wiley, who was still climbing mountains in Nepal or someplace well into her sixties, who once insisted on mixing us martinis at 11 AM on a Sunday morning when I dropped by to borrow a ladder. Tommy Gibbons, the ex-highway patrolman turned quintessential police reporter.

Ron Goldwyn, a superb writer, an out-of-towner who fell in love with Philly, who soaked up its soul and reveled in it. David Taylor, my partner in crime on the metro desk, a tireless ally in more battles than I want to remember.

Suzy Gordon, the first person I ever hired, a pantheon human being, a remarkable journalist who did everything well, who did everything that needed to be done, and who never worried about the limelight. She was and remains so far beyond that.

While there is no shortage of themes in the reminiscences that lie just ahead, three jump out, at least to me.

First of all, many of the pieces hearken back to an era when journalism sure was fun. Much has gotten better since then. The field is filled with the best and the brightest, people who in the past would have been lawyers or investment bankers or something sensible. There's much more enterprise reporting, much more analysis, much more depth. There's much more concern for ethics.

But something wonderful has been lost.

The characters are gone. The Damon Runyon or "Front Page" spirit is outta here. The zest, the flavor, the wisecracks, the sheer shot and a beer of it all—lost as irrevocably as the 1953 Studebaker.

In 1966, as an *Inquirer* reporter, I was assigned to cover the courts. I was based in the City Hall press room, Room 212, a place where there was always a pinochle game in progress. Room 212 had a marvelous cast: Don McDonough, the "affable prexy" of the Philadelphia Press Association, a man with more moves than a clock; Bill Fidati, a marvelous City Hall reporter whose real passion was the racetrack; Harry Karafin, with his endless string of cynical one-liners ("It could have been worse. It could have been me."), who later was convicted of using the *Inquirer* to shake people down and who died in prison; Dave Racher, who has now covered the criminal courts for the *Daily News* for more than three decades, but who was even better known for his bottomless supply of stock tips, virtually all of which ended badly (I'm still recovering from the Spokane National Mining fiasco).

And, of course, Wally Malone, a reporter for the *Daily News*. He was from a little Irish neighborhood near Center City Philadelphia called Schuylkill, and he was a treasure trove of tales and throwaway lines and corner-boy wisdom. Wally didn't like to be alone, and when he had an errand to run, he'd invariably turn to me and say, "Walk me."

I had more laughs in a walk with Wally Malone than you'd have in a lifetime with most people.

"Kid," he said to me one late night/early morning in some questionable bar somewhere, "I'd give anything to be 32 again." After that I began counting the days (and there were maybe 2,700) until I turned 32.

There aren't many Wally Malones left in the business anymore. This book captures the spirit of the time when they were everywhere.

The *Bulletin* reflected its community big-time. It was relentlessly local. Its prudishness, its discomfort with aggressive reporting, its on-the-one-hand/on-the-other-hand editorials, its guest-in-the-house mindset—they really did resonate with Philadelphia, or at least with a big chunk of it. (Though that does seem somewhat hard to fathom today, given the city's current image as the place where they threw snowballs at Santa Claus and booed the Easter Bunny—the place, one columnist once wrote, whose motto should be: Whatta you lookin' at?)

And finally, all that worry over fairness could look weak, faint-of-heart, the antithesis of the kick-ass-and-take-names spirit of the great crusading newspapers. The squeamishness that led a major newspaper to refuse to publish a story on the famous Kinsey sex survey can seem awfully lame.

But in the current era—with investigative series that get into big trouble by asserting far more than they can prove, in a tabloid-drenched media world where virtually nothing seems beyond the pale—the idea of a little restraint really doesn't sound so bad.

Chapter 1

Nearly Everybody Read It

By Peter Binzen

JOIN THIS NEWSPAPER WRETCH for a trip back in time. Way back, before the computerized newsroom and the videocam. Before *USA Today* and CNN and *Hard Copy*. Before newspapering became an elite profession and investigative journalism became its mantra. Before corporate juggernauts gobbled up family-owned papers or closed them down.

Return with me to an earlier period when the nation's urban areas were far safer than they are today, when their ethnic neighborhoods were still stable and full of newspaper readers, when nearly every city of any size had at least two fiercely competitive papers, and newsboys hawked late editions on virtually every corner.

Accompany me back to yesteryear when newsrooms were noisy, crowded and chaotic, a cacophony of clattering typewriters and teletypes and cries of "Copy!" from rewritemen on deadline—all in stunning contrast to the sterile soundlessness of today's electronic work stations.

Let us go then, you and I, back to an era when the staffs of metropolitan dailies included many reporters who went to work right out of high school. Their blue-collar backgrounds matched those of the subscribers and, as a result, there was an affinity between reporters and readers. Whereas many of today's college-educated journalists grew up in relative affluence somewhere else and are strangers in the cities where they work.

Hearken to a time when newspaper publishing was almost exclusively a white man's game that reflected the racism and sexism of the world outside.* When reporters' salaries were absurdly low, their benefits were almost nonexistent and their line of employment was not highly valued by the upper classes.†

When readers trusted their papers to print the news without pushing hidden agendas—in contrast to today when public confidence in all newspapers appears to have eroded.‡

When most newspapers were respectful of the institutions of society and took pains to sustain them, even when some probably should have been torn down and their misdeeds exposed.

* * *

Perhaps more than any other metropolitan daily, one now-defunct Philadelphia newspaper displayed all the genuine strengths and serious weaknesses of the old journalism. That paper was the *Philadelphia Bulletin*, my employer for more than 30 years.

The *Bulletin* closed in 1982, less than three months short of its 135th birthday. It was the dominant paper in Philadelphia for 76 years and for much of that time it was the largest evening newspaper in North America with a circulation of well over 700,000.

It was not only the biggest paper in its field, it was also the most unusual. H.L. Mencken wrote that all successful newspapers are "querulous and bellicose." The *Bulletin* was neither. Its editorial writers were such notorious fence straddlers that when they endorsed a mayoral candidate one year, his reaction was, "How could you tell?"

And the paper was prudish, opposing sensationalism in any form. It refused to publish its own writer's account of Alfred Kinsey's 1953 report on female sexual behavior for fear of offending its readers' sensibilities. For the same reason, it sometimes airbrushed clothing on lightly clad figures in its comics section.

---

*New York Times correspondent Harrison E. Salisbury, returning to the home office in 1954 after many years abroad, found "no blacks in the newsroom, none on the advertising staff nor in the circulation department. The whiteness of the *Times* was glaring, but I did not notice it. This was the way things were. Nor did I notice the scarcity of women. The *Times* employed two or three female reporters in the city room, but most women, except secretaries and clerks, worked in the ghetto of the 'women's department.'" (Harrison E. Salisbury, *A Time of Change: A Reporter's Tale of Our Time*, Harper and Row, 1988, pp. 8-9.) The same situation prevailed then in virtually all big-city newsrooms, the *Bulletin*'s included.

†"In 1947, newspaper work was for life's losers. Men who dreamed of big money and rich wives went in for medicine, law, business or engineering...Newspapermen, by contrast, occupied the social pit. Respectable folks did not want their daughters to marry one." (Russell Baker. *The Good Times*, William Morrow, 1989, p. 51.)

‡A poll conducted by George H. Gallup for the Nieman Foundation in 1995 concluded that the basic principles of journalism were declining and that the public was losing confidence in the media. (See also "Under Siege," *American Journalism Review*, September 1995.)

As late as the 1950s, this peculiar paper used homing pigeons to fly photos to its sports department from racetracks and ballfields. It banned liquor advertising from its pages long after its peers had welcomed such revenue. It employed police reporters who couldn't write, which was not unusual in those days, but one on the *Bulletin* staff couldn't speak English very well, either. His marvelous malapropisms were the talk of the newsroom.

Yes, the *Bulletin* was provincial. But it had every reason to be for it was published in a city often derided as "America's Biggest Small Town."

At the turn of the century, Lincoln Steffens put the knock on Philadelphia as "corrupt and contented," and its evening newspaper, though never corrupt, was perhaps too contented with the status quo to function effectively as a journalistic watchdog on a consistent basis.

To its critics, the *Bulletin* seemed stodgy, dull and overly cautious, and they probably had a point. In more cosmopolitan quarters, the paper was a laughingstock. It certainly lacked glitz, and it was slow to adjust to changes that eventually doomed most of the nation's evening papers. But Mencken notwithstanding, the Old Lady was very successful for a very long time. Its readers found it to be dependable, prudent, accurate, fair and comprehensive. They trusted it to cover the news without pandering to low tastes or base desires. That's why nearly everybody read it for so long.

As the *Saturday Evening Post* once observed, the *Bulletin* was "tailored to the city" of Philadelphia, but when the city declined in power, prestige and population, so, alas, did its evening newspaper stumble and fall.

* * *

Recent years have not been kind to print journalism. The newspaper death rate seems to have spun out of control. The *Houston Post* is gone. The *Arkansas Gazette*, the *Anchorage Times*, the *Pittsburgh Press*, the *Tulsa Tribune* and the *San Antonio Light* are merely a representative sample of the papers that have closed down in the 1990s. And in such cities as Indianapolis, Milwaukee and Providence, formerly competitive papers have merged.

Surviving daily newspapers in city after city are now controlled by giant media corporations whose stockholders keep demanding greater profits. As a result, the papers are obliged to slash payrolls, close bureaus and reduce "news holes." They're steadily losing ground to C-Span and the Internet, to home computers and fax machines. Equally troubling is the industry's spiritual malaise. "In the new corporate culture of the newsroom," Howard Kurtz, the *Washington Post*'s media critic, has written, "editors hold endless meetings and cook up prefabricated story ideas. Prose is squeezed through more and more hands into ever smaller receptacles. Controversial ideas are pasteurized and homogenized until most of the flavor has been drained."*

---

*The *Washington Post National Weekly Edition*, May 3-8, 1993, p. 10.

His colleagues tell Kurtz that the newspaper game isn't much fun anymore, and he doesn't disagree. In the view of many reporters, he says, newspapering has "all the romance of a fast-food kitchen stamping out Big Macs."

"There is a growing sense too," writes Kurtz, "that we have gotten dangerously out of touch with the readers we struggle to serve. Journalists have become part of a top-drawer professional class, a virtual adjunct of the political establishment. Many newspapers have taken on an insurance-company atmosphere, with serious young people churning out serious stories as if they were legal briefs on product liability. The oddballs, louts and curmudgeons of yesteryear are a dwindling presence."

Phil Gaily, editorial page editor of the *St. Petersburg Times*, puts it succinctly: "The soul has gone out of the business."

I submit that the *Bulletin*, for all its faults, had a soul. Like so many other exemplars of the "old journalism," it also had its full quota of oddballs, as readers of these essays will discover. Working for the *Bulletin* was a lot of fun, and that's why my former colleagues and I reflect on our years there with such affection. It's my guess that our reflections will find resonance wherever much-loved papers have died. They're gone but they should not be forgotten.

* * *

The *Bulletin* was founded in 1847 by Alexander Cummings who called it *Cummings' Telegraphic Evening Bulletin*. It used the system of dots, dashes and spaces just developed by Samuel Morse, which enabled telegraphers to send news rapidly by wire.

From 1860 to 1895, the *Bulletin* was owned by several stock associations with constantly shifting membership. The paper was biased toward the Republican Party and, like its 20th-century successor, it was a bit dull. It had its moments, however. The *Bulletin* gave Lincoln's Gettysburg Address good notices when most newspapers pronounced it too short and superficial. And a tough *Bulletin* editorial on July 6, 1876, denounced the American government for its war against the Sioux at Little Big Horn. It termed General George Custer's death "the direct and inevitable result of the wanton, unnecessary and indefensible violation of one of its own treaties by the government of the United States."

"Ours is a crime and a disgrace, and it is to us that retribution has come swiftly and terribly," thundered the *Bulletin*.

The record will show that *Bulletin* editorial writers did very little thundering after William L. McLean, business and circulation manager of the rival *Philadelphia Press*, borrowed $17,000 to buy the paper in 1895. Maybe that's why his *Bulletin* caught on. Or maybe it was McLean's genius that explained the journalistic miracle that was about to unfold.

When he bought it, the *Bulletin* was the smallest of the city's 13 dailies. It had a staff of six and a circulation of 6,300. But in his opening statement, the new publisher expressed confidence that his paper would win support from "a constituency which will appreciate the development of a clean and reputable journal on the highest lines of independent and progressive journalism."

McLean knew his audience. In ten years under his ownership, the *Bulletin* became Philadelphia's premier paper with a circulation of more than 200,000. From last to first in one decade. And first it would remain for three quarters of a century.

In 1905, an executive of N.W. Ayer, McLean's advertising agency, came to him with an idea for a promotional slogan. Since the *Bulletin* had taken over leadership in the city, the adman suggested that it proclaim, "In Philadelphia, Everybody Reads The *Bulletin*." The publisher demurred. He settled for, "In Philadelphia, Nearly Everybody Reads The *Bulletin*."

And that was the *Bulletin*'s slogan ever after. It gained international currency through Richard Decker's cartoons in the *New Yorker* magazine. When Robert L. Taylor, a later publisher, interviewed Indian Prime Minister Indira Gandhi in 1968, she said: "You're from that paper with the famous slogan."

On William L. McLean's death in 1931, his son, Robert, took the reins of a paper with an average circulation that year of 558,184. Father and son reflected their Scottish descent: reserved, frugal with words and money, soft-spoken. No one ever heard Robert McLean, whom his staff always referred to as "the Major" because of his service in World War I, raise his voice in anger.

The Major believed in hiring the best people he could find for the *Bulletin*'s news and business operations and giving them full authority to run their departments. He rarely entered the newsroom but had a clear vision of what the *Bulletin* stood for. It was a family newspaper with standards of taste and decency that would be welcome in any home.

The Major once put it this way: "I think the *Bulletin* operates on a principle which in the long run is unbeatable. This is that it enters the reader's home as a guest. Therefore, it should behave as a guest, telling the news rather than shouting it."

He was wrong, of course. His principle failed to survive a collapse in the nation's standards of journalistic taste and decency. And yet in his time he was absolutely right, as the *Bulletin*'s rising circulation proved.

Robert McLean was fond of quoting C.P. Scott, editor of the *Manchester Guardian*, to this effect: "Comment is free but facts are sacred. The voice of opponents, no less than that of friends, has a right to be heard. Comment is also justly subject to a self-imposed restraint. It is well to be frank; it is even better to be fair."

The *Bulletin* came to be criticized for many things but rarely for lack of fairness.

Unlike some of his contemporaries, Robert McLean, although a moderate Republican himself, made sure that his paper left politics to the politicians. For years, the Chandler family's *Los Angeles Times* was, in David Halberstam's view, "a manifestly unfair newspaper," one that was "intensely, virulently partisan."

"The *Times* was not an organ of the Republican Party of Southern California, it *was* the Republican Party," Halberstam wrote in *The Powers That Be*.

At the same point, Philip L. Graham, publisher of the *Washington Post*, was a wheeler-dealer whose liberal activism was carried out, Halberstam charged, "at the price of the paper's essential integrity." When Lyndon Johnson was the Senate majority leader, the *Post*'s publisher became one of his top unpaid advisers, speech writers and promoters. "He was, very simply, Lyndon's man, and to the degree that he could tilt the paper toward him, he did," Halberstam wrote of Graham.*

Under Robert McLean, the *Bulletin* steered clear of such partisanship. In a staff memo in 1973, he criticized an editorial in his paper that urged President Nixon to take certain actions in the Watergate crisis.

"The whole section dealing with what the President 'should' do, and what other actors in the drama 'should' do, is unprofessional and adventitious," McLean wrote. "By its nature, a newspaper is an observer, not a participant...we are not qualified to direct the affairs of government and we should have the humility to recognize that fact."

Such a view, that the press should function solely as an observer of government, irked those who wanted the *Bulletin* to be more daring and activist. They wanted it to stake out strong editorial positions on controversial issues and argue for them forcefully. And sometimes it did. But not often enough to satisfy its critics. Yet the Major never wavered, even though his policy often made the *Bulletin* appear bland, timorous and weak-kneed.

He saw the press as a watchdog of government but not as an adversary. Elsewhere, newspapers became more adversarial at the time of the Vietnam War and Watergate, and a generation of young reporters yearned to work for those papers that challenged the government's war policy and helped to destroy a flawed presidency. The *Bulletin* failed to attract such journalists, nor did McLean want them. In the same memo in which he cited the press's role as observer rather than participant, he said that offering "gratuitous advice" to the nation's leaders "sets a bad example for the young reporters who would like to be activists." And he added: "Example is more important than precept."

Yet McLean's position was unpopular among many of his own reporters and editors who wanted the *Bulletin* to come out swinging on critical issues. I include myself in that crowd, but I grudgingly admired the Major for taking a stance which ran counter to that of many of the nation's biggest and most influential papers.

I'm convinced he adopted his position not out of fear that activism would offend readers or advertisers but out of journalistic conviction. He held with Lord Macaulay that the free press was "the fourth estate of the realm," that it was part of the machinery of self-government, that its job was to observe and criticize when criticism was justified, but not to set itself up in opposition to the other branches of government.

---

*In her memoir, *A Personal History*, Katherine Graham acknowledged that her husband's closeness to Johnson troubled her. After she succeeded him as publisher, she never practiced journalism that way.

And if the *Bulletin*'s refusal to join the pack in attacking government made it dull and boring, so be it. At least it was honest. And the Major valued honest reporting over every other quality. In defining what it meant for a newspaper to be operated on good principles, he once wrote:

"It means, of course, we are honest; honest with our readers, honest with our advertisers, honest with the public. It means that we use good sense in making decisions and take into consideration the long-range effect of anything we do—not just the momentary advantage of what seems expedient. When we have determined what in our judgment is good policy, we can then throw ourselves wholeheartedly behind it and turn on the heat with confidence."

The Major's views on how the press should function proved popular in Philadelphia, a city of generally quiet-spoken, self-effacing citizens who frown on flamboyance. The *Bulletin*'s circulation rose steadily under his leadership, exceeding 600,000 in 1942 and 700,000 in 1946. The following year it peaked at a yearly average of 773,943, a total it would never reach again.

In April 1947, the *Bulletin* celebrated its 100th birthday with a party for its 1,700 employees and their families at Philadelphia's Convention Hall. There was a six-foot-high birthday cake but no strong potables. And that was in keeping with the paper's ban on liquor advertising.

To mark its centennial, President Harry S. Truman wrote a letter to Robert McLean that went beyond the usual pleasantries. "The long and honorable history of the *Evening Bulletin* commands respect," the President wrote. "That it commands affection also is attested by the *Bulletin*'s remarkable circulation figures. This respect and this affection could not have been attained had the *Bulletin* not built up over the years a reputation for the highest integrity. It has differed with me and the political party I represent, but I have never known it to hit below the belt."

Certainly, the *Bulletin* then appeared to be at the top of its game. Just two months earlier it had purchased J. David Stern's *Philadelphia Record*, which had been crippled by a long strike. The purchase gave the *Bulletin* vitally needed entry into the Sunday newspaper field. It picked up the *Sunday Record*'s syndicated features, comics, columns and newsprint contracts.

Included in the $13 million deal with Stern was radio station WCAU, which had just begun a television operation as well. There were only 14,000 TV sets in all of America in 1947, and WCAU was losing money. Soon, however, it became profitable. By 1957, with the TV habit spreading across the country, WCAU-TV was making $4 million a year, far outstripping the *Bulletin*'s earnings. In 1958, the McLeans sold the television and radio stations to CBS for $20 million. WCAU-TV was first in its market at the time and the sale price was dirt cheap. Had the family held on to the property for another 10 or 15 years, it might have gotten $200 million or more, thereby gaining the money needed to strengthen the *Bulletin* when its competition with the *Inquirer* heated up in the 1970s.

The McLeans also acquired from Stern a smaller South Jersey daily, the *Camden Courier-Post*, but the U.S. Justice Department forced its divestiture on the grounds that a *Bulletin-Courier Post* combination would constitute monopoly control over the region. This ruling, which was bitterly opposed by *Bulletin* lawyers, undercut the paper in subsequent years as South Jersey grew in population and business activity. Family members believe it was a key factor in the *Bulletin*'s ultimate closing.

Of course, no one was thinking of closing the paper in 1947. It had added thousands of readers during World War II when the only source of detailed information on the fighting was in the nation's newspapers. Moreover, the *Bulletin* had already begun adjusting to changing demographics. Recognizing that many of its readers were moving out of Philadelphia, it started publishing suburban editions in the 1940s.*

From Stern's *Record*, the *Bulletin* hired Walter B. Lister and made him managing editor. Lister, cool, detached and totally professional, had been an editor in New York at the age of 25. He knew the business and knew the English language. J.A. Livingston, who was a cub reporter at the *Brooklyn Eagle* when Lister was city editor there and later joined him at the *Bulletin*, recalled once being sent out to cover a major fire. A man died in the blaze, but Livingston's story never got into the paper. He soon found out why. "Mr. Livingston," said Walter Blister, as the staff referred to the city editor, "you can burn a man to a cinder, you can burn him to a crisp, but you can't burn him to a pulp."

To run the *Bulletin*'s business operations, the Major chose Richard W. Slocum, who had been the newspaper's lawyer. Slocum was a hard-driving, outgoing executive with wide contacts in the city, and he was brilliant in his expanded role. He knew how to cut a deal with the Teamsters Union to keep the *Bulletin*'s trucks rolling. He also knew how to persuade the John Wanamaker department store to advertise in the new *Sunday Bulletin*, over the fierce opposition of Walter Annenberg's *Inquirer*, which until then dominated the Sunday field in Philadelphia.

So the *Bulletin* was never stronger than in 1947. It was true that the 100th birthday greetings from *PM*, the left-of-center New York afternoon paper published by Ralph Ingersoll, were cheerless. *PM* described the *Bulletin* of that period, probably with some accuracy, as "rich, self-satisfied and Republican."

But *Time* magazine took a more generous view. Reflecting on the *Bulletin*'s position as the nation's No. 1 afternoon paper, the news weekly observed: "McLean put it there by giving Philadelphians what they want. All the news (no matter how trivial), sold in good time and told in good taste. Lest his *Bulletin* track mud into the neat row houses where it was a daily guest, he forbade it to muck-rake. When syndicated comic-strippers took to stripping their girls, he had his art room paint their clothes right back."

---

*For example, the *Bulletin* of August 6, 1945, reporting on the atomic bombing of Hiroshima, carried on its front-page "ear" the notation: "Night Extra Suburban Edition Delaware County News."

Time disagreed with critics who said that "only in Philadelphia would nearly everybody read the *Bulletin.*"

"The *Bulletin* may be unspectacular," said *Time*, "but it is a good newspaper."

In 1948, Robert McLean was elected chairman of the board of the Associated Press. He had joined the cooperative news agency's board in 1923 and would head it for 20 years.

On his retirement as board chairman in 1968, the *New York Times* devoted a full page to his career. It said he never believed in loud talk but spoke for "truth, fairness and decency." And the *Times* added: "In the newspaper profession nearly everybody knows 'the Major.'"

* * *

When I joined the *Bulletin*'s staff in 1951, the newspaper was thriving and the City of Philadelphia seemed to have a lot going for it, too. Its population had risen steadily from just over one million in 1890 to over two million in 1950. It was the nation's fourth largest city, and it totally dominated the region. It was home for America's largest railroad, the Pennsy, as well as the tiny, spunky Reading. It was home for the most popular magazine, the *Saturday Evening Post*, and the largest evening newspaper. Two large oil companies, Atlantic Refining and Sun, had their headquarters in the city. So did one of the largest manufacturers of railroad cars, the Budd Company. Stetson hats, Philco radios and Disston saws were made in Philadelphia and sold all over the world. Two major-league baseball teams played in the city. Horn and Hardart, the nation's first fast-food chain, operated its automats in numerous downtown locations. Five department stores competed there, and all five advertised heavily in the *Bulletin*.

Three decades later, virtually all of those institutions had moved out of town or gone out of business. Philadelphia became a different, less inviting place. But how was anyone to foresee that in 1951? For back then public attention was focused less on urban economics than on Communist subversion. It was a time of black lists and guilt by association. Senator Joseph R. McCarthy was naming names. And the *Bulletin*'s city editor, Stanley G. Thompson, couldn't be too careful. At my job interview, he asked outright if, by any chance, I was a member of the Communist Party. I was comfortable answering that question in the negative since I voted Republican in those days, like my father before me.

But the city editor still wasn't satisfied. Later that day he telephoned the pastor of the Presbyterian church I occasionally attended in Upper Montclair, New Jersey, to make sure that he wasn't hiring someone who advocated the violent overthrow of the government.

My first assignment involved a water-main break at a downtown hotel. It was a minor break that caused little damage but tied up traffic, and my story made page one in the late editions that day. It was timely local news, just the kind the *Bulletin* liked to put in the paper.

As I settled into the newsroom, City Editor Thompson, a crusty Kentuckian with an unkempt shock of gray hair, a watch fob in his vest pocket and total commitment to the *Bulletin*, loomed ever larger in my life and that of my young family.

Early on, he told me that in a choice between family responsibilities and responsibilities to the *Bulletin*, the newspaper must always come first. And that's how it was at our house and at the homes of virtually all *Bulletin* reporters. I doubt if any editor would dare issue such a mandate today. He (or she) might be sued for harassment. But at that time and with that editor, who earned our total loyalty, nobody challenged the edict.

I soon discovered that the *Bulletin*'s policy was to cover every aspect of life in the Philadelphia region. It covered every nickel holdup, every grassfire, every meeting of the city's zoning board and its park commission. It covered the courts very closely as well as the Register of Wills. Accuracy was its watchword. In exposing wrongdoers, Thompson once told me, the paper preferred the scalpel to the meataxe. It rarely overreached or claimed more than it could prove. This cautious approach was never more evident than in a series that the *Bulletin* published across the top of page one in January 1952. Entitled "I was a Philadelphia Bookmaker," the series disclosed how city police and politicians conspired with numbers writers to violate the law and share the profits. It was not only very readable but very revealing. It had prize possibilities. In typical *Bulletin* fashion, however, a disclaimer accompanied each article in the series. It read as follows:

"These articles make public, perhaps for the first time, the life of a bookmaker. They are designed to inform, not expose. For obvious reasons, the author conceals his identity, and other names and some localities have been altered. Certain payoffs to police and politicians are described; here it should be borne in mind that the author dealt with those who are corrupt, not with the great number who are honest and upright."

In other words, aside from a few rotten apples, Philadelphia's police force and its political establishment consisted of men of integrity who could be trusted. The corruption that the *Bulletin* uncovered was spotty, not system-wide.

The disclaimer may or may not have been accurate. The point is that the *Bulletin*, with its fairness credo, was wrecking its chances of winning awards for investigative or crusading journalism. But then Major McLean never coveted journalism prizes. Indeed, he viewed them with suspicion.

The bookmaker series had actually been written by City Editor Thompson with legwork by a police reporter. Like Walter Lister, Thompson had come to the *Bulletin* from the *Philadelphia Record*. The two worked well together. With Dick Slocum in the counting house and the Major in overall command, the *Bulletin* fielded a talented management team. Late in the 1950s, however, the team began to fall apart. Slocum died of cancer in 1957 at the age of 55. In 1959, Thompson died at 61. And in 1963, Lister suffered a disabling stroke which led to his death four years later. Lister had sometimes disagreed with Robert McLean's views, but he admired the publisher. He once told another *Bulletin* executive: "The Major doesn't always know what he's talking about, but there's nobody I would rather work for."

In 1964, Robert McLean's purchase of Thomas M. Storke's *News-Press* in Santa Barbara, California, removed him from day-to-day oversight of the *Bulletin*. After winning a Pulitzer Prize for an editorial denouncing the John Birch Society, Storke had broken with his son, whose wife was said to be a Bircher. Because of the family breakup, he decided to sell his paper, and the only publisher who met his standards was McLean. As conditions of the sale, the Philadelphian was required to establish part-time residence in Santa Barbara and put someone close to him in charge of the paper.

McLean complied with both conditions, moving to California and naming Stuart Taylor, whose mother was the Major's sister-in-law, as publisher of the *News-Press*. At the same time, Stuart Taylor's brother, Robert, who had succeeded Slocum as the *Bulletin's* general manager in 1957, was named its publisher. The *News-Press* proved to be a valuable acquisition. The Major bought it from Storke for $9 million; his heir sold it to the *New York Times* 21 years later for close to $100 million.

Although the Major continued as the Bulletin Company's board chairman after moving to California, he gave up daily contact with the paper, and the business side suffered from his absence. The newsroom was another matter. Stanley Thompson's successor, columnist Earl Selby, proved to be an enormously effective city editor, driving his staffers hard but none harder than himself. He was never beloved, but he galvanized the newsroom. While Stanley Thompson's bookmaker series had been "designed to inform, not expose," Earl Selby sought to do both by putting strong emphasis on investigative reporting. Unlike the Major, he desperately wanted to win journalism prizes, and he did. Selby directed the coverage that gave the *Bulletin* its first Pulitzer—the first ever won by a Philadelphia newspaper—for an exposé of police corruption in 1964.

* * *

William B. Dickinson, a superb newsman who succeeded Walter Lister as managing editor, was a Kansas farmboy whose first newspaper job was with the *Kansas City Star*. He won a Nieman Fellowship at Harvard before World War II and during the war served as a United Press correspondent in England and Australia. He covered the Japanese surrender for the UP and, after the war, headed the news service's bureau in New York City. That's where he was when Lister recruited him.

Under Dickinson, the *Bulletin* broadened its coverage, digging deeper into science, medicine, education and arts reporting, and sending staffers overseas on special assignments. So impressed was *Philadelphia Magazine* that it published an admiring profile of the *Bulletin* in January 1967 entitled "Depth in the Afternoon."

With a touch of hyperbole, the article described the *Bulletin* as "a paper that's willing to spend money to cover news anywhere in the world." By contrast, it noted that Walter Annenberg's *Inquirer* rarely sent staffers on national or international assignments.

Three months after its glowing tribute to the *Bulletin*, *Philadelphia Magazine* broke the story of an *Inquirer* reporter, Harry J. Karafin, who had shaken down news sources by threatening to run slanted articles about them if they didn't pay up. Karafin, who often had boasted of his close ties to the *Inquirer's* publisher, was convicted on 40 counts of blackmail and unlawful solicitation. He died in prison.

Annenberg's reputation was that of a ruthless press lord who used his rag—it really was a rag under his ownership—to help his friends and smear his foes. There was never a hint that he knew of or condoned the criminal activity of his staff's extortionist, but the episode must have shaken him.

In November 1969, less than three years after Karafin was exposed, Annenberg sold the *Inquirer* and its smaller sister paper, the tabloid *Daily News*, to Knight Newspapers for $55 million. He then went off to London as the Nixon Administration's ambassador to the Court of St. James's.

What followed in Philadelphia was a titanic struggle between a family-owned newspaper with limited financial resources and a giant Miami-based chain with, in the current idiom, deep pockets.

From the *Bulletin's* perspective, this is a sad story, and I don't intend to dwell on it. Suffice it to say that the *Bulletin* began the competition with a big lead in daily circulation—647,000 versus 487,000—but that the gap narrowed with almost every passing year. When their losses became too great, the McLean family sold the *Bulletin* in 1980. Its final owner, the Charter Company, closed it down on January 28, 1982.

One wag said the *Bulletin* died of "circulatory" disease, but the fact was its circulation exceeded that of the *Inquirer* until the final six months.

There were any number of theories as to what caused the paper's collapse:

That as television changed the leisure-time habits of Americans and increasing numbers of people started following the evening news on TV, evening newspapers gradually became extinct.

That rush-hour traffic congestion made late-afternoon newspaper deliveries ever more difficult.

That too many of the *Bulletin's* readers, and even more importantly, its advertisers, fled to the suburbs and lost interest in a city paper.

That the *Bulletin* was hurt by self-destructing labor unions.

That its management lacked the flair and imagination needed to cope with changes impacting the industry.

That Knight Newspapers, later Knight Ridder, had vastly greater staying power than the McLean family and was able to sustain losses longer than the McLeans could.

That the *Bulletin* was simply the victim of the free enterprise system: beaten by an all-around better newspaper that overtook it first in advertising and, finally, at the very end, in circulation.

I would never concede that the *Inquirer* was a better paper than the *Bulletin*. But it was certainly far better under chain ownership than it had been under Walter Annenberg. And more than anyone else, the man who made the *Inquirer* better was Eugene L. Roberts, who was named executive editor in the fall of 1972.

Gene Roberts, whose shuffling walk and North Carolina drawl disguised a razor-sharp intelligence, had been the *New York Times'* national editor. At the *Inquirer*, he put his years of experience to work in methodically improving one department at a time. He recruited top editors from other places and quickly gave his paper a cohesiveness that it had lacked. Bright, young, ambitious reporters flocked to Philadelphia just to work for Gene Roberts.

Investigative journalism was at full throttle in America in the 1970s, and Roberts' *Inquirer* proved to be very good at it. His reporters wrote provocative stories and his editors packaged them brilliantly. Soon the prizes began coming in. The *Inquirer* won its first Pulitzer Prize in 1975, and before Roberts left in 1990, it had collected nearly a score of them.

Occasionally, the paper overreached. It was sued for libel quite often, and one plaintiff was awarded more than $30 million, the largest libel award in the history of American journalism. (The case was finally settled out of court in 1996, but the settlement price was not disclosed.)

The *Bulletin* faced fewer lawsuits but won fewer prizes. Although the quality of its reporting remained strong, the paper never learned to package its product very well. And even after the Major moved to California, his opposition to investigations by "activist reporters" was honored by upper echelons of the *Bulletin*'s management.

The paper lost its ace prober when Earl Selby departed. Later, key executives apparently concluded that he had overdone it. Bill Dickinson indicated as much in a 1967 interview. He first commented that Selby was undoubtedly the best investigative reporter he had ever known. After being named city editor, Dickinson continued, Selby had kept his focus primarily on investigative reporting. And then the *Bulletin*'s executive editor offered this curiously ambiguous reflection:

"It might possibly be said—although I would not say it—that perhaps there was a little overemphasis in that area."

In making that statement, which could only be construed as a condemnation of investigative excesses, Dickinson may have had Major McLean's strong views in mind. He may also have been thinking of a *Bulletin* probe in 1963 that nearly landed Robert Taylor and City Editor Selby in prison. Based on information from an anonymous informant, the paper had published stories detailing widespread municipal corruption. Philadelphia's district attorney demanded that the source of the stories be identified, but the *Bulletin* refused to comply. The case then went to court where both Taylor and Selby were found guilty of contempt, fined $1,000 each and sentenced to five days in jail. By this time, the *Bulletin*'s battle to protect its source had made national headlines, and when the convictions were overturned by the Pennsylvania Supreme Court, the newspaper known for its caution was widely hailed as the defender of a free press. Another paper might have sought to capitalize on this acclaim in its promotional efforts for readers and advertisers. But not this one. A disgruntled Earl Selby left the following year for the *Readers Digest,* and only toward the end of its life did the *Bulletin* again put strong emphasis on investigative reporting. By that time, it was too late.

* * *

Not long ago, I revisited the last home of the evening newspaper that nearly everybody in Philadelphia once read. It was the *Bulletin*'s sixth home and it was billed as the world's most modern newspaper plant when it opened on six acres at 30th and Market Streets in 1955.

It consisted of two buildings connected at lobby level. One was the two-story publication facility. An underground freight line ran into the basement of this building, and 14 freight cars loaded with paper could stand at a siding there. A cable "towveyor" a third of a mile long carried the paper to underground storage space and to the presses which were in two lines, each longer than a football field. The presses could turn out 50 complete newspapers in a single second, close to 250,000 an hour.

The other building stood four stories high directly across the street from the Pennsylvania Railroad's mammoth 30th Street Station. This building housed the *Bulletin*'s executive offices, its advertising and circulation departments, its typesetting and engraving operations and its newsroom.

I had worked in that newsroom from the sparkling day in the spring of 1955 when it opened until the gray winter day in 1982 when it shut down. After the *Bulletin* ceased publication, the office building was sold. At the time of my visit much of it was being leased to Electronic Data Systems Corporation (EDS), the computer services firm founded by Ross Perot that was later sold to the General Motors Corporation.

The giant fourth-floor room where the entire news staff of the nation's largest evening paper toiled in close proximity to one another for so many years had been broken up into scores of joyless work stations. The sight depressed me. The crowded newsroom, filled with characters not cut from any mold, had been a noisy and exciting workplace. As I strolled through it, memories flooded back and I encountered ghosts from the *Bulletin*'s storied past.

There was Al Simon, who performed an essential function, cleaning the commodes, and Edie McCully, the telephone receptionist, always cheerful, always smiling, despite tragedies in her personal life. There are no Edie McCullys in newsrooms any more; callers to newspapers now are usually greeted with electronic announcements.

There were standout photographers Don Pasquarella and Charlie Higgins, and also Fred Meyer, who shared in the *Bulletin*'s first Pulitzer. There were sportswriters Don Donaghy, who wrote about baseball under the name "Lynn C. Doyle," and Jack Fried, whose byline covering boxing and wrestling was "Matt Ring."

There were reporters George R. Staab, Peck's bad boy of the newsroom, and Raymond C. Brecht, its consummate gentleman.

There was rewriteman Joe Reichwein, whose list of weird newsmakers in *Bulletin* stories included Gracious Outlaw, Filmore Fuddy, Seemy Drinks and Orville Cluck.

There was former City Hall columnist John C. Calpin, whose knowledge of the workings of municipal government was encyclopedic. Calpin had started as a police reporter at $15 a week in 1925, when Nelson Eddy, later to make his name in Hollywood, also worked for the *Bulletin*.

There was a remarkable team: Fred McCord, the Shakespeare of the rewrite bank, and sobsister Rowland T. Moriarty, who could not write but was a master at wheedling information from people in trouble. The immensely readable Sunday stories produced by this pair were invariably slugged either "heartbreak" or "moola."

There were Sam Boyle and Phil Schaeffer, two fine editors who epitomized the *Bulletin* at its best. There were George R. Packard, B. Dale Davis and Craig Ammerman, the *Bulletin*'s last three executive editors, so very different from one another in personality and style, but each committed to the paper and each, ultimately, unsuccessful.

There was Assistant City Editor Iz Lichstein, who dealt so expeditiously with a hilarious but potentially devastating in-house incident one Friday night in the 1940s that to this day hardly any *Bulletin* alumni know of it. Iz was working the night desk when a special-delivery letter for Managing Editor Dwight Perrin arrived from New York. Expecting a news release, he signed for the letter and opened it—only to find himself reading a juicy love note from Perrin's secret inamorata in Manhattan. With his job on the line should Perrin discover that the night side was reading his private correspondence, Lichstein and his assistant, Henry Yocom, got an envelope like the original, retyped Perrin's name and address on it and sent a copy boy on a train to New York to remail the letter by special delivery. It arrived the next day and the managing editor was never the wiser. Iz Lichstein, one of the *Bulletin*'s most devoted operatives, kept his job. In fact, he later went on to edit the *Bulletin Almanac*, an indispensable compilation of Philadelphiana.

There was Ruth Seltzer, who chronicled the comings and goings of high society in Philadelphia but was under instructions never to mention the McLeans in her column.

There was, finally, Orrin C. Evans, a man of great dignity and the only black reporter in the *Bulletin*'s newsroom until the coming of Claude Lewis, whose essay concludes this volume.

* * *

Someone once said there is no history, only historians who interpret the past differently. That's probably true. But the contributors to this volume have not written a history of the *Bulletin*, nor have we explained in any detail why it ultimately failed. Rather we have looked back, nostalgically in some cases but realistically, I think, at the paper when it was in its prime half a century ago. Even now we keep meeting people who say they still miss the *Bulletin*. This book is for them. But it's also for younger readers who may be unaware of how dramatically journalism has changed in our lifetimes. Readers will find each contributor reflecting on a different aspect of the *Bulletin*'s operation. If there is a common thread running through these essays it is the affection that all the contributors felt for the paper. Until near-ly the end, the *Bulletin* was family-owned, and most of us who worked there felt like family. In countless cases, the individual subscriber spoke of *my Bulletin*. Our readers were also part of the *Bulletin* family. In too many cases, that feeling is missing in today's newsrooms and among today's newspaper readers.* More's the pity.

*A Pew Research Center survey in March 1987 found that only 27 percent of Americans say they look forward to reading the paper each day.

Chapter 2

Nothing was Too Trivial

By Robert J. Williams

WHEN I BEGAN AT THE *BULLETIN* nearly 70 years ago, newspapering even in the largest American cities was a hard-scrabble trade rather than an elite profession. What is spoken of now as "journalism" was often dismissed back then as the "newspaper game," a recreational pursuit that wasn't to be taken very seriously. In the public mind, reporters and stage actors alike were dismissed as low life whom respectable people wouldn't open their front doors to. It was the servants' entrance for them. Certainly, at a starting salary of $15 a week for cubs, the pay attracted few college graduates into newspapering.

With an evening circulation of more than 500,000 copies, the *Bulletin* was the largest of seven daily papers in Philadelphia then, and it must have been very profitable. Yet its newsroom looked like a second-hand furniture store. Reporters sat at battered wooden desks that might have been hand-me-downs from other departments of the newspaper where appearances mattered. If two chairs matched, it was an accident. Beside most desks were spittoons for tobacco-chewing reporters. Nearly everybody smoked and stamped out their butts on the floor. Occasionally, wastebaskets caught fire from carelessly tossed cigarettes and matches.

Every desk had a telephone jack but no real phone, just a primitive headset with an earpiece held by wire clamps across the scalp. Reporters padded their clamps with copy paper (newsprint cut into letter-size sheets) to avoid minor concussions. But these clumsy devices served a useful purpose. With headsets rather than hand-held telephones, rewritemen could type out stories as the details were phoned in by police reporters and then summon copy boys to rush their copy to the city desk in short "takes" of two or three paragraphs at a time. In the frenzied competition of those days, such speed was essential.

Most of the *Bulletin*'s staffers were two-finger pounders and most of the typewriters were ancient Underwoods. On each reporter's desk was a pointed metal spike where "dupes" (copies) of his stories were stored. The spikes were embedded in bases made in the composing room of the same lead alloy used for the typesetting machines. Spikes were lethal weapons, and the *Bulletin*'s medical department specialized in treating punctured fingers. "Spike" also entered the language as a verb. If an editor spiked a reporter's story, he killed it.

Scattered throughout the room were glass glue pots with small brushes. Once an edition was published—and the *Bulletin* published seven every day from about 9 o'clock in the morning until roughly 6:30 in the evening— reporters would paste up on copy paper the stories that required changes. They might give a story a "shave," striking out paragraphs to make room for fresher news in later editions, or lengthen an important story by marking the place for a typed "insert." Or they might eliminate "typos" by making corrections in the margins of the glued copy paper. This low-tech practice was common at big-city papers for many years. Not until the coming of computers did glue pots vanish from newsrooms.

* * *

I first set eyes on the *Bulletin* Building on November 11, 1918, the day the Great War ended. My family was living in a boarding house at Broad Street and Montgomery Avenue in North Philadelphia. From there in 1917, I had watched hearses carrying victims of the influenza epidemic to their graves. Six days before the Armistice, I marked my sixth birthday, and on the day itself I walked down Broad Street with my parents to see the celebration at City Hall. The *Bulletin* was then published at Juniper and Filbert Streets, diagonally across from City Hall's northeast corner. Vaguely, I recall hearing a lot of bells and whistles, but the image of the *Bulletin*'s white-domed building remains undimmed after more than three quarters of a century. There were big signs on its facade that my dad told me gave news of the war; that we'd won it.

Just over a decade later, I obtained a summer job at the *Bulletin*. It was July 1929, three months before the stock market crash launched the nation's worst depression. I had just finished 11th grade at Northeast High School, and my job was to clip and file stories in the *Bulletin* library (nobody called it the "morgue") off the eighth-floor newsroom. Near the elevator door sat a stern-faced woman of middle years. She was stationed there to guard the "gate," the newsroom entrance, and a muscular bouncer couldn't have been more effective. She flagged all outsiders with two exceptions—the office bookie and the office bootlegger. Congress had amended the Constitution in 1919 to prohibit the "manufacture, sale or transportation of intoxicating liquors" anywhere in the country, or the importation thereof. But of course anyone wanting booze during Prohibition could get it. Many bootleggers offered door-to-door delivery. The *Bulletin* newsroom's supplier was better dressed than the reporters. His merchandise was contained in the briefcase that he carried like any businessman.

It's probably safe to say that the police charged with arresting violators of the 18th Amendment and the reporters who covered them were rarely short of hooch themselves. After raiding illicit stills, the cops were supposed to test the confiscated stuff at the police lab to make sure it was, in fact, "intoxicating liquor" and then set it afire in the boondocks somewhere, generally in the presence of newspaper photographers. That's what they were supposed to do. But in fact a lot of the liquor never reached the bonfires. Once they determined it wasn't made with poisonous wood alcohol, the police and the press consumed it.

* * *

After finishing high school in 1930, I became a member of the *Bulletin*'s news staff, and so I would remain for more than four decades. I soon discovered that the denizens of the paper's newsroom in the Prohibition Era came in all shapes and sizes, human animals in a zoo without cages. I'll never forget George Grossman, the assistant city editor responsible for editing the paper's first edition. He was astonishingly quick at scanning pages to see what changes were needed. Many editors were skilled at this process but Grossman had a special talent, and for a special reason. Moving copy at top speed gave him the time to concentrate on the serious business of his day—betting on the horses. He invariably backed losers at the track, however, and he was always broke. One day a sportswriter gave him money to bet on a long shot, but Grossman placed the wager instead on a horse of his own choosing, figuring the long shot wouldn't win and he could pocket the bet. When the long shot won and the sportswriter discovered what the editor had done, he threatened to kill him. But Grossman dissuaded him from committing murder in the newsroom.

Once in a while, Grossman, after losing at the track, would threaten to jump out one of the newsroom's grimy windows. And, of course, that threat was the cue for someone to open a window. But he never jumped.

As the cub reporter whose absence from the office mattered least, I became Grossman's errand boy when his losses got him in trouble with his gorgeous, dark-haired wife. Once he handed me a wad of bills with instructions to rush to his apartment where the iceman was holding her hostage until she paid their long-overdue bill. My arrival with cash ended that crisis. Another time he sent me racing to a loan office. He had assured his wife that he had made the monthly payment, but he had not. I forked over the money before she learned the awful truth. Grossman borrowed from almost everyone in the office. Finally, he sat down with one of his creditors, made a list of what he owed and declared a dividend. His first payout was the last. He left the *Bulletin* for a public relations job on a cruise ship and later worked for a PR agency. That concluded this colorful deadbeat's newspaper career.

Another assistant city editor had a split personality—before and after drinking his lunch. In the morning, Don Brooke was all business; in the afternoon, he was loud and belligerent, and he didn't care whom he talked back to, even if it was Charles Israel, the paper's revered—and feared—city editor. When a VIP jumped to his death from a mid-city office building one afternoon, the *Evening Ledger* beat us to the story because our central city police reporter, Ted Wilcox, outwitted himself. Wilcox had posed as a detective to get into the office building, but the cops discovered his ruse and wouldn't let him leave or phone in his story. Israel, furious at the *Evening Ledger*'s scoop, told Brooke to fire Wilcox. "You hired him, you fire him!" Brooke bellowed in the presence of stunned staffers who had never heard anyone yell at the city editor. Wilcox, instead of losing his job, was promoted to the most envied of all assignments—Washington correspondent. He got a Navy commission in World War II and became press aide to Admiral William F. (Bull) Halsey, whose fleet sank four Japanese aircraft carriers and a battleship in the Leyte Gulf engagement, crippling the enemy's navy.

Later, Brooke, as head of the *Bulletin*'s copy desk, abruptly ended a reform that had bedeviled the entire staff. Management had hired an "expert" to improve writing at the paper, and the "expert" kept demanding shorter leads. Brooke listened for just so long. And then, after a motorist died in a downtown auto collision, he rewrote the story's lengthy lead to make it read: "A man was killed in an accident today." Only a few details followed. That was the last we heard both of shorter leads and of the writing "expert."

Israel, the editor to whom all staffers had to answer for their sins, spent most of his working hours reading carbon copies and proofs of all the local stories. Unlike Brooke, he never raised his voice, but his words were often more penetrating than a stiletto. And when he left his rolltop desk for the multi-position desk where his assistants worked, it usually meant trouble for someone. One day I received the dreaded summons to appear before him. Israel handed me the expense account I had submitted for the previous week as a district police reporter. The *Bulletin*'s expense account form listed "Trolley Trips" as the sole means of reporting transportation for reporters, and I included a slew of them.

"Williams," the city editor said, "if you had ridden so many trolleys, you would not have had time to cover a single story." He okayed the slip and offered me a rare smile. "After this," he said, "use your imagination." I soon learned that with salary raises prohibited because of the straitened economic times, expense account fiction was the editor's way of keeping the staff reasonably happy. That's why *Bulletin* expense accounts came to be called "swindle sheets." And the larceny went on and on, even after World War II.

* * *

In the 1930s, the United States was predominantly a nation of farms and small towns. Fewer than one in 20 adults were college graduates and 60 percent dropped out of school before ninth grade. City dwellers tended to cluster together in blue-collar ethnic neighborhoods, and this was especially true in Philadelphia. The *Bulletin* knew its audience and played to it more skillfully than any of the other daily papers it competed against. It approached the news as if Philadelphia were a rural village. Nothing was too trivial. Rarely would a day pass without publication in the *Bulletin* of a paragraph on the golden wedding anniversary of some unknown couple out there in the great city. The *Bulletin* regularly published lists of all marriage licenses issued and divorces granted and, in small type, the names of all local high school and college graduates. Without fail, the sighting every spring of the region's first robin would be announced on the front page. (Of course, we knew that most robins never flew south of South Philly.)

It's certainly true that the old *Bulletin* reported minutiae, and it was often ridiculed for this practice. Yet in their coverage of major stories *Bulletin* staffers proved themselves capable of producing copy of the highest quality. They did it time and again. I'm thinking particularly of unflappable Harry G. Proctor, who wrote the cleanest possible copy and made it look easy. Proctor covered one of this century's most dramatic newspaper stories, the execution of Bruno Richard Hauptmann, at the state prison in Trenton on April 3, 1936, for the kidnap-murder of Charles A. Lindbergh's infant son.

Hauptmann was put to death at night, allowing reporters for evening papers plenty of time to compose their stories before their deadlines the following morning. So driving back to Philadelphia from Trenton, Proctor stopped for a lobster dinner. On reaching his desk, he put on his eyeshades—he was addicted to eyeshades and cigars—pulled a bottle of whiskey from a drawer, set it on the desk and began typing. His impeccable account began:

By Harry G. Proctor
(Staff Correspondent of The *Bulletin*)

Trenton, April 4—Bruno Richard Hauptmann has kept, at long last, his rendezvous with death.

At 8:43 o'clock last night, in the death house of the New Jersey State Prison, there shot through his stalwart frame the first of three shattering stabs of man-made lightning.

At 8:47, the incisive voice of Dr. Howard Weisler, the prison physician, sounded through the awful hush that sat upon the close-packed ranks of witnesses: "This man is dead."

Thus, an obscure German carpenter paid his debt to society for one of the most infamous crimes of all time, the kidnapping and murder of Charles A. Lindbergh Jr., and thus was written "curtain" to at least one act of the tragic Lindbergh drama.

All the furor and turmoil of months that had attended the unprecedented battle to save him wound up in a deathly silence in a brick-walled room measuring 18 by 20 feet, and in the space of four-and-one-half minutes.

He walked to his death as he had walked in life, lithely, alertly, almost defiantly.

He needed no assistance, and he got none. He was to the last as much master of himself as any human being could be in the clutches of the law.

He made no statement. He left no confession. He uttered no complaint. Just once, as he was strapped into the electric chair, his lips moved slightly.

A guard said afterward that he muttered a word or two in German. But the guard knew no German, and the meaning of that final utterance was lost forever.

Thanks to a tip in the toilet, I got a scoop in the Hauptmann case, but the *Bulletin* didn't print it. The execution had been scheduled for the night of April 1, 1936, and the entire country awaited news from Trenton. I had been sent there as Proctor's gofer. In the State House men's room that afternoon, the fellow in the adjoining urinal happened to spot the press card in my hatband. He whispered that Hauptmann was not going to be put to death that night after all. I quickly taxied to the courthouse and there confirmed this information. The governor had indeed postponed the execution for two days pending the outcome of a grand jury investigation into a warning by Burlington County Detective Chief Ellis Parker, a notorious headline hunter, that the wrong guy was about to be fried. The delay was expected to be announced any minute. I immediately telephoned the office, gave the story to a rewrite man and emerged from the phone booth as reporters swarmed in. The delay was official and I had a world beat!

Scooping the opposition even by a couple of minutes was huge in those pre-television days, and this was especially true in a matter of such magnitude as the Hauptmann execution. Next morning, I was told that Managing Editor William B. Craig wanted to see me. Instead of congratulations, however, he offered apologies. It turned out that the *Bulletin*'s editors, not trusting the word from their rookie, had awaited the wire-service flash before reporting that Hauptmann wouldn't be executed that night after all.

* * *

A couple of months later, President Franklin D. Roosevelt, after being nominated for a second term at the Democratic National Convention in Philadelphia, delivered his acceptance speech at Franklin Field, the University of Pennsylvania's football stadium. FDR's text had been released in advance, and the *Bulletin* published an "extra" to sell to the crowd entering the stadium. An army of "little merchants," as the *Bulletin* labeled its newspaperboys, had been deployed to hawk the special edition, and copies sold as fast as the kids could hand them out. But not because people wanted to read the President's speech. It had rained most of the afternoon and the boys kept crying, "Get yer *Bulletin*. The seats are wet and dirty."

* * *

The term "media circus" had not been coined in the 1930s, but Philadelphia played host to a dandy one. Late in 1932, Z. Smith Reynolds, heir to his family's tobacco fortune, had been found shot to death in his North Carolina mansion. His pregnant widow, Libby Holman, the famed Broadway torch singer, said her husband had committed suicide. So did Reynolds' male secretary. The authorities did not agree; they charged the pair with killing Reynolds to collect his millions. The two were indicted and ordered to stand trial. Before hearing testimony, however, the trial judge threw out the charges for lack of evidence and released them. It was rumored but never proven that the powerful Reynolds family had intervened to make sure its soiled linen was not displayed in public.

Shortly after winning her freedom, Libby Holman entered the Lying-In Division of Pennsylvania Hospital at 8th and Spruce Streets, where DuPont and Roosevelt babies would later be delivered. Reporters flocked to Philadelphia from all over the country before the birth of Christopher Smith Reynolds in January 1933, and they stayed for Libby Holman's lengthy post-partum hospitalization. It was an irresistible story, not just for the tabloid press but for all the papers. In addition to the baby's millionaire father, his mother Libby had popularized such hits as "Moanin' Low," "Body and Soul" and "Something To Remember You By." Her biographer, Jon Bradshaw, described her as "slumber-eyed, raven-haired, petulant-lipped, husky-voiced." The press reported breathlessly on the condition of mother and child, and the *Bulletin* carried front-page stories almost every day. "Holman Stork Expected Here." "Libby Holman Baby in Incubator." "Reynolds Baby Has Dark Hair." "Baby Reynolds is Gaining." "Libby To See Son Soon." "Libby Can't See Baby for a Week." "Baby Is Great, Says Libby's Dad."

The torch singer remained at Pennsylvania Hospital for three months to recover from what doctors said was a nervous breakdown, and many out-of-town reporters stayed in Philadelphia, too, hoping vainly to talk to her. Finally, just before leaving the hospital, she granted a mass interview, but the only news that came out of it was that her infant son's hair was blond, not dark.

Tragedy dogged Libby Holman and Christopher Smith Reynolds for the rest of their lives. She tried to make a comeback on Broadway but failed. At the age of 17, her son was killed in a mountain climbing accident. And at 71, she committed suicide by inhaling carbon monoxide in the front seat of her Rolls Royce, parked in her garage. According to Bradshaw, she left over $13 million, most of it to charities.

* * *

Shortly after 6 PM on September 6, 1943, the Pennsylvania Railroad's crack Congressional Limited derailed in Philadelphia's Frankford section while traveling at high speed from Washington to New York. The Pennsy was the nation's biggest railroad and this was its deadliest wreck: 79 persons killed and dozens injured.

It was Labor Day and the *Bulletin*'s newsroom was virtually empty when word of the derailment came in. It fell to me, the only editor there at the time, to assemble the staff to cover the disaster. I need not have worried. As reporters heard radio reports, they phoned me to say they were on their way to the scene and to hospitals. Writers and editors appeared unannounced at the office. I guess you'd call it *Bulletin* esprit-de-corps. Or more likely the reporters' burning desire to cover big stories and to demonstrate once again their major-league caliber.

At the time of the wreck, the only reporter in the newsroom was a newly hired assistant to the *Bulletin*'s religious editor. He was seated at a desk in a remote corner of the big room. I knew his name was Bayard Brunt and I knew he had never covered a hard-news story, but he was the only body available. I told him to get to the wreck at once by whatever means. I didn't hear from Brunt for many hours after that, and when he finally phoned I chewed him out for not keeping us informed. He told me to shut up and let him explain. In the derailment, one of the train's passenger cars had been sliced in half, lengthwise, after slamming into the support tower of a signal bridge. Brunt got there before police lines had been set up. Spotting the severed car, he managed to enter it and found himself amidst dead and dying passengers. One of the woman passengers was still conscious though pinned under twisted steel. Firemen were working to free her. Brunt squatted down beside the trapped woman and sought to comfort her. Though finally removed from the wreckage, she died later in a hospital.

When Brunt finally got back to the office, he wrote a dramatic story which was published on page one the next day. I doubt that any reader who started that story missed a single word. The religion editor had to find a new assistant.

* * *

During World War II, countless American families started backyard "Victory Gardens" to produce vegetables for their own use. In almost every Philadelphia neighborhood there was a competition to see who could grow the biggest tomatoes. In this atmosphere, the *Bulletin* printed a communication in its "Letters" column from a man who claimed to be the tomato champion. He grew record-size tomatoes, he reported, by fertilizing his plants with the bodies of dead cats. Cat lovers immediately flooded the paper with angry protests. No sooner had the furor died down when the letter writer submitted a progress report on the continued effectiveness of feline corpses in improving garden output. After that, nothing more was heard from him. What the paper's irate subscribers didn't know was that the *Bulletin* had encouraged its staff members to contribute controversial letters as a means of enlivening the page. Let the record show that the dead-cat letters were an inside job. However, those of us who knew the source vowed to remain mum forever. And we have.

* * *

Publisher Robert McLean never permitted news of his family's private activities to be reported in his paper, and he rarely visited the newsroom himself. I remember once, though, when he stopped by after his annual summer vacation in Maine. On that occasion, he asked the managing editor if, in his absence, we had printed an obituary of one of his close friends. He had heard that the death was actually a suicide that had been covered up. If that was so, the publisher's orders were to run a second story explaining the cause of death. At the managing editor's direction, I found the obit and discovered that we had, in fact, attributed the death to natural causes. A reporter dug out the facts. The truth concerning the suicide of the publisher's friend was finally printed.

In a world rife with coverups and lies, one had to silently cheer.

Chapter 3

Blood on My Shoes

By Pierre C. Fraley

WHEN I DECIDED, after graduating from Harvard in 1938, that I wanted to be a newspaperman, my father made an appointment for me to see Robert McLean, who was an old friend of his. The *Bulletin*'s publisher told me he never got involved in hiring. He referred me to the managing editor, Bill Craig, who asked if I had been to journalism school. I confessed somewhat sheepishly that I had not, thinking that was the end of my chances. "Good," said Craig. "We won't have to retrain you."

He hired me as a copy boy at $15 a week. After running copy for several months, I was promoted to general assignment reporter and given a $3 raise. I soon learned that everybody on the paper was underpaid, probably even Bill Craig. John Calpin, a long-time assistant city editor and political writer, later told me that he didn't get a raise for 17 years.

I was working on rewrite in 1950 when Stuart Taylor, the new city editor, tapped me as the paper's science and medical writer. It was an exciting time to be covering medicine. In the course of my work, I interviewed both Alexander Fleming, who accidentally came upon penicillin, and Selman Waksman, who discovered streptomycin. Sir Alexander was a cheerful, round-faced man who chain-smoked cigarettes. He was continually and ineffectively brushing ashes off his rumpled blue shirt. It was easy to see him as the kind of man who would carelessly leave his Petri dishes around so that they might become contaminated.

But it was also clear that he had the kind of mind that would wonder what had happened to the dishes and hence discover penicillin. He was an example of Louis Pasteur's aphorism that in science, chance favors the prepared mind. Sir Alexander's mind was certainly prepared. On the other hand, Waksman, who was later involved in controversy over the awarding of the Nobel Prize, was quick, organized and intelligent, anything but sloppy.

Dramatic advances in heart surgery were taking place in this period, and much of the action was in Philadelphia. The last bastion in the human body to hold out against the developing skill of the surgeon and his sharp scalpel was the human heart itself. No surgeon had yet devised a safe, sure way to cut into a beating heart to repair congenital defects such as a hole in the septum or to correct a leaky heart valve.

In 1942, a team of thoracic surgeons at Hahnemann Hospital in Philadelphia opened a partially closed valve inside a heart, in a procedure called a mitral commissurotomy. The surgeons made a small incision in the wall of the patient's beating heart. One of them, Charles P. Bailey, attached a thin scalpel blade to his finger, carefully eased it through the hole and gently cut open the tightened leaflets of the valve.

Because Bailey was working in Philadelphia around the corner from the *Bulletin*, I went several times to his operating suites to interview him. Bailey was an innovator, an impetuous experimenter, not afraid to take risks in devising new operations and techniques. And he wasn't averse to publicity—so long as it was favorable.

Before heart-lung machines were perfected, thoracic surgeons searched for ways to slow the patient's heart rate, thus making it easier to operate. One procedure that Bailey tried was to cool the patient's body down close to hypothermia. In experimenting on the drug chlorpromazine, the French had induced what they termed "artificial hibernation." Bailey picked up this idea. Hypothermia reduced body metabolism, allowing Bailey to slow the heart beat for as long as eight minutes without damaging the brain. Normally, damage could occur in three minutes.

I saw one of his heart patients lying in a large tub filled with a slush of ice and water. When he first tried this technique, he filled a canoe with ice water and placed his patient in it. The patient I saw was in a large chest that looked like a freezer.

One day Bailey told me that if I wanted to continue reporting on his operations, I should be present in the operating room and watch the procedure firsthand. A patient with an atrial myoma, a small tumor growing inside one of the chambers of his heart, had been referred to Bailey for treatment. The growth interfered dangerously with the flow of blood. The patient was near death.

Charlie offered to let me observe the surgery, the first of its kind ever attempted. But he set one condition. If the operation succeeded, I could report it exclusively to the *Bulletin*. But if the operation failed and the patient died, I must promise not to write a word about it. Such a Faustian bargain would probably be viewed as highly improper today, but it was based on mutual trust between doctor and reporter, the kind of trust that is not always present in the current climate of medical journalism.

I agreed to Bailey's condition. I told the city editor only that I was going to Hahnemann Hospital to investigate a possible story. On the appointed day, I showed up at the hospital's surgical suites about 7 AM and received instruction on how to scrub my hands and how to put on the green surgical uniform. Then I tucked my wallet inside one of my socks and, with notebook in hand, entered the crowded operating room.

Charlie found a place for me just behind his right shoulder where I would have a good view of the operation but would be out of his way. The technical problem was one of life and death. It would be relatively easy for the surgeon to cut the tumor loose from the heart wall. But if it then floated freely into the blood stream, the resulting obstruction would almost certainly kill the patient. Bailey planned to avoid this eventuality by catching the growth before it entered the blood stream, and removing it.

To do this he had fashioned a tiny net, resembling a fisherman's net but much smaller, not much more than an inch in diameter. Bailey called it a guppy net. The frame was metal and the net was made of orlon-type material. The mesh openings were large enough to allow the passage of blood but small enough to capture the tadpole-shaped tumor hanging down from the heart wall.

As I labored furiously to take notes on my small pad, Bailey's team sewed a circular piece of sheet rubber to the outline of the heart. The top was fastened to a metal frame with a handle held by a member of Bailey's team about six or eight inches above the heart. It formed a kind of dam to hold the blood that would flow in the surgery.

When everything was in place, Bailey made an incision in the heart wall just below the spot where the tumor was attached. Blood welled up in the rubber dam and rose three or four inches. Perfect. Bailey then started to insert the guppy net through the well of blood and into the heart through the incision. The net was almost in place when the anesthesiologist called out that the patient's blood pressure was dropping dangerously.

Bailey withdrew the net until circulation and pressure came back. He said he'd had the net tantalizingly close to where he wanted it before cutting the tumor loose from the heart wall. After a few minutes, he tried again. As he placed the net into the heart opening, the anesthesiologist barked another warning. Believing he had time to complete the procedure, Bailey continued briefly but had to stop when the patient went into shock. In this emergency, he knocked the well of blood out of the way so his team could inject medication directly into the heart muscle. Blood spurted over the operating room, on the doctors, the nurses, on me. The floor became slick with spilled blood. Doctors screamed out conflicting orders, but it was too late to save the patient's life. He died on the operating table.

I fled the chaotic scene and retreated to the locker room. One of Dr. Bailey's principal associates soon came in. His locker was next to mine. He sat down heavily on the bench and put his head in his hands. I said I wanted to say something to Dr. Bailey but didn't think this was the time.

"No," he said, "Charlie goes to pieces when he loses a patient. He'll go off for four or five days to be by himself. Call him in about a week."

It was evident that such tragic outcomes were, if not the rule, not the exception, either. "Some day I'm going to write my autobiography," the associate said. "I'm going to call it 'Blood on My Shoes.'" I looked down at his white operating-room shoes. They were crimson with blood.

I kept my small notebook, encrusted with blood, for several years, even if I couldn't draw on its contents because of my promise to Charlie. I never wrote the story—until now. I never even knew the patient's name. But in one of the last stories I wrote for the *Bulletin*, Charlie Bailey acknowledged that he had been wrong about the functioning of the mitral valve. The historic operation he had attempted in my presence was based on a complete misunderstanding of its mechanics.

* * *

One of the most fascinating "sex stories" of the postwar generation broke on my beat in 1953, but the *Bulletin* never published my account. Here's what happened. In 1948, Alfred C. Kinsey, a relatively unknown zoologist at Indiana University, had published the first comprehensive study of male sexual behavior in the United States. His study, which was based on thousands of interviews, proved to be a startlingly frank examination of matters which had rarely been discussed in public, and it caused a furor. Without advance publicity, Kinsey's book sold 300,000 copies, and was attacked and defended around the world.

In the early 1950s, word circulated that he and his colleagues were ready with their eagerly awaited sequel, *Sexual Behavior in the Human Female*. In today's environment, the author of a titillating sex book can expect to sign a multi-million-dollar deal with a slick publisher who will hire publicists to hype the writer nationally and get him on *Oprah* and *Geraldo*.

Not Dr. Kinsey. And not in 1953. He had doubtless welcomed the first book's sales, but he disliked the notoriety that went with best-sellerdom, and he was determined to control advance publicity for the second book. So hush-hush were his methods that his Philadelphia publisher, W.B. Saunders, referred to the book by a code name and locked the manuscript in a safe every night.

The usual practice among publishers is to send review copies of their books to newspapers, magazines and other potential reviewers in advance of publication. No advance copies of Kinsey's study of sexuality in the human female were circulated. Instead, as the publication date approached, science and medical writers like myself were forced to enter into a unique compact with Kinsey.

Under his ground rules, only those writers who agreed to attend several days of briefings by Kinsey and his staff at Indiana University's Institute for Sex Research could read advance page proofs of the book. Our reviews had to be written on the premises and then submitted to the Kinsey staff for correction of any errors of fact or interpretation.

Here was an author demanding—and getting—the right to read and edit reviews of his book before they were published. In today's more liberated society, such control over the press would be unthinkable. Any contemporary journalist who put up with Dr. Kinsey's strictures would be drummed out of the profession. But this was a different time. And so intense was the interest in his research that the most prestigious newspapers in the country meekly surrendered to the man whose specialty in the field of zoology had been in the classification of gall wasps.

In August 1953, I traveled to Bloomington and checked into Indiana University's Student Union where most of the science and medical writers were assigned bedrooms. With the other reporters, I attended the required briefings on the statistical methods that Kinsey's team had used in drawing conclusions from the interviews they had conducted. Only then was I allowed to see the page proofs. Like the others, I signed a document stipulating that I would not duplicate any of the materials, would not remove them from the Student Union or show them to outsiders.

It was one of the hottest weeks of that summer, and I spent much of the time lying in a bath of tepid water, seeking relief from the 100-degree temperatures while reading proofs of the 842-page book. The story I wrote was dutifully submitted to the Institute's staff and was approved with only one or two suggestions for minor changes. I made the changes, went back to Philadelphia and turned in my story. It was set in type for use on the book's publication date. Then I went on a cool vacation in Maine.

On August 20, 1953, the Kinsey report on female sexual behavior was officially released. But the *Bulletin*'s huge readership never saw what I wrote. Prudish editors spiked my story, fearing that its subject matter might offend the delicate sensibilities of Philadelphians. Instead, the *Bulletin* ran a four-paragraph editorial noting that the findings required thoughtful study and could not be summarized by the newspaper "without giving unnecessary offense to many in its large family of readers."

And so my labors in Bloomington were all for nought. By contrast, my friend Earl Ubell, science writer for the *New York Herald-Tribune*, was jubilant. His story not only landed on the *Trib*'s front page, but for the first time in that illustrious paper's history, it printed a six-letter word referring to the climax of sexual excitement. Of course, the *Bulletin* would never use that word which began with o, and I won't either.

* * *

My most important "beat" as a science/medical writer concerned the effectiveness of a new drug, Thorazine, in the treatment of psychotic patients. Again, it was my contacts that got me onto the story.

Thorazine (the trade name for chlorpromazine) was brought to this country by SmithKline, a well-established Philadelphia pharmaceutical firm. One of those testing the drug on patients was a psychiatrist named William Winkelman and, as it happened, his father was a good friend of mine. The elder Winkelman tipped me off that his son was studying an important, perhaps revolutionary, drug. I obtained a preliminary copy of young Bill's report and told him I was preparing a story for the *Bulletin* based on his study.

Bill was very upset. He pointed out that if the *Bulletin* carried a story before his scientific report appeared in an accepted medical journal, his reputation would be damaged. He would be labeled a publicity seeker, anathema in the medical profession. He implored me to hold off until his account was published in the *Journal of the American Medical Association*.

As I had with Charlie Bailey, I reached an agreement with Bill Winkelman, one that today's journalistic purists might find abhorrent. We agreed that I would prepare my story but embargo it for release simultaneously with his article in *JAMA*. In the meantime, he would check my story for accuracy and give me additional background. My story would thus be more complete and it would contain the first public report on the revolutionary drug, just as Winkelman's article would be the first for the medical profession.

We both did as we had promised. My story was carried in the *Bulletin*'s first edition on the same day that the *JAMA* issue with Winkelman's article was mailed to doctors. He concluded that chlorpromazine was "especially remarkable in that it can reduce severe anxiety, diminish phobias and obsessions, reverse or modify a paranoid psychosis, quiet manic or extremely agitated patients, and change the hostile, agitated, senile patient into a quiet, easily managed patient."

Thorazine, while admittedly no panacea, did help relieve overcrowding in the nation's psychiatric hospitals. And the first account of its potential appeared under my by-line in the *Bulletin*. I got my exclusive and Bill Winkelman abided by medical ethics. Maybe this isn't the way journalism is practiced today but I'm convinced that the public interest was served by our arrangement.

* * *

In June 1954, I persuaded the city editor to let me cover the American Medical Association's annual meeting in San Francisco. It's lucky I did because big news came out of the meeting. Two scientists from the American Cancer Society—E. Cuyler Hammond and Daniel Horn—reported for the first time that cigarette smoking was killing men.

Based on a study of 187,766 white men between the ages of 50 and 69, they declared that those with a history of regular cigarette smoking had "a considerably higher death rate than men who have never smoked or men who have smoked only cigars or pipes." The researchers found a "definite association" between smoking habits and deaths from heart disease and lung cancer.

The tobacco industry immediately hired the New York public relations firm of Hill and Knowlton to play down the significance of the report. (More than 40 years later, the cigarette makers continue to deny the existence of a link between smoking and fatal diseases.)

Leonard Zahn, an affable and gregarious Hill and Knowlton associate, frequented press rooms at medical meetings, developing personal relationships with science writers. He made a point of always smoking cigarettes while chatting with us, as if to demonstrate his disdain for the scientific evidence.

Earl Ubell noted that Zahn was the only "secret non-smoker" he knew. The only time Len does not smoke, Earl said, is in the privacy of his own room.

At one press conference, Cuyler Hammond reported on a survey of smoking habits. The survey asked such questions as "Do you smoke before breakfast? At bedtime? When you are having a drink?" Another question was: "Do you smoke after sex?" One respondent seemed confused by that one. He answered: "I don't know. I never looked."

* * *

Wilton Marion Krogman was Professor of Physical Anthropology at the University of Pennsylvania and one of the most engaging men I ever met. Besides his scientific and academic work, he loved his role as "bone detective," a kind of Sherlock Holmes for cadavers. Whenever a body or even a few scattered bones were found in a lonely spot, Bill would examine the remains and reconstruct the dead person's age, race, gender and even his or her socioeconomic background. After writing several pieces about him, I asked Bill if I could look over his shoulder the next time police called him in to identify a corpse.

Several weeks later, Bill phoned to say a badly decomposed body had been found in a remote "Lover's Lane" in Philadelphia's western suburbs. The district attorney's office was claiming that the corpse was that of a woman who had been raped and murdered. Bill had the remains in his office. "Come on over and watch," he said.

When I arrived, Krogman was taking measurements with calipers and other equipment. His first words to me were: "I wish the D.A. wouldn't make these dramatic announcements before he knows what he's talking about."

As he worked on the remains, he explained to me what he was doing and finding. What he found was that the body was not that of a woman who had been violated but a white male about 35 years old who apparently had lived in reduced circumstances. He had recently suffered a broken arm that had not healed properly; certainly it had not been set by a doctor. Some of his teeth were missing; others were in poor condition with many unfilled cavities. He was probably a drifter, a bum. The D.A. looked silly.

* * *

One afternoon a woman phoned me to report that while her daughter was undergoing surgery at the Children's Hospital of Philadelphia there had been an explosion in the operating room. She was very upset because the hospital wouldn't tell her what had happened. I took her name and the number of the hospital room she was calling from. Then I phoned Dr. C. Everett Koop, the Hospital's renowned surgeon-in-chief, whom I knew on a first-name basis. The woman said he had operated on her daughter.

I told Chick Koop what I had heard and asked for details. He said it was a minor matter. The patient's family didn't want any publicity, Koop insisted, so he couldn't say anything about it.

Half an hour later I was at Children's Hospital talking to the patient's family. They told me what they knew, which wasn't much. On a piece of copy paper, I drew up a one-paragraph release for the family to sign. It authorized me to write a story about the explosion for publication on the day the girl was released. I suspected that the hospital might stonewall me and, sensibly as it turned out, made sure the family was on my side.

The mother called on the morning her daughter was released from Children's Hospital. I went immediately to Chick Koop's office, told him I was preparing a story and asked for comment. When he repeated that the family wanted to avoid publicity, I produced the signed release. He then said that the family did not understand the adverse reaction to such a story. It might scare people away from needed operations, he said.

I told him that I intended to write the story and submit it to my editor who would decide whether to run it or not. Koop said he would call my editor and tell him not to use the story. I said fine, if the editor chose not to publish the story that was his responsibility. I told Koop my duty was to write the story as carefully and accurately as I could. That is what I did. I called several leading authorities, including Bob Dripps, Professor of Anesthesiology at the University of Pennsylvania, for background on operating-room explosions, how frequently they occurred and how many patients were affected each year. Dripps' low-key factual material helped soften the impact of the Children's Hospital episode. I don't know whether Koop called the paper, but the story ran the day after I turned it in. Although the explosion had not affected the surgery, I still thought it was newsworthy.

Chick Koop later went on to do an outstanding job as the outspoken and often controversial Surgeon General of the U.S. Public Health Service. It was Koop who insisted that health warnings be printed on every pack of cigarettes.

* * *

One year the American Dental Association held its annual meeting in Philadelphia. Discussion centered on strange statistics coming out of a small town in Texas. Dental caries, better known as cavities, was the most prevalent and widespread childhood disease in America. Yet for several years there had been no recorded cases of dental caries in the tiny Texas town. At first, researchers assumed that there had been an error in reporting. Then it was found that the town's water supply had a high content of sodium fluoride. Studies showed that the fluoride was hardening the teeth and protecting Texas children from cavities. I reported these findings which were made public at the dental association's annual meeting.

A controversy soon developed between those who wanted to fluoridate water systems and those who feared that fluoride might be toxic or cause other health problems. Some opponents argued that fluoridation could serve as an opening wedge for the introduction of potentially dangerous or hazardous additives to the public water supply. Those on the lunatic fringe warned of a Communist plot to poison the population of the United States as a prelude to a Russian takeover of this country.

In the summer of 1954, Philadelphia's progressive mayor, Joseph S. Clark, and his enlightened health commissioner, James P. Dixon, decided to fluoridate the city's public water supply. They announced that minute amounts of fluoride would be introduced into the system on Labor Day. I wrote the story for the *Bulletin*. Fearing that some residents might think the fluoride was making them sick, Clark and Dixon held a mock ceremony on a certain date, presumably marking the introduction of fluoride. Although fluoride was not added that day, the city received phone calls from a few hypochondriacs who insisted that the phantom chemical had made them sick. Several weeks later, the fluoride was actually added without fanfare and without complaints of ill effects. Ever since then, Philadelphia children have gotten fewer cavities.

* * *

One day in 1946, I visited Byberry, the notorious state hospital for the severely mentally ill. Its budget was so low that the hospital was nothing more than a human warehouse. Byberry was in the farthermost reaches of Philadelphia. Out of sight, out of mind. The state neglected it. On this day, I joined a group of state legislators on a tour of the woefully underfunded institution.

The hospital director, Dr. Eugene Sielke, took us into Ward B, a snakepit for the most violent and uncontrollable patients. It was usually locked and closed to the public. The effect on me was shattering. After phoning in a routine story on the legislators' visit, I returned to the office and poured out my feelings in a personal account. My story, "The Shame of Byberry Jolts a Case-Hardened Reporter," was published on the *Bulletin*'s editorial page. It was rare for the paper to allow one of its reporters such latitude. The story won an award from the Fourth Estate Square Club and earned me a $5 bonus.

Byberry was a horrible hospital and its mistreatment of patients reflected public attitudes toward the mentally ill in those days. Yet I remember one incident there that was truly funny. Dr. Francis C. Grant, one of the country's most eminent brain surgeons, often operated without charge on Byberry patients—pro bono publico. After a lengthy, difficult operation one day, he felt the need to unwind outdoors. Still in operating garb and with his green mask pushed back over his forehead, he walked out of the building and strode briskly around the grounds to the main gate on U.S. Route 1.

Two Philadelphia policemen happened to be driving by in their patrol car. They stopped and asked him who he was and what he was doing.

"I'm Dr. Grant," said the man whom everyone called Chubby. "I have just completed a brain operation on a patient and I'm relaxing and getting some fresh air."

Sure, of course, said the cops. Just get in the car and come along quietly with us.

Chubby said, "No, I really am Dr. Grant and I did just finish a brain operation."

Yes, yes, said the cops. Come along quietly. Chubby got into the patrol car and returned obediently to Byberry's main building where the policemen discovered that he really was Dr. Francis C. Grant, the prominent neurosurgeon.

That's another story I couldn't write for the *Bulletin*.

Chapter 4

A Leek in the Soup is Worth Two in the Garden

By Rex Polier

HIDDEN AT ONE END OF THE L-SHAPED NEWS-ROOM of the old *Bulletin* Building like discarded bric-a-brac in a dusty attic was "Features," a repository of everything deemed unimportant by the news staff. From this outpost issued film and theater criticism, symphony reviews and a television column as well as columns on cooking, gardening, home furnishing, society news and other matters of special interest to women, for in those days "women's news" was segregated in the *Bulletin* and in most other big-city papers.

It was in this atmosphere in 1942 that I began my career with the quaint evening paper that became successful by focusing on the humdrum. As I quickly discovered, appearances can be deceiving. Deployed among the baggage in our journalistic linen closet was a staff of delightful, unconventional characters who made my apprenticeship a joy and produced a lifetime of fond memories.

To begin with there was Paul Cranston, the features editor who was regarded as an eccentric genius by the publisher but as Satan on earth by some of his aggrieved staff. Though he dressed fastidiously in a homburg and tailored topcoat and was said to have descended from the family for which the town in Rhode Island was named, Cranston delighted in posing as tough, sardonic and cynical, the *Bulletin*'s Humphrey Bogart. He had once been stage manager for George White's "Scandals" on Broadway, or so we were told, and his reputation in "Features" was that of a ladies' man and a regular at the city's night spots.

Cranston spent as little time as possible creating features. He needed to complete the job quickly so that he could indulge his fancy for racetrack wagering. Betting on horses seemed to be an obsession with this editor. On most days, he would arrive at his desk shortly before noon and immediately start writing assigned stories. He was superbly organized and carried in his head what needed to be done and who should do it. One by one, he would summon staffers to his side, make assignments and give copy deadlines. In a matter of minutes, with everything in place for the next day's paper, he would turn over responsibilities to his faithful assistant, a gentle newsroom veteran named Jack Fleet.

After that came the real substance of Paul Cranston's day. A short, pudgy figure would shuffle into the department shortly after noon, eyes almost closed from poundings he had taken as a lightweight boxer. Clutching the *Daily Racing Form,* he would stumble toward the editor's desk, his few remarks unintelligible to all but Cranston. Once seated, Harry Blitman, to give him a name, would open the horseplayers' bible, and the two would pore over the day's races at nearby tracks. Woe betide anyone who might attempt to interrupt this communion. About 12:30 PM, Cranston and Blitman would leave for the track...never to return that day. The rest was up to the good soldier, Jack Fleet.

There was never any question about Cranston's intelligence, although he went to great lengths to conceal it. He was both an editor of exceptional flair and a fine writer. Every so often we would see in a magazine a beautiful piece that he had written, and the contrast between his tough-guy image and the lyrical writing which revealed his warmth and humanity was a continuing source of wonderment. He once got a tiny duck for Easter, raised it in his bathtub and wrote a wonderful magazine piece about it. When the duck outgrew the bathtub, Cranston put it in his car and drove to a farm in New Jersey where he gave the farmer $50 in exchange for a promise to look after the duck as long as it lived.

Such a colorful figure could only exist in a grandiose manner, and Paul Cranston did.*

* * *

Another editor I'll never forget was a bald-headed pixie named Dudley Jenkins, who read copy, checked crossword puzzles, scrutinized the comics for off-color art and handled myriad other details on the Features desk. Jenkins was said to have been the black sheep of a prominent family in a Philadelphia suburb. I remember him as an iconoclastic cherub who gossiped

*He collapsed at Garden State racetrack on May 3, 1951, and died that night in a hospital. He was 45 years old. For another view of Paul Cranston, see "Escaping the Monkey Cage," by Polly Platt.

endlessly about the scandalous behavior of Philadelphia's first families and the venality of its politicians and whose repudiation of all governments and organized religions was offered nonstop to all who would listen as he chain-smoked cigarettes.

Outside the office, he led a curious, lonely life. Divorced from an attractive Japanese woman, he showered affection on their daughter, Patsy, a Broadway actress. He drank a great deal but held booze admirably. He was often short of money and on one occasion, flat broke and in need of a vacation, he spent two weeks living with a clam digger in the digger's shack at the New Jersey shore.

It's a shame that his talents were wasted. There was a publishing house in Philadelphia that paid $25 for one-act plays, and it bought many from Dudley Jenkins. Whenever he was short of money, he would dash off a one-acter and sell it at the publisher's cut-rate price. I always thought of his transactions as the literary equivalent of selling blood.

Just when Jenkins seemed beyond redemption, he met a woman of his age whom he might have been expected to scorn. She was a Christian gentlewoman who never used alcohol. She was also well educated, like Jenkins, and charming, and as he began taking her to films and concerts, his personality changed. His opinions, previously outrageous, became tempered with reason and his perverse outlook on life mellowed. There was even talk of marriage. It is wonderful to report that his few remaining years were happy ones. On a beautiful autumn afternoon while the two were motoring up the West River Drive in Philadelphia, their vehicle was struck head-on by an approaching car. Dudley Jenkins and his beloved died instantly.

* * *

Joan Woollcott, a young Features reporter with a freckled face, a pug nose and a lot of zip, enlivened the department in her few years there. She was full of bright conversation but never mentioned her illustrious uncle, Alexander Woollcott, the sharp-tongued journalist, drama critic and writer for the *New Yorker* magazine. George Kaufman and Moss Hart created a colorful, Woollcott-like character in their 1939 hit play, *The Man Who Came To Dinner*. Woollcott's niece was Dudley Jenkins' favorite combatant. She was an outspoken liberal, while Jenkins stood firmly on the side of conservatism. That was strange considering the unconventional life he lived. She was immensely fond of the little man with the neat mustache and called him "Popsy," which seemed to please him. You might say she played Sissy Spacek to his Topper. The pair would have been smash hits on radio and TV talk shows had such shows existed then.

Joan's husband was a school teacher active in the teachers union, which Dudley insisted was a creation of the Politburo. She was addicted to cigarettes and seemed to be constantly enveloped in clouds of smoke. She also appeared always to be well along in perpetual pregnancies. Bets were that Joan's next would be delivered in the city room. Cranston even proposed that the paper buy him rubber gloves in anticipation of the blessed event, but they weren't needed.

* * *

For many years, a *Bulletin* staffer whose byline was "R.E.P. Sensenderfer" wrote its theater reviews. It was a part-time job; Sensenderfer was regularly employed in the Sports department. With his full crop of white hair and benign smile, he could have made a career playing Santa Claus. And in fact that was how he was perceived by the New York press agents. Sensenderfer reported on potential hits at Philadelphia's six legitimate theaters, and his reviews were always gently phrased. He seldom had a sharp word for any production, no matter how terrible it might have been. It is no wonder that the press agents spoke of him as "good old Bob down there in Philadelphia." But the day after a show's premiere, Bob would be back in the Sports department.

To my knowledge, Bob Sensenderfer never panned a show but Al Bendiner often did. Not with words but with drawings. Bendiner, a brilliant artist and a theater addict, delighted in sketching stage goings-on for publication in the paper on the day after a show's opening. He was skilled at tipping off readers when he witnessed a stinker. His favorite signal was the faint outline of a cat, obviously defunct, lying on its back with its legs stretched stiffly aloft. The cognoscenti looked for the poor creature; it was Bendiner's way of telling them that the tryout at the Schubert was no good.

Naturally, his cats brought protests from the theater producers, but to no avail. Although Bendiner enjoyed the occasional brouhahas, they made poor Jack Fleet's life a nightmare. Early every morning after a theater opening, he would dash to the composing room to inspect Bendiner's panel for signs of the offensive cat. There was no censoring Bendiner, a nationally recognized caricaturist, but checking his drawings before publication was just one of Fleet's numerous chores. He actually seemed to enjoy his purgatory and spent more and more time fussing over details. A passionate music lover, Fleet once built his own piano. On his retirement, he left a file about 18 inches high with countless memos and other paperwork dating back to the 1940s.

* * *

For many years, the *Bulletin*'s film critic was a native Chicagoan named Laura Lee. An independent soul, she disguised herself as a man to march in the New Year's Day Mummers Parade in Philadelphia back when only men participated. She was well known and widely respected in Hollywood. When Lucille Ball, the red-haired comedienne, learned that the *Bulletin*'s critic did not own a television set, she pleaded with her to accept the gift of one for the sake of her "education." But Laura Lee declined, saying she saw no reason to own one. Shortly after the passing of her beloved artist husband, this vivacious woman, alone and despondent, committed suicide one New Year's Eve in Florence, Italy.

* * *

I remember Barbara Barnes as a fluttery, soft-spoken woman with a slight tic like actress Billie Burke. She might have been a Philadelphia socialite dabbling in journalism. But in her case as in that of others in this weird and wonderful cast of characters, appearances were deceiving. Born in 1898, she had grown up in a posh suburb of Philadelphia, attended an exclusive private school and studied at the Pennsylvania Academy of the Fine Arts. In the 1920s and '30s, while raising two sons, she ran a business whose workers handpainted lampshades, and she served as an official of the Works Progress Administration (WPA).

When she was nearly 40 years old, she prepared for a career in journalism by writing stories at home and then reading them aloud to her cook. If the cook questioned a word she had written, Barbara crossed it out and inserted another. Journalism was a man's world then, but there was no stopping Barbara Barnes. During World War II, she worked overseas as a freelance correspondent and covered the homefront with reports on women toiling in munitions factories. She also prepared a radio series on the postwar work of the American Friends Service Committee.

When I got to know her after the war, her focus at the *Bulletin* was on home furnishings. Her writings in that field won numerous awards. But her boss, the malevolent Cranston, seemed to resent everything she did. He would look up from her copy and order Barbara to come to his desk. Tossing her story back at her, he would snarl:

"Barbara, what is this shit?"

Barbara always retained her ladylike composure just as Agnes Irwin girls have always been taught to do. But back at her desk, she would exclaim: "He's the foulest-mouthed man I have ever heard."

Although Barbara Barnes was her *Bulletin* byline, her actual full name was Barbara Mifflin Borie Murdoch.*

* * *

Three other women staffers helped to create a marvelous working atmosphere at the *Bulletin*. Frances Blackwood, handsome, patrician and white-haired, instructed Philadelphia ladies in the culinary arts for many years. She not only wrote authoritatively about cooking, but answered readers' questions by telephone. Much merriment ensued in Features when a frantic reader once phoned to say that she was baking a cake for a dinner party and Frances' recipe wasn't working. It was up to Frances to stave off the impending social disaster, which she did in a calm manner that reflected her breed-

---

Editor's Note: Barbara Barnes died at 98 in 1996.

ing. There were numerous such episodes. However, Frances was not only charming but naive. She failed to recognize occasional double entendres in her writing. On one occasion, for example, she began a piece: "A leek in the soup is worth two in the garden." That sent Dudley Jenkins and another copy reader named Jack Brady into paroxysms of laughter.

Blanche Krause, the fashion editor, was a feisty dame fond of one-liners. Returning from Manhattan one afternoon, she proclaimed: "New York career women look like they eat their young." Such a bald statement wouldn't raise an eyebrow today, but back then few women spoke that way. Especially in staid Philadelphia.

Blanche delighted in taking sly digs at Cranston, making sure he didn't overhear her. Every so often he would tell a struggling staffer how to write a story. His advice was always the same: "Pretend you're writing a letter to someone. Write 'Dear Joe' and then just go on from there." Blanche never needed help with her stories but, observing the scene, her brown eyes would sparkle mischievously. "Did he tell you to write a Dear Joe letter?" she would inquire of the reporter, choking with merriment.

The fashion editor did not suffer fools gladly, but she enjoyed exposing the ignorance of some of the *Bulletin*'s top editors, all of whom, of course, were men. She often repeated the story of a none-too-bright assistant managing editor who questioned a story on furniture that she had written. The paper had cautioned its writers not to give products a free ride by mentioning them gratuitously. In her article, Blanche had referred to furniture by Duncan Phyfe, the Scottish-born American cabinetmaker whose 19th-century shop was one of the first to use factory methods of furniture construction. However, the reference was lost on the dim-witted editor.

"Blanche, you've been around here long enough to know our policy," he said. "Who is this guy Duncan Pife?"

Helen Mankin, who worked next door in the Sports department, was one of the first women in the nation to be hired as a sportswriter. Her coverage was limited generally to women's tennis and lacrosse. She scurried about our end of the corridor radiating good cheer and amusing her grizzled male counterparts. They loved her, tolerated her and, without admitting it, were terribly proud of her.

She also was wonderfully innocent. Covering an out-of-town tennis match one day, she wired that play had been interrupted by "two pigeons fighting above the court." The sports editor could not resist wiring back: "Look again, Helen. Those pigeons are not fighting."

Late in life, Helen married a widower named Stanley Lovegrove. He had been a staff artist at the *Bulletin*. She returned from their honeymoon bubbling with good spirits. Asked about details, Helen chirped: "We did everything the old-fashioned way."

Roars of obscene laughter arose.

* * *

About the time I joined the paper, Max de Schauensee became the *Bulletin*'s music critic. From the late 1940s to the 1970s, he served in that role, and his knowledge of classical music made him one of the country's premier critics. Like many other members of the staff, however, he was more interesting in himself than much of the stuff he wrote about.

Austrian-born Max was the consummate European in background, education, cultural outlook and values. His father was a Papal Knight, and Max and his brother were both barons. But Max's fascination with baseball reflected his Americanization. He was a slim man with a long, lean face and thinning black hair. His horn-rimmed glasses gave him the look of a pedagogue and his clothes were unpretentious. He spoke in a soft, cultured voice with the slightest trace of an accent.

I happened to be at my desk late one afternoon when I first saw Max. He was hunched over an old typewriter, hunting and pecking out an employment application. My first impression was that of a drifter down on his luck looking for a job. I would never have guessed the truth. Nor did Max make a show of his knowledge of the classical music world.

He lived as a bachelor in a downtown apartment surrounded by recordings, books and baseball memorabilia, for the game was his second love. He knew most of the leading musical artists, and many would visit him. But regardless of who his visitors were or what they did, Max greeted them as if they were royalty.

My favorite story concerns a visit by a once outstanding Italian opera singer who had fallen on hard times. Max took him to lunch in a hotel dining room and summoned the waiters to his table.

"I want all of you to meet one of the great singers of our time," he said, pointing to his guest. Then he introduced him. I'm told the poor old fellow rose, sobbing, and embraced Max. I'm sure he was sent on his way with a few lira. But how much more important for his self-respect was the recognition accorded him by Max de Schauensee, a fine music critic and a marvelous human being.

Chapter 5

Of Pigeons, "Peanuts" and "Pogo"

By James Smart

FROM THE 1920s TO THE 1950s, more than two dozen graduates of one Philadelphia high school—Northeast at 8th Street and Lehigh Avenue—became top *Bulletin* reporters and editors. In that period, the city's public schools were highly regarded nationally. And all-male Northeast was one of the best.

A single *Bulletin* editor was largely responsible for the school's journalistic aura. William B. Craig emigrated from Scotland as a boy and was graduated from Northeast at age 15 in 1895. He then began working as a reporter for the *Evening Call* at a salary of nothing a week. A year later, the *Call* became the first evening paper to dissolve under pressure from the booming McLean *Bulletin*.

Craig moved to the *Star*, was paid actual money and saw the paper collapse in 1900. He joined the *Bulletin* briefly, jumped to the *North American* as assistant city editor, but two years later was back at the *Bulletin* for good. He was named city editor at 26 and managing editor at 41.

Craig became a *Bulletin* hero with a career-risking move in 1918, when the telegraph wires hummed with a false report that the Great War was over. The other Philadelphia dailies rushed extra editions onto the street. Craig's instinct was to hold back on the story, despite objections from subordinates. Late in the afternoon, when the truth was announced in Washington, the other newspapers had journalistic egg on their faces, while Craig's *Bulletin* front-page headline smugly announced, "Armistice Not Signed; False Rumor Stirs Nation."

Encouragement from Craig brought aspiring journalists from Northeast High School to the *Bulletin*, year after year. Most started at rock bottom as copy boys, running newsroom errands and, especially, carrying copy from the staff typewriters to the editors' desks. (The school is co-ed today and in a different location, and no newspaper persons of note have emerged since the *Bulletin* folded, but, perhaps significantly, the school has produced one Philadelphia television news anchor, three TV sports reporters and one radio news reporter.) Craig retired in 1948, just before I got my diploma from Northeast and started running copy at the *Bulletin* for $25 a week.

About 25 copy boys, most of us self-anointed writers waiting to be "discovered," did a variety of jobs. We made sure that every staff member had on his desk a spike on which to impale his notes and carbon copies. We cleared the spikes daily and filed each writer's work. We kept a filled glue pot on every desk, and gave the gummed-up pots and brushes a weekly scouring in hot water, a messy job.

Even messier was making "books," on which deadline news stories were written. A book consisted of an 8 1/2 by 11-inch piece of cheap wood-pulp copy paper, folded in half; inside were placed six 8 1/2 by 5 1/2-inch sheets of thin tissue paper and four thick pieces of double-sided carbon paper. Books were used by rewritemen to grind out copy in short "takes," accelerating the news production process. The copy boys took the folded-over original and carbon to the city desk, dumped the gummy carbon paper into a basket for reuse, and stuck the six other carbons on spikes for distribution to top editors, the Associated Press office downstairs, and to WCAU radio, owned by the *Bulletin*, for use in writing radio news.

Copy boys tore sheets of incoming copy from the clattering Teletype machines and took it to the proper editors; the machines typed out news that arrived over telephone lines from city, state, national and international sources, through press services and the *Bulletin*'s own people in Harrisburg and Washington.

One boy stood in the "slot" behind the chief copy reader, inside a ring of copy readers at a circular desk. When the slot man finished with a piece of copy and gruffly snapped "Boy!" the copy boy grabbed the copy, folded it in a deft motion we all learned quickly, stuffed it in a leather cylinder and dropped it into a pneumatic tube. A pull of a lever sent it to the typesetters one floor above.

There were dozens of other details taken care of by copy boys. We brought writers "clips," files of clippings of previously published material, from the library (the *Bulletin* never was so undignified as to call its library a "morgue"). The library was one floor below the newsroom; writers' request slips were sent down and the envelopes of clips brought up on a hand-hauled wooden dumb-waiter.

We ran errands between the newsroom and *Bulletin* offices in City Hall and local and federal courthouses. We went to the bus or railroad terminals to get packages of photos or manuscripts sent by distant correspondents, slipping a few bucks to the conductor or bus driver who acted as courier.

Copy boys who had been identified as self-starters were given such tasks as punching the endless paper tapes that sent news headlines scrolling in electric letters along the five Flashcast signs the *Bulletin* operated at important intersections around the city. The copy boy cooped up in a tiny darkroom processed incoming wirephotos from the United Press news service. Various departments—sports, features, photo, art, editorial page—had their own boys with specialized jobs.

We were elements in an intricate set of activities that produced seven daily editions—more than 750,000 copies ranging usually from 64 to 96 pages. The process astonished me.

Suppose a writer finished a front-page article and yelled "Boy!" at the 9:20 AM deadline for the first edition. A boy took the copy to the city desk, where decisions like headline size were made. Another copy boy moved it to the slot man, who tossed it to a copy reader to check spelling, punctuation, grammar and style and write a headline. The slot man next handed it to the boy who sent it to the composing room. The "copy cutter" chopped it into short lengths and it was distributed to several Linotype operators to speed up the typesetting process. The still-hot lines of type were assembled in order and placed in position in the metal front page.

Like other pages, the heavy type form was moved on cumbersome rolling tables to big machines that made mats, cardboard-like molds, of the pages. The mats were dropped down chutes to the sub-basement pressroom, where they were used to mold curved metal plates that fastened on the rollers of the three-story-high presses. The presses printed the newspapers, which rolled out on conveyors to be bundled and loaded into waiting trucks.

And that news article, finished at 9:20, was on sale at downtown news-stands at 10 AM.

In September 1948, I was offered an unusual job. The *Bulletin* had a feature called Heigh-De-Ho, which published daily contributions by school children, mostly high schoolers. It had been started in the 1930s by Harold Fox, under the punny pseudonym of Hy High, Jr. Fox was discharged because of a scandal that, in the sedate *Bulletin* tradition, I will discreetly not detail. The editorship, and the sobriquet Hy High, Jr., was assumed by his assistant, Dorothy Bomberger, daughter of a former president of Ursinus College.

Dorothy's office was always open to school kids, and particularly on Saturdays, was full of aspiring teenage writers and artists, whom she encouraged and influenced. Many became professionals. It was another example of *Bulletin* involvement with its readers.

Dorothy was assigned a copy boy to help her. Ed Lohan, the head copy boy (another Northeaster who soon left to join the staff of *Women's Wear Daily*), asked me if I would like to replace the Heigh-De-Ho copy boy, who was leaving. Some colleagues advised me against it on the grounds that the Heigh-De-Ho office was on the 11th floor, out of sight of the newsroom and therefore out of mind for editors inclined to promote copy boys. The upside was that the job had some autonomy and would provide an opportunity to edit copy, write headlines and work in the composing room supervising make-up.

I made the move, which proved to be a good choice. Working with the typography and layout of the column, I learned a lot that helped me later. Apprentice compositors were assigned to work with me on make-up, and I became friends with fellows my age who would later become composing room foremen. If there was a composing room problem with my column, I could go there and get friendly cooperation, often to the astonishment of editors who had never made friends among the composing room crew.

The Heigh-De-Ho office was shared by Charles J. Love and about 50 of his thoroughbred homing pigeons. Love had been brought to the *Bulletin* partly for promotional reasons and partly for practical ones. Promotionally, he went around giving talks.

At schools, Love would end his talk by handing out "Pigeon-Gram" forms on which children wrote messages. The papers were put in capsules on pigeons' legs, and a delegation of children would go to the schoolyard to watch Love release the birds.

The pigeons headed back to the *Bulletin* at 50 or 60 miles per hour, and came into their loft through a window in the corner of the office. (Another 350 homers lived in a loft on the roof.) I would catch the arriving birds and remove the messages. Soon there would be a call from a phone booth full of giggling kids, asking if Harry's message had arrived. I would read the text, "Harry loves Joan," and there would be screams of appreciation.

The practical reason for the homing pigeons was that World War II had consumed wire and other components needed for the relatively new field of transmitting photographs by wire. Homing pigeons were an old-fashioned but reliable alternative. Negatives of photos of horse races at a distant track, or an Athletics or Phillies game at Shibe Park, could be placed in containers strapped to pigeons' backs for a quick trip to the *Bulletin* Building.

Some corporate cost-cutting eroded Heigh-De-Ho, and Dorothy Bomberger saw an end coming. She suggested that I ask to fill an impending opening as copy boy in the Features department. Heigh-De-Ho was suspended not long after I moved to Features. Miss Bomberger ended her career in the *Bulletin* library.

In Features, I did the typical copy-boy chores—running errands, going down to Corson's luncheonette in the lobby to buy coffee for the staff, ordering supplies, and carrying proofs and copy up and down stairs. But the job included editing the comic pages. This was mostly detail work, organizing material sent from syndicates and making sure it got into the paper at the right place on the right day. The crossword and other puzzles had to be marked for typesetting, and checked for errors. I composed the cryptograms myself.

Mats of comic strips had to be taken to the foundry on the 10th floor to be cast in metal. Comics contents had to be watched; editors expected to be alerted to any transgressions of the unwritten *Bulletin* propriety code. Cartoonist Al Capp, for instance, tended to draw voluptuous women in his

"Li'l Abner" strip, sometimes in astonishingly skimpy garments. Consultation among features editors often resulted in my having to ask the art department to add material in strategic places to the clothing of Capp's beauties. Once, when "Brenda Starr" was depicted taking a shower with only the streaming water concealing her unclad form, my immediate supervisor studied the problem and told me to have an artist add more drops of water.

An editorial crisis arose when a woman in the "Gasoline Alley" strip became pregnant and her waistline started to increase. There was discussion of retouching the woman's abdomen, or even suspending the comic strip during her pregnancy. Finally, four editors and I met with managing editor Walter Lister on the emergency. I spoke up for the woman on the grounds that even Philadelphians were aware of where babies come from, that motherhood had not yet been ruled obscene and that I, in my formative years, had observed my mother enlarge while expecting my sister without suffering any deleterious effects that I was aware of. Lister laughed and allowed the pregnancy to be depicted. Some weeks later, he asked me, "How does it feel to be responsible for the first pregnant woman in the *Bulletin*?"

Lister, who had come to the *Bulletin* from the *Record* when it folded in 1947, had been named managing editor about the time I was hired. He was a Cleveland native who had been a top editor at seven newspapers by then, and was probably the only man ever to be city editor of three New York City newspapers, which he called "a doubtful distinction." He was a shrewd, tough, fair boss whose steely, blue-eyed stare demanded the best. Lister winced at cliché journalism, and would paternally suggest to young writers that sentences rarely needed to start with "however," "of course," "meanwhile" or "nevertheless," and that automobiles that "failed to negotiate a curve" actually just plain ran off the road. How some newsmen viewed him was expressed by a young reporter who pleaded to be hired. "Why don't you go back to Ohio and be happy?" Lister advised. "I don't want to be happy," said the reporter. "I want to work for you."

Unlike many American newspaper editors who considered the comics frivolous and juvenile, Lister was strongly interested in them. He was among the first editors in the country to run such future winners as "Peanuts," "Pogo" and "Dennis the Menace." At one point in my tenure, we redesigned the daily layout of the comic pages. A few days after the change, Lister tossed a letter on my desk. It was from a reader who said he had been clipping the "Gasoline Alley" strip and pasting it in scrapbooks every day for some 30 years. Its new position on the page fell right on the fold, and it became wrinkled. Could we possibly change it? "Maybe I'm crazy," said Lister, "but let's move it." So the *Bulletin* rearranged a daily page format to please one reader.

Another of my responsibilities was editing the Ethical Problems column. It consisted of letters from readers asking questions about their social behavior, and answers and advice from other readers. This was one of several columns started in the early years of McLean ownership of the *Bulletin* at the turn of the century. Those columns were journalistic pioneers in reader interaction. There were columns like Answers to Queries, replying to questions of general interest from readers, and Legal Queries for questions about law. There was Motor Pathfinder, in which early motorcar owners wrote asking how to drive their Hupmobile or Pierce-Arrow from their residences to some distant town in an adjacent county. The *Bulletin* printed precise directions.

Answers to Queries and Ethical Problems had survived into the second half of the century. Originally, Ethical Problems responded to the new concerns of the rising working class, earning better wages and having more leisure (with a reduced 48-hour work week). Turn-of-the-century problems were along the lines of whether it was correct to wear a tuxedo at an afternoon wedding, or proper to eat raw oysters while dining out with a young woman. By the 1950s, the column had become mostly a teenage forum, with exchanges of opinion on kissing on the first date or the seemliness and control of "petting." But as before, it was the *Bulletin* providing information readers wanted. I devoted more time to selecting controversial letters than some of my predecessors and increased the mail for the column, which my bosses noticed.

Laura Lee, the long-time film critic, did a weekly column answering readers' questions about the movies. She had the Features copy boys research the answers. Most had just jotted down facts; I began submitting answers to her in full written form. Before long, I was writing the column, although her name was still on it.

Ultimately, I was promoted to staff status. The only changes in the job were a higher salary and a copy boy to relieve me of the errands and routine office duties.

In 1952, my bosses made a great fuss because Frank Brookhouser was joining the staff. Frank had been a *Bulletin* reporter before he went over to the *Inquirer* and became its major daily columnist. His column was mostly about entertainment, crime and political gossip. He was an excellent writer, with one published novel and many short stories of merit, although his column rode more on content than style. After a falling-out with *Inquirer* management, he jumped to the *Bulletin*. I was told to prepare a desk, coincidentally in an area right next to mine, supply it with office necessities and give Mr. Brookhouser anything he asked for. When he arrived, the only thing he asked for was a smaller wastebasket. Frank proved to be totally down-to-earth and became a pleasant mentor, discussing writing with me and in some ways treating me like a son. He once insisted on giving me a box containing the books that influenced him as a boy, mostly classics and poetry. I still treasure them.

Frank subscribed to every major magazine, and when he was finished with them he always tossed them over to me. This was a real boon to a heavy reader who had two small children and one small salary, and would not have been able to afford all those subscriptions.

I had learned to read early. Though my father was a textile worker who went only to the eighth grade, he was a constant and eclectic reader. By the time I was in fourth grade, I had waded happily through his complete sets of Dickens and Mark Twain, as well as Sinclair Lewis, his modern favorite, plus most of his assorted novels about detectives, spies and the Northwest Mounted Police.

I also devoured newspapers from front to back. We had two delivered, the *Record* and the *Bulletin,* and my father often brought home one or two more after work. (The *Inquirer,* the *Daily News* and the *Evening Ledger* were the other dailies.) But I never read all the news weeklies and literary magazines regularly until Frank Brookhouser provided them.

As a young reporter, Frank had covered the stage shows at the downtown theaters and met many musicians, singers and performers early in their careers who got to be well-known entertainers. Often when celebrities were in Philadelphia, they would give Frank a friendly call and his column would be the only mention that they were in town.

One evening in June 1954, there were only three people still at their desks in Features: Frank, editor Jack Fleet and I. Frank's phone rang. It was singer Dinah Shore, whom he had known since she was a young band vocalist. At the time she was the star of a top-rated television series sponsored by Chevrolet. Frank called over to Jack and said that we could get an exclusive interview with Dinah, but he couldn't do it because he had to broadcast his thrice-a-week radio program.

"I don't have anybody," said Jack.

"How about Jimmy?" Frank suggested.

This was obviously a new thought to Jack. "Think you can do it, Jimmy?" he asked. Any reader who doesn't know my answer hasn't been paying attention.

Chapter 6

I Loved Every Minute

By Adrian I. Lee

ON THE DAY IN 1948 when I entered the *Bulletin*'s newsroom seeking employment, the paper was on deadline for the largest of its seven editions. Its "home circulation" One Star hit more doorsteps than any other afternoon edition in the country, and the presses were scheduled to start rolling any minute. I saw Stuart Taylor, the city editor, signal to a rewriteman by drawing a finger across his throat, a gesture that meant: "Get off the phone and write what you've got, we're running out of time."

So this was it, I said to myself. This was Robert McLean's legendary *Philadelphia Evening Bulletin*—it had reached peak circulation of 774,000 the previous year and would never get that high again.

What fascinated me that day was the rising tide of noise, the increasing tempo of the typewriters, the sense of urgency that permeated the room. Over the years, typewriters would give way to computers, and the racket would give way to a genteel quietude. Raising your voice in a latter-day newsroom is like shouting in church. But in the deadline rush that day, some in the *Bulletin*'s big newsroom were yelling.

It all reached out and enfolded me in its embrace. I couldn't have escaped if I had wanted to. I was hooked. Where before I had wanted to work for any paper that would hire me, now the *Bulletin* was *the* paper. I desperately wanted to be a part of that scene.

Over the next 35 years the ways of that newsroom would become as familiar to me as the ways of a much-loved woman. I would discover the crankiness of the typewriters and the tyranny of the clock. My discarded cigarettes would burn holes in my wooden desk, but I would wear the standard uniform of that earlier day: a suit, white shirt and tie. Finally, I would come to understand how a paper that paid as little as the *Bulletin* could inspire such loyalty. I loved every minute, and I would go back to those days and do it all again, just as it happened.

* * *

The *Bulletin* was a family newspaper and when Stuart Taylor learned that a cousin of mine had worked there, he hired me on the spot as a $35-a-week police reporter. I was down to about $50 of the $800 I had saved in the Navy, but I had cracked the door and slipped through and that was all that mattered.

Some relatives put me up until I had saved enough to move to the Germantown Y, where I met a fellow lodger, Jake Cassel, a reporter for the *Philadelphia Daily News*. His room was lined with books by Jack London, John Galsworthy, Poe, Dickens, Descartes. I stared in astonishment. Descartes yet. Why should I have been leery of informing editors that I had majored in classical Greek at a small college in Alabama?

After a month or so in the city room, I was sent to the police reporters' hangout in Room 619 of City Hall to spell the ageless Bob Hofford for a day. While it was difficult to be reverential about a room as unswept as that one, I was at least respectful. After all, it was the room where the sudden, violent deaths of such storied Philadelphia gangsters as John (Big Nose) Avena and Pius Lanzetti had been phoned in to the paper. The big break in the South Philadelphia arsenic murders—a group of wives poisoning their husbands to collect their life insurance—had been reported from 619. This was historic ground...if only the phones could talk. The place was straight out of "The Front Page"—Chicago-style crime reporting.

Outside the sun was shining but there was perpetual twilight in 619. The windows looked as though they had never been washed. Scattered in the room were half-eaten sandwiches, girlie magazines and empty bottles—soda pop, not booze. There was a tacit agreement among the competing police reporters not to drink on the job. If you were drunk when you checked in, chances were somebody would cover for you, but there was to be no boozing in the room after you got there.

Besides, the days of hard drinking in the news business were coming to an end. Years earlier, the *Bulletin*'s night city editor routinely reported for work with a bottle of whiskey in one paper bag and a quart of milk in another, and you could never tell whether he was drunk or sober. Such spectacles were now rare. And, in any event, the night editor was fired not for drinking but for ignoring an upstate murder.

I switched on the lights, got out my notebook and pencils and braced for the worst—anybody who took Bob Hofford's place even for a day was regarded as a usurper, not only by the other denizens of 619 but also by the cops who dealt with the police reporters on a regular basis.

Suddenly, I heard a horrendous scream coming from the Central Detectives office which was down a dimly lit corridor from 619. "Don't hit me!" a voice cried out. There followed the whap, whap of somebody being struck with a hard object. "Talk, damn you, it's your last chance. It'll be the hot seat for you." More whap, whap.

I reached for the phone. Was this a news story or were the cops putting me on? I had to know. I ran down the hall to Central and blurted out what I had heard. The detectives looked at each other. "A scream, you say?" In the back of the room one officer sought to strangle a laugh. He was getting red in the face. I went back to 619.

But my hazing wasn't over. Half an hour later, a detective ran into 619, unzipped his fly, made as if to relieve himself in the waste basket, zipped himself up again and ran out. Thus did I get my baptism in big-city police reporting.

* * *

For someone who grew up in a place called Lemon City with its roomy stretches of palmettoes and saw grass in South Florida, Philadelphia was a revelation. I marveled at its compactness. Up close, it was a rowhouse mosaic of differing nationalities, a web of blood and in-law relationships. There were Irish wards, Italian wards, Polish wards, German, Lithuanian, Ukrainian, Armenian, and more. Families lived and died in their wards. They were buried from their wards' churches, some of them adorned with icons, some with powerful, bigger-than-life statuary and some dating back to pre-Revolutionary times, totally unadorned.

For a long time, these ethnic Philadelphians almost always married within their nationality groups, but as the neighborhoods reached out to each other, people began marrying across neighborhood lines. The city was in transition from a confederation of nationalities to one vast neighborhood called Philadelphia.

For the *Bulletin*, the significance of this transition was that people showed interest not only in what was happening in the neighborhood they were born and raised in, but in their "second" neighborhood, the one they married into or moved to for work.

A fire that drove a family into the freezing night in Manayunk would command interest in Wissinoming, Olney or Fishtown. People all over the city awaited the soft thud of the *Bulletin* hitting their doorsteps with accounts of virtually every fire, every stickup.

That kind of saturation coverage doesn't exist today, nor could it. The Philadelphia metropolitan area now sprawls over too wide an area. It is too complex. No longer can a newspaper blanket an area in the manner that an admiring rival cited in 1918: "When a housewife sees the firewagon racing down Second Street in the morning, she can pick up the *Bulletin* in the afternoon and learn where it went, what was afire, and whether anyone was killed or injured."

Although it wouldn't be possible for any news-gathering operation, print or electronic, to promise that kind of coverage now, the old *Bulletin* did it, day after day, edition after edition. I don't think any paper in the country played to its neighborhoods the way we did.

On any given day we had at least six police reporters or "district" men on the street. Plus Hofford at Central Detectives. This represented an uncommon allocation of manpower for any paper, no matter how large.

The corps of district men was a mixed bag. For newcomers it was a testing ground. For veteran reporters it was a career. The oldtimers had their districts "sewed up" and when news broke, the cops would see that they were alerted.

I began my days with a pocketful of dimes for phone calls, a hunk of copy paper folded to fit my coat pocket, a Philadelphia Transportation Company map and a handful of trolley tokens. I didn't have a car. If I was rushing to the scene of a murder or an armed robbery and couldn't wait for a trolley, I'd hitchhike. And when drivers learned that I was a *Bulletin* police reporter, they would actually drive blocks out of their way to drop me off at the scene. Amazing? Not really. It reflected the trust and affection that Philadelphians had for *their Bulletin* in those days.

Thanks to those motorists, I would sometimes beat the Green Hornet to the crime scene. The Green Hornet was Harry Camp, dean of the *Bulletin*'s police reporters. He drove a green car equipped with the latest in police and fire radios and a telephone to the newsroom. He could drive like a demon and was often "first in" on big breaking crime stories no matter where they occurred.

While the rest of us were assigned to specific districts, Harry had the whole city as his beat. And he was a very good reporter. Once at the scene he could assimilate facts faster than anybody I knew. It was embarrassing to have him swoop down into your district and snatch up your best story in weeks. He kept us moving. Which is probably what the *Bulletin* had in mind when it souped him up with all that new-fangled electronic gear.

On most papers, I guess, police reporting was scorned, but not on the *Bulletin*. Feeding those omnivorous seven editions a day with as much new stuff as you could find was exciting work. It was demanding but never dull. Police reporters got about as close to the grittier side of life as you could get, observing at first hand the endurance, loneliness and incredible patience of those who live on the edge.

If the work was often exciting, it could also be heartbreaking. Knocking on the door of a rowhouse to ask the family for a photograph of their child who had just been killed in an accident was about as much as even Harry Camp could stand. To hear a family member murmur, "Mother, it's the *Bulletin*, they've come for a picture," and then hear the response, "Yes," as if the *Bulletin* had been expected and it was all right, was one of the most astonishing experiences I had as a police reporter. It was as if the *Bulletin* itself was a member of the grieving family. A newspaper that could inspire such a response, that could enjoy such acceptance, should never have died.

* * *

Instead of writing their own stories, the *Bulletin*'s district reporters telephoned the city desk and then "unloaded" on rewritemen who produced virtually all of the copy for each edition. Newspaper rewriting is now a lost art. Today's college-educated reporters want to write their own stuff, preferably big-dome "think" pieces. Their interests extend into esoteric areas far removed from the petty crime news and precinct political reporting which made Robert McLean's *Bulletin* one of the great publishing successes of the century. They don't want their pristine copy to be tinkered with, and many would view the entire rewrite process as an invasion of their freedom of expression.

That was certainly not the case when I started at the *Bulletin*. Some of its very best newspapermen worked on its rewrite bank. Just as police news was the paper's life blood, so effective rewriting was the key to its reputation for accurate, comprehensive and timely reporting.

Once years ago, an editor of the competing *Philadelphia Daily News* said of news reporting, "Don't believe it until you read it in the *Bulletin*." It was the ultimate tribute to the *Bulletin*'s insistence not only on getting the story but "getting it right."

The paper's main defense against error was its superb line of rewritemen. They knew how to write within the exact limits of the information they were given. They never embroidered, they never stretched the facts. If it was a political story they were writing—and they wrote much more than police news—they never allowed their personal feelings to intrude. And yet, and this was proof of their talents, they could breathe life into seemingly mundane stories, making them interesting for a wide readership.

In the *Bulletin*'s newsroom, rewritemen sat like oarsmen in a racing shell, one in front of the other along a narrow table a few feet from the copy desk. Instead of an oar, each had a telephone headset and a typewriter on a shelf that extended out at an angle from the table. I was to get to know all of them—Fred McCord, Adolph Katz, Jerry Dietz, Bayard Brunt—and later I put in a stint on rewrite myself.

One among them was a tobacco chewer and he was easily identifiable. While taking notes from me over the phone, he would quit typing every minute or so and I would hear a tinny "pling." In my three years of unloading police news on Jerry Dietz, I never heard a "splat." His aim in the spittoon was true to the end.

Fred McCord's byline rarely made the paper because rewritemen operated anonymously. Yet he was one of the finest newspaper writers of that or any other generation. He once wrote that the soles of Depression-era job seekers were worn so thin they could feel the difference underfoot between a nickel and a dime. Although McCord's stories were pure poetry, he never took himself seriously. He liked to tell of his earlier years with Hearst, covering the Spanish Civil War from his desk in New York.

He was sent out to buy a map of Spain so that he could write up all the battles from a distance of 3,000 miles. "I did all right with the map," he recalled. "I made only one mistake. I took Barcelona two weeks before it was overrun, but nobody seemed to notice in the office or out among the readers. It was the time of innocents."

We had a somewhat cynical saying, "Let the story sing and put the facts in the sidebar." Fred McCord was a master at letting stories sing but at the *Bulletin*, if not with Hearst, he always stuck to the facts.

Adolph Katz was an emotional man and when huge plumes of smoke billowed from his pipe, you knew he was writing a big story on deadline. Katz nursed an ambition to be an archeologist. When news broke of an exciting discovery by University of Pennsylvania scientists at Tikal, he wangled an assignment to the Guatemalan jungle. They liked him at the digs and, on his return to Philadelphia, they sent him progress reports and photographs. After that, on slow days in the office, he would write feature pieces on the Mayan past in loving detail.

Bayard Brunt was even-tempered—angry all the time. It was an education to hear him extract very detailed information from a police reporter, even for a three-paragraph item that didn't require such precision. "What gauge shotgun was it?" Brunt would demand in his nasal drawl. "Well, go back and find out."

In his telephone interviews with news sources, Brunt's *modus operandi* was like the water torture, one drop at a time. In his sing-song voice, he would dole out each question phrase by phrase with silences in between. It might take him a minute and a half to finish a question. At the other end, the suspense must have been awful, especially if the interviewee had something to hide. Brunt was mesmerizing. I don't remember anybody ever hanging up on him.

Memories of Dietz, McCord, Katz, Brunt and company have dimmed with time, but what I will never forget is how they bent to their labors. For very little money they produced a prodigious amount of copy every day. You'd never see them in the *Bulletin* lunchroom. Instead, they reported for work with a thermos of coffee and a sandwich in a paper bag, and ate at their typewriters. With what the *Daily News* columnist Tom Fox called those "delicious slices of city life" pouring into their ears, the rewritemen were not an appendage of the *Bulletin*, they *were* the *Bulletin*.

* * *

Police reporters tended to stick to their assigned districts. They rarely showed their faces in the newsroom. One particular visit of mine I'll never forget. I had stopped to talk with a rewriteman about our policy on suicides. It was quite explicit: cover 'em. I understood that, but what puzzled me was why we bothered. A suicide seldom amounted to much more than a "nine head"—two or three paragraphs. Considerable reporting was required. Along with routine name and address there were questions: whether the deceased left a note, whether he turned up the gas in the oven and sat with his head inside, or shot or hanged himself, and, if shot, what caliber weapon was used, and if hung, was it with a piece of rope or electric cord, and who discovered the body, when and where.

As I rambled on, I realized I had another listener, the assistant managing editor, Hugh McMillan, who rarely—and I mean like never—spoke to anyone save his immediate assistants. McMillan wore an artificial hand to replace the limb that he reportedly lost in a pressroom accident. He seemed unrelievedly dour, yet if you caught a glimpse of him as the edition was going to press, you would see him direct a smile to one of his news editors, Iz Lichstein. "Well, Isadore"—McMillan was the only one who addressed Iz by his full name—"That's it." That was all, and the grayness that seemed to envelop McMillan would close in again.

Iz, a bachelor, was totally devoted to the news business. Time never blunted his enthusiasm for it. He studied every piece of copy that came under his pencil with childlike wonder and excitement. And McMillan, too, may have secretly enjoyed working in such an environment, though you never would have known for sure. Indeed, his last day on the job was memorable for the manner of his departure. He locked his desk drawer, dropped his keys on top and walked out. Few in the newsroom were aware that he would not be coming back.

McMillan's commitment to the paper was reflected in the remark he made after overhearing my conversation with the rewriteman on the matter of suicide stories. He called me over to his desk. "I think you should know," he said, "this paper was founded on stories like that." His tone was mild and that was all he said. But no more words were needed. A top editor whom I had approached with fear and trembling had taught me a lesson without ever raising his voice. And that was typical of the place. The *Bulletin* was a great teacher, better than any school of journalism I could ever imagine.

* * *

Bulletin police reporters were not issued handbooks on how to deal with the cops they covered. There was no established policy. Each district man came to terms with police in his own way. If there was any rule it was that you were to get the story, get it fast and get it right. Was there police corruption back then? I'm sure there was; in fact, the *Bulletin* won a Pulitzer Prize for exposing an instance of it. Was there brutality? No doubt. However, I no more believed that all cops were sadistic and that brutality was "systemic" (as our competition, the *Philadelphia Inquirer*, later claimed) than I believed that all politicians were crooks.

Brutality could be inferred, but conclusive evidence was usually lacking. I'm thinking of a black defendant brought up before a magistrate early in my time as a police reporter. His head and face were a mass of cuts and bruises, and blood was oozing through pads of gauze that covered his wounds. Even the magistrate (and magistrates were a tough breed back then) expressed concern. "What happened to this man?" he asked. The arresting officer, who was also black, had a ready answer. "Your Honor, he tried to escape and ran in front of a trolley car." It was the cop's word against the defendant's. I had my suspicions but the evidence was inconclusive, and the magistrate didn't pursue the matter.

Early on, I bummed a copy of *The Magistrate's Handbook*, which reformers distributed to magistrates with much the same hopes that the Gideon Society entertains in distributing Bibles, that they might induce recipients to tread paths of rectitude. I read the handbook, but I doubt if many magistrates read it or paid heed to its strictures.

One particular magistrate comes to mind. He was an undertaker on the side. Before him was a man who identified himself as "Major Sneed." It appeared to be an open-and-shut case of numbers writing. Major Sneed—his moniker, not his military rank—had been observed writing numbers and stuffing the slips in his overcoat pocket. As the police closed in, he had vainly sought to throw the slips in the gutter. They totaled some $350, a decent pinch in those days. Yet as the police gave their testimony, Major Sneed bore the relaxed look of a man confident of vindication.

Did Major Sneed have anything to say? He did. He said he had been framed; somebody had sneaked the slips into his pocket when he wasn't looking. What an outrage, said the magistrate. Imagine a law-abiding citizen subjected to that kind of thing. "Gimme those slips," he said. "I'll get to the bottom of this."

The numbers slips were passed to the bench. At the following week's hearing, however, the magistrate insisted that they had been stolen from his car. The incriminating evidence was gone. Major Sneed walked, a free man. He smiled all around as he left. As well he might. For Major Sneed was the magistrate's cousin.

A new state constitution drafted in 1967 wrote the magistrates into oblivion on the grounds that they weren't lawyers. Whether the public is getting a better quality of justice from their replacements, I don't know. My years as a police reporter left me with the impression that many Philadelphia magistrates, though short on law, were long on human nature. They did not believe in the perfectibility of man, but they were a stabilizing influence in some pretty tough neighborhoods. And their lectures to youthful lawbreakers, while their mothers stood by weeping and exclaiming in Polish or Italian, were classics of their kind.

I remember a fire in a slumlord's $1-a-night tenement in the center of the city that burned out the building and killed two people. The smell of charred wood and sodden bedding penetrated as far as City Hall. It was an indictment of municipal indifference to the festering problem of flop houses. This same slumlord had a number of other firetraps in even worse repair. Perhaps because these awful places offered the only shelter for down-and-outers in the Depression, the city hadn't bestirred itself to enforce the fire code.

A hearing on a string of citations against the slumlord was held before Magistrate Nate Beifel, a man of honest indignation. Where other magistrates developed thick skins, Beifel was visibly affected by other people's misfortunes. The slumlord appeared with not one but two expensively dressed lawyers who were clearly uncomfortable in such dingy surroundings. By their disdainful expressions, one could see that they thought the court smelled bad, which, in fact, it did. It had been raining that morning and there's nothing to beat the stink of an unwashed raincoat when it gets wet. There were a lot of unwashed, wet raincoats in Beifel's courtroom.

The hearing went badly for the magistrate. The lawyers ensnared him in the intricacies of the fire code. Beifel twisted and turned in his seat. It was as if the constraint was physical. Apoplectic with rage, he suddenly burst out: "Coffins!" It was as though he had found the one word that perfectly described the slumlord's awful housing. "You don't have ten tenements there," he cried, "you have ten coffins."

The lawyers were stunned. "Most inappropriate," they expostulated.

"Coffins," Beifel roared again. "Coffins, I say."

I could still hear him bellowing as I ran to the phone to make the One Star. My story ran under the headline, "Ten Coffins." I believe it won Beifel reelection. There were worse magistrates.

* * *

At most magistrates' hearings, I would take notice of a certain presence, a generally inconspicuous player in the courtroom drama to whom the magistrate would lend an attentive ear, usually in private. The player was the neighborhood committeeman. He was there to look after the interests of his constituents, and his mere presence was often enough.

Among reformers the neighborhood committeeman symbolized everything that was wrong with the political system. He was viewed as a seedy figure scurrying from exposure, his pockets bulging with fixed tickets and his influence undermining honest government. But of course nothing was as simple as the reformers thought.

I had no illusions about the system of patronage and political activity by city employees that existed until enactment of Philadelphia's reform city charter of 1951. There was a lot wrong with that system (but a lot of good, too) that the reformers either didn't see or chose to ignore. Whatever, they introduced civil service and other changes that effectively destroyed the basic structure of ward politics, vastly decreasing the role of the political parties and of the local committeemen in the lives of the citizens.

What happened was that a political system that had absorbed successive waves of immigration from Ireland, Italy and Eastern Europe was swept away just as the massive change from white to black in the city's demographics, especially in its working-class wards, put African Americans in a position to benefit from that system. Patronage jobs were not there for blacks when it was their turn, and they needed the employment.

The charter-writers traded patronage for a sanitized civil service that set up needlessly tough qualifications for city jobs. Many blacks, no matter how conscientious, couldn't qualify, and earlier immigrants couldn't have, either. In any event, the jobs didn't carry with them any responsibility for improving life in the wards that constituted the *Bulletin*'s strongest support. The jobholders under civil service could pass every house on a block without worrying, as a committeeman would, about the families inside. The charter stood for the new politics of disassociation.

In 1948, however, when I began covering the cops and the magistrates, Philadelphians were still voting Republican, city employees were allowed to hold political positions, and the old order seemed secure.

Just as magistrates ranked at the bottom of the legal system so committeemen represented the lowest rung of the political ladder. And yet most of the committeemen I observed back then were good at what they did. True, they sometimes intruded in the legal process, putting quiet pressure on magistrates, but only for what they believed were good and sufficient reasons, and then always judiciously. They knew which of their constituents were worth rescuing from the toils of the law and which ones deserved to disappear in the direction of the county prison.

They also knew that with the bang of the gavel discharging a defendant, he was passing into their keeping, and that they were responsible for his behavior. Magistrates were not inclined to free bad actors, and the committeemen did not intervene on behalf of poor risks. It was a nice balancing of forces, all to the end of maintaining neighborhood peace and harmony.

Committeemen performed many of the chores that are now assigned to publicly funded social workers. But their responsibilities extended far beyond bureaucratic social work. A committeeman could bestow jobs on deserving constituents, but he also could take them away. He could obtain a stay of taxes for a widow without means. He could go downtown to pay a gas bill for a constituent without a car or a checking account—people were still mattressing money in those days—and maybe add a couple of dollars from the ward treasury if the constituent came up short. If somebody was shaking down the neighborhood *Bulletin* paperboy, he would stop it. Not that the committeeman was particularly enamored of a paper he perceived as trying to put him out of business, but shakedowns impaired the quality of life in his division.

When a good committeeman died, his division went into mourning.

* * *

On a cold winter night, Coroner Joe Ominsky's morgue was a refuge from the wind whistling up Broad Street. Over the front door was an angel carved in stone and inside a violinist sawed away. He was Ominsky's night man, a short, barrel-chested figure with his fingers crooked to the strings. The night's contingent of police reporters would listen to him playing sprightly Hungarian dances while phoning out for hoagies. It was not a Hungarian precinct.

You always knew when an I.D. was in progress. As the bereaved disappeared to the back of the morgue to view the deceased, the violinist would play faster and faster. As the stretcher was pulled out of the wall and the rollers rumbled and screeched, Ominsky's violin man would beat it down. On their way out, the bereaved would bob their heads to him in acknowledgment.

I doubt very much that the new morgue in West Philadelphia would know what to do with a violinist. It's all glass and stainless steel and glazed tile. Reporters ducking in out of the cold? Phoning for sandwiches? Playing a couple hands of poker? They'd call the cops.

* * *

I always looked forward to the turn of the swing man's wheel that took me to South Philadelphia on Nate Kleger's day off.

There, deep in the Italian wards, was the committeeman's committeeman. Dave Moskowitz ran a division that purred like a milk-sated cat. His division was a regular campaign stop for Richardson Dilworth, the charismatic liberal Democrat who won two terms as mayor of Philadelphia and later served as president of its reform school board.

When Dilworth piled out of his caravan, Moskowitz, chewing on a cigar, would invariably confront the candidate. "Ah, *Dilsworth*, again," he would say, and nothing about Moskowitz seemed to irk Dilworth more than the deliberate mispronunciation of his name.

Tapping ash on Dilworth's shoes, Moskowitz would then make a prediction. "I'll tell you right now how many votes you're going to get in this division," he'd tell Dilworth. "You're going to get one vote." And that's generally what Dilworth got.

Moskowitz studied Dilworth reflectively, and I think he was genuinely puzzled. He couldn't comprehend what sort of man it was who would destroy what Moskowitz viewed as a system of service to constituents.

Later, on my return to the newsroom as a rewriteman, I found it easy to slip into the conventional thinking of committeemen as sleazeballs. For all its supposed awareness, a newsroom can be an insular place. And as I laughed along with the others at the standard caricature, I knew that we had it wrong. The reform elite had taken us over. I wondered how we could be so dependent on the good offices of committeemen in maintaining law, order and a sense of community in their divisions, yet so ignorant of what kind of people they really were.

* * *

The *Bulletin* gave me many opportunities to cover great events, but nothing taught me more than my years as a police reporter.

When John F. Kennedy was shot, the paper put John G. McCullough, who would later edit the *Bulletin*'s editorial page, and myself on a plane to Dallas. Like me, McCullough had done police reporting many years earlier. And despite the passage of time, both of us still knew how to cover a police story. For that was what the Kennedy assassination was. It was a homicide—the most important one in this century, perhaps—but still a homicide.

According to the tersely written affidavit signed by Dallas Detective J.W. Fritz, Lee Harvey Oswald "did voluntarily and with malice aforethought kill John F. Kennedy by shooting him with a gun." The affidavit didn't identify the President. It didn't say anything about him except that he was dead by another man's hand. There were 25 lines under that entry, but as far as Fritz was concerned, there was nothing more to say. He left the lines blank.

You might say that my career as a police reporter for the *Bulletin* started with nickel-and-dime holdups in Philadelphia and ended with the murder of a President in Dallas.

But I go back to the early days before the paper's core readership broke up and stampeded to the suburbs. The *Bulletin* blanketed its region then and seemed as deeply rooted in the city's affections as were its presses in the bedrock at 30th Street. Over time, though, the society that the paper served vanished, and so at last did the *Bulletin*.

One thing I'm sure of: there will never be another paper like it.

The last word comes from the junk dealers who, salvaging what was left of the pressroom, found the footings for the presses so embedded that they couldn't be dug out. And those footings for long-silent presses are all that is left of Robert McLean's *Philadelphia Evening Bulletin*.

Chapter 7

Escaping the Monkey Cage

By Polly Platt

MRS. TROTTER, THE SOCIETY EDITOR at the desk behind me, was humming. Bad sign. Either she wanted to leave early, which meant my staying late, or she was missing a deadline.

I hurried through the day's 29th engagement story. It was 1949 and the *Bulletin*'s form was rigid:

"Mr. and Mrs. Horatio Pennypacker IV, of Harvard, announce the engagement of their daughter, Miss Penelope Rittenhouse Pennypacker, to Mr. Montgomery Morrison, Jr., son of Mr. and Mrs. Montgomery Morrison, of Chestnut Hill."

I handed her the copy plus two carbons. She read it, humming. Then:

"You forgot the P! It's Mr. and Mrs. Horatio *P.* Pennypacker! P for Patterson, of course. Mr. Pennypacker's mother was a Patterson! Oh!" She let out a shriek and jangled her bracelets loudly. "Oh dear, it's Mr. and Mrs. *Morrison Montgomery*, not Montgomery Morrison! Oh!"

Mrs. Trotter was a flighty sort of person who wore flowing dresses that seemed to flutter, lots of perfume and *lots* of makeup. She couldn't type a sentence without three typos, but she had an eagle eye for mine. As far as I could see, that was the only quality justifying her position, for her writing, when she tried to be lyrical about a special wedding or a ball, was as bad as the spelling. I didn't know what she was doing on a newspaper at all. If she needed the job, as was rumored, I wondered why she didn't open a gift shop or something.

Miss Reinhardt, at the desk just behind her, grunted and glared at me. Miss Reinhardt liked to think of herself as the Cholly Knickerbocker of the *Bulletin*. She did the daily telephoning that the Evening Chat column depended on. She tirelessly dialed the telephone numbers in her new and already much-thumbed 1949 Social Register to ask what she called "my people" if they had any "news"...a dinner before the Saturday Evening Dance? A visit from an out-of-towner? Something happening at the Merion Cricket Club? Nothing nasty. Certainly nothing scandalous—that wasn't the *Bulletin's* tone.

Once a year, speaking close into the phone in deepest confidence, she could ask her people what they were wearing to the Assembly, the white-tie ball then still exclusively attended by the descendants of its founders in 1745—Philadelphia's answer to the Princes' Ball in Munich. While I felt such telephoning to be shameful, growing a terrible blemish on my soul, and went to great lengths to avoid it, Miss Reinhardt thrived on it. It put her "in" with what she called "la creme de la creme" of her people, and showed them that she knew who she was.

Miss Reinhardt spoke lovingly of her people, and hated Mrs. Trotter, whom she considered unfit for the job of handling them. Mrs. Trotter had only been at the *Bulletin* a few years. Furthermore, Miss Reinhardt was secretly convinced she was only in the Social Register through the accident of her marriage, not her birth. She felt that Mrs. Trotter didn't *care* for her people, and that she, Cecilia Reinhardt, had been unfairly passed over as Society Editor after 30 years of noble news-gathering. She may have thought that this was because she was short, squat and plain, in fact undistinguished by any of nature's gifts. She tried to distract attention from this by wearing dreary dark dresses and no makeup. She must have been around 55, then, and seemed old as the hills to me. I was 20, and had been at the *Bulletin* for six long months of excruciating boredom writing engagement and wedding announcements.

When Mrs. Trotter was out of the office, Miss Reinhardt insinuated to me that Mrs. Trotter knew who was who not from *knowing*, because of 30 years of research on the subject, like Miss Reinhardt, but from having memorized the Social Register. Miss Reinhardt was not in the Social Register, which perhaps explained her reverence for those who were—by birth. For her, my sin of forgetting a middle initial was not to be taken lightly. As for reversing the names... The only reason she didn't cut me dead after this, the only reason there was hope for me, was that my name, because of my family, was in it.

So she limited her signs of disapproval to clicking her tongue several times.

* * *

Mrs. Trotter jangled her bracelets and fretted under her breath. I didn't have to turn around to see the sort of face she was making behind my back. She suspected that I hated being in Society. She also knew that she would be in trouble if I quit. Miss Reinhardt refused to handle a typewriter, and there weren't many young suckers around just out of Wellesley who, with visions of "Front Page" glory some day, were willing to put up with her humors and the utter vapidness of the daily assignments. So instead of complaining, she would deliver the Punishment.

"Do it over quickly! We'll miss the Sunday edition! And then I want you to call up some of your mother's friends and ask them what they're wearing to the Charity Ball."

"My mother doesn't go to the Charity Ball and doesn't know anyone who does."

"Don't be silly, dear. Now just do it." She added under her breath, "This is the kind of thing they don't like telling Miss Reinhardt."

There was another world at the *Bulletin* I could see from my desk. Not the newsroom—that was another planet, the other leg of the L of the 9th floor, invisible to us. (It felt off limits as well. We never went there, and the inhabitants of that planet never came near us.) The Society department was a big enough room for the four desks (one empty) in it. It seemed suffocating, and not just because of Miss Reinhardt's interminable phoning and Mrs. Trotter's humming and fretting, supposedly to herself but loud enough so that one was obliged to hear, and the fact that it had no window. The suffocating part was the "work" that went on in it. In addition, it was cut off from the rest of the world—the world I longed to join—by a door that Mrs. Trotter kept shut.

* * *

The upper half of one whole wall of the office was glass. My desk, like Mrs. Trotter's, was next to the glass. From this cage, like the monkey I felt, I could look out to a vast room full of light and air, with big windows and lots of space between the desks, where real people were doing real jobs, writing real stories. This was the area of Sunday and Daily Features, separated from Society by an aisle and sealed off by the glass wall and the closed door. I could see Jack Fleet, the features editor, sitting at his desk, his long beagle face frowning with the importance of the proofs he was reading. The cooking and gardening editors were phantoms, I hardly ever saw them. Blanche Krause, the big and oddly awkward-looking fashion editor, occasionally appeared, when she wasn't covering fashion shows. Barbara Barnes, the women's editor, swept through often, her long, full skirts cut on the bias rustling past the desks, sometimes touching the cage wall. She always seemed to have clusters of fascinating-looking people around her. She was gracious and charming to them, like a hostess at a tea party.

Toward the far wall was the Sunday Features department. This was three men—Dipper Wilson, Dudley Jenkins and Paul Cranston, the Sunday editor. Dipper and Dudley saw to the mechanics of the Sunday features, preparing stories for being set in type, proof-reading them later, conferring with the Linotype machine operators upstairs and solving mysterious layout problems.

Cranston had the only private office in this leg of the L. It was the same size as Society, also with a half-glass wall toward the rest of the room. The similarity ended there. The large window at the end of the L, onto Juniper Street, was right next to it and seemed to be part of it. The door was almost always open. And there was just one person in it—the boss. Cranston was the brains and the artist of the whole operation. He thought up the stories, and assigned and edited them. He ordered the art work and created the layouts.

You could see him sitting at his desk, alone in his office, gazing for long periods out the window. When this happened there was bound to be an exciting assignment for someone.

* * *

Not much went on in Sunday Features on Monday morning. Dipper and Dudley spent it chatting at their desks until Cranston showed up, usually around noon.

Then things began happening. When Cranston walked down the aisle by our office to his, everything changed. The whole place—Sunday and Features, his private fief—came to life. It's not an exaggeration to say that he electrified everyone. He walked slowly, with a short, heavy body. He was bald, with a face he referred to as an "ugly mug." Such was the energy and charm of his presence, the grace of his mind and the nimbleness of his wit that his looks were as unimportant as the skin of an orange. He was compellingly alive, an infectious leader. Already a legend, to the office he was god, and being in his favor was to bask in light. Whether they called him "Paul" or "Mr. Cranston," they pronounced the words with the respectful care one would reserve for "Sire."

* * *

Paul Cranston, then around 45, came to the *Bulletin* in the '30s as a reporter and instantly made a name for himself, both with his strong and sometimes even lyrical writing and his panache. He would get the story, if it meant disguising himself, camping outside the mayor's office or renting an airplane. Everyone at the *Bulletin* had their favorite stories about his escapades. Once he made a sensation in Harrisburg. He managed to see and persuade the Governor to delay the execution of a man Cranston believed to be wrongly accused by landing on the Governor's lawn in a balloon. The Governor decided that a man landing in a balloon was a man to be listened to. The prisoner was later proved innocent.

During World War II, he was war correspondent for the *Bulletin* with the U.S. Army in Europe. When he came back, his aura was that much greater. He wrote his own ticket. He demanded the post of Sunday Editor, with the salary of the Managing Editor (a huge concession, which made the Managing Editor, Walter Lister, hit the roof when he found out about it) and his hours to put in as he saw fit (sometimes, it was said, at the racetrack). One of his conditions was that Dipper Wilson be brought back from retirement to be his aide-de-camp.

Dipper, silver-haired but nearly bald, looked exactly like Humpty Dumpty, but this Humpty Dumpty was never seen to be even close to cracking up. He could rise to any newspaper catastrophe. He was always pleasant and calm, totally unflappable no matter what copy was lost in the composing room or what irate reader had been let loose in the Sunday department.

Monday mornings Dipper seemed hardly present, sitting immobile at his desk. From my desk inside the cage, I could tell when Cranston was spotted at the angle of the L, heading down our way, by Dipper's face lighting up. I could see him turning to Dudley. "Paul's here," he would say. The two of them would jump to attention and rush to Cranston's office to hear the plans for the week. This would take about an hour, interspersed with hearty gusts of laughter. Cranston was known for his bawdy jokes.

Mrs. Trotter called him "Mr. Cranston." When she had to ask him a question, she hopped about like a bird rushing from her office down the aisle to his. When he walked back down the aisle on his way out to lunch, she fluttered an uncertain smile, coquettish but carefully not too much so—Mr. Cranston was a dangerous Lothario, she let it be known. I supposed the message was more for me than for Miss Reinhardt, but I found it equally irrelevant. Cranston was for worshipping at the feet of, as an editor, rather than flirting with.

My ambition was somehow, some day, to get out of Society and write features for him. I spent a lot of time thinking up stories I could do on my own time. I had already handed in four. I put them on his desk when he wasn't there, with a note and my name. They had been printed without comment, with a fake by-line and changes which transformed them from wooden exercises into funny essays. I blushed when I saw the changes, and learned. I wondered if he knew who wrote them. So far he hadn't acknowledged my presence on the staff.

Something happened a week later. Dipper came to the door of Society. "Paul wants to see you," he said.

"Me?" I said.

"You," Dipper said.

Cranston was sitting on a chair away from his desk, leaning over layouts and other papers spread out on the floor.

"You're the youngest around here," he said, without looking up. "I need to know what someone your age thinks of this."

He indicated some cartoons on the floor of a little boy caught in mischief.

This wasn't what I had been preparing for. I had hoped I'd learned something about writing features while working for the *Wellesley College News*. I had found out I didn't know much. Now I was being asked to go out on a limb about something I *knew* I didn't know anything about, by the intimidating editor I was pinning my professional hopes on. I had read a lot of the Cranston articles in the morgue. I thought I had better say something.

I picked up three cartoons from the floor and sat down in another chair without being asked. I looked at them for a long time.

"I think they're great," I said finally.

"Good. So do I."

It was a cartoon called "Dennis the Menace." Cranston was the first to buy it.

* * *

The ice was broken. Now from time to time when Cranston walked by the cage, he would nod absently in my direction as well as Mrs. Trotter's.

Two weeks later, the chance came that I'd been dreaming of—a story assignment—but as is so often the case, not in the form of my dream. I almost refused it. I had a feeling that if I did, I'd be in limbo until the end of time.

He called me into his office. "We need something different for this Sunday," he said. "Carrie Trotter tells me you're one of the golden girls allowed into the Assembly. I'd like you to do a first-person story about what it's like."

"Oh, but—there's nothing to tell, really." I hunted desperately round for evasion tactics. "It's just like any other dance, only more boring, all the old grandmothers sitting around."

"Don't you have to show up in long white kid gloves to the elbow? Drop a court curtsy to the ladies receiving? Eat an eight-course dinner starting with terrapin?"

"Couldn't I interview someone instead? Like Mrs. Roosevelt—or..."

"Mrs. Roosevelt I was thinking of for next week."

"You were?"

"I want to make some changes around here. Would you like to move out of Society?"

"Would I like to move out of Society?"

"I thought so. I need someone out here to write features for the Sunday edition. I told Carrie I wanted you. She's kicking and screaming. I told her we were going to give her a shot in the arm—Tom Lewis."

"Tom Lewis? In *Society*? But he's on the city desk. People say he's the best rewriteman on the East Coast."

"That's right. He has a lovely way with words, too. But rewrite burns people out; he needs a rest. Society needs someone who can write. You have a few things to learn. Maybe we could handle that part together. So you'll write that story about the waltzing fossils?"

* * *

So it was that Tom Lewis, a great bear of a lovely man who had never been down our leg of the L before, who had never been to a dance and called his wife Mom, who had the fastest, sleekest style of any rewriteman on deadline, and the swiftest grasp of any breaking story, from international finance to the latest Mafia contract, came to sit at the empty desk in Society. I was there with him for another month until we broke him in to our various minuets. He smoked a lot of cigarettes but I think he actually enjoyed the stillness of it all. He turned out to be a lesson in what a gifted writer can do. His elegant, skillful writing with its surprises and light-hearted, well-turned phrases made it actually fun to read what the bride wore and what bouquet she carried.

And so it was that I escaped from the monkey cage to the fresh air of delightful people doing delightful things, going out as the *Bulletin*'s feature writer and coming back to the office to write it up, and then going over

Cranston's corrections word for word. I did interview Mrs. Roosevelt in New York—a remarkable woman, a great lady who excused herself to a 20-year-old journalist for being 10 minutes late. She had only 15 minutes for me, but packed in so much that I could fill up half of the first page of the Sunday Feature section.

After a year or so, there were fewer corrections and then barely any, until the terrible day every newspaper writer dreads when I was blocked on deadline. I was to write about Frank Lloyd Wright's visit in town, an architect I had long so idolized that he was beyond any words I could find. Paul Cranston took over the story and in a flash wrote a masterpiece under my byline. Lister, the managing editor, gave me his first compliment on it.

* * *

That this was just about totally unknown I learned later as a reporter for the *New York Post*. Lister had been city editor there before coming to the *Bulletin* and had daily terrorized the staff. "He never said a kind word to anyone," one of the reporters told me. "He used to pillory the worst stories on the bulletin board with gashes of red crayon." Lister was milder at the *Bulletin* and gave me more compliments from time to time—on stories that I had actually written. It was he who years later gave me the reference to the editor of the *Post*, where I found out what it was like to be a street reporter chasing murderers and celebrities in disgrace; and later, after I married and moved to Vienna, it was Lister who sent me to Monaco to cover the wedding of Grace Kelly.

But it was at the *Bulletin* that I learned whatever I know about writing from the best editor of all. I owe a lot to the *Bulletin* and everything to Paul Cranston. He resigned, after I'd been there about three years, to write a biography of Narcissa Whitman, the first woman to cross the Rockies. He was in awe to the point of infatuation with this remarkable woman, and writing her story was something he'd wanted to do for a long time. He had very high blood pressure and knew that there wasn't much time left. I felt desolate. He was the only editor I'd ever had. Dipper Wilson comforted me. "If you can write for Paul, you can write for any editor in the country," he said.

Paul Cranston had finished *To Heaven on Horseback* about six months later, and soon after fell into a coma. When the word flew around the office, Jack Fleet asked me if I would like to go to the hospital with him. I was grateful. In fact, the whole of our leg of the L went, including Mrs. Trotter—everyone except Miss Reinhardt. I found out later that almost the whole newsroom and all the top brass went too. He died the next day.

* * *

P.S. I don't mean to be nasty about Mrs. Trotter and Miss Reinhardt. They were both good eggs in their way and kind to me. With almost 50 years distance, I can appreciate them as an impatient 20-year-old was unable to do.

Chapter 8

The Bulletin Killed the Best Unpublished Story I Ever Wrote

By James M. Perry

I GREW UP IN PHILADELPHIA in, of all things, a Democratic family, and the paper we loved before and during World War II wasn't the good, gray *Bulletin*—it was the piss-and-vinegar *Record*. The *Record*, as I remember it, did what I think great newspapers do—expose the guilty, ridicule the charlatans, deflate the windbags, report the news—and, all the while, have a little fun.

The *Record* was there when Philadelphians came back from the Big War, and these young men (and women) decided they had seen enough of a city that clearly was still "corrupt and contented." Led by Dick Dilworth and Joe Clark, they threw the rascals out. This was a testing time for newspapers, and I don't remember the *Bulletin* playing much of a role. I may be wrong—this was a long time ago—but I'm sure it was the raffish little *Record*, the only liberal voice in the city, that measured up, until it was shut down in 1947 by a union strike (to this day I can't forgive the Newspaper Guild for putting it under).

After the *Record* folded, the *Bulletin* got their funnies (and a Sunday paper), and Stanley Thompson and Walter Lister as news managers, too. But I don't think the *Bulletin*, even with this transformation, ever got the *Record*'s sense of a paper's need to get *involved*. I can only offer one explanation: the McLean family. They didn't want to be associated with that kind of paper.

Still, we should be grateful for what the *Bulletin* was. It was decent, fair, accurate, honest (most of the time, and far more than Walter Annenberg's *Inquirer* ever was), well-written and handsomely edited.

I joined the *Bulletin* in 1952, after working for two years on the *Hartford* (Connecticut) *Times*. I still remember vividly one of my early days at Juniper and Filbert, probably 40 years or more ago. I was a rewriteman that awful morning when a police reporter called in with a routine story about an automobile accident. I thought I heard him say one of the drivers was dead on arrival at the hospital.

So I wrote a five-paragraph story, sending the poor fellow to his eternal reward. The police reporter spotted my mistake when an early edition hit the street; he called the city desk to get the story corrected. Len Murphy, the assistant city editor who had handled the story, rumbled over to my desk and exploded in anger. Stanley Thompson, the city editor, dropped by—a rare desk-side personal appearance—and cleared his throat furiously. It was his distinctive way of registering displeasure. Fortunately, just before the final deadline, the unlucky driver chose to make us look good. He died, and we all felt better.

In its glory days, in the '50s and '60s when it was the largest evening paper in the land, the *Bulletin* was a local newspaper specializing in the coverage of local news, and it cared—a lot, much more than most newspapers do today—about getting the facts straight.

Those of us who worked for the *Bulletin* back then tend to forget how good we were, and just how honest the paper tended to be as long as it was dealing with the everyday flow of news in one of the nation's most interesting and colorful cities. A major reason the newspaper was so good at its self-appointed news-gathering task was, I'm sure, the city desk. It was a great city desk, the most accomplished collection of spot-news editors I have ever seen in one room at one time. My colleagues tell wonderful tales in these essays about the people who reported the news and wrote the stories for the *Bulletin*, but I would put in a word for the men (no women worked on the city desk) who made it all possible: Sam Boyle, Frank McBride, Phil Schaeffer, Bob Williams, Willard West, Joe Reichwein, Izzy Lichstein, Vernon Groff, and many, many more. I didn't see their likes again until I joined the *Wall Street Journal*, and never in such numbers.

These days, newspapers put reporters through what are called annual "performance reviews." I work for the biggest one of them all, the *Wall Street Journal*, and I have a recent performance review in front of me. The nub of it is a huge box in which every reporter is rated on such things as "quality of work," "oral expression" and being "receptive to new ideas." There are check-offs for "exceeds requirements," "meets requirements" and, kiss of death, "does not meet requirements in most areas."

The *Bulletin* didn't put up with that kind of nonsense. Mr. Thompson would tell you about a raise in a handwritten note on cheap copy paper stuffed in your mail slot. I still have one of them. "Perry," it says, "effective this week, your pay is increased $10 a week as recognition of faithfulness and progress. Thompson." Faithfulness? What a wonderfully old-fashioned concept. Now, we flit from paper to paper, or paper to magazine, or paper to TV, or paper to all three, and some reporters even demand signing bonuses, like a running back for the Eagles.

And if you were being transferred within the newsroom, Mr. Thompson told you about it the same way. I have one of those notes, too. "Perry," it says, "we are going to make a swap, effective April 12, which will put you in financial for six months. The experience will be of value to you, I think, and the young man who comes to us (Burton Chardak, from financial) should benefit by the experience here. Thompson."

The transfer, of course—I hated the idea—was non-negotiable. Reporters did what they were told in those days, and if one of us had said we wanted to sit down and have a long chat about our career goals, the editors would have thought we were mad. Now, reporters routinely confer with their editors for hours to discuss their careers. Some reporters hire *agents* for these negotiations.

Maybe reporters in the '50s and '60s weren't so fiercely ambitious the way so many reporters are today. For most *Bulletin* reporters back then, the paper was a career. You started there, you ended there, and day to day there wasn't a hell of a lot to talk about, career-wise, as they say. The *Bulletin* employed "lifers" like Eph Gorenstein and Rowland T. Moriarity and Slim Sawyer and George Staab and Jean Barrett Lit. Those of us who came to the *Bulletin* after the war from Yale and Penn and Trinity (and the Army, the Navy, the Marine Corps and the Air Corps) tended to look down, just a little, at those colleagues without the benefit of our vast erudition.

But it was these "lifers" who knew the city best. Gorenstein had once been a uniformed usher at a downtown movie theater. When things were slow in the newsroom, he flogged wristwatches. He was a master of malapropisms; his were called "Ephisms," and Bayard Brunt kept a notebook full of them. Once, in a story about power outages, he reported that "high Tennyson" wires had been blown down. Eph described one poor fellow as "only a little *clod* in the wheel." He said that someone suffered from "*very close veins.*" Another time, he called his rewriteman from the scene of a ship collision in the Delaware River. "My God," he said, "you ought to see it. People are philandering around in the water." He called me once to say a man had been shot and the wound was in his "thig." "Thig?" I queried. "Thig, dammit," he retorted, "You know, just above the knee."

The story was told—and it may even be true—that when Eph was covering Camden, across the river in South Jersey, some of his colleagues dreamed up a prank in which an editor ordered him to look into a report that a "Papal bull" had somehow gotten loose and was making its way south on the Black Horse Pike. Cops at police stations along the way were alerted to tell Eph, by now in hot pursuit, that the bull had just roared through town. Eph, it is said, caught on that his leg was being pulled and called off the chase. But the joke really was on the perpetrators, for Eph became a legend among the Roman Catholic hierarchy and when they had a good story to break, they called their Jewish friend at the *Bulletin*.

Reporters for big regional and national newspapers are fairly accused these days of being disconnected from ordinary working stiffs. That was never a problem at the *Bulletin*, or, I suppose, at most big papers back then. As often as not, we were sitting next to a working stiff, probably a graduate of one of the city's public or parochial high schools.

Some of these reporters never wrote a story during their entire careers. Moriarity, for example, would come into the office on Fridays and unload his notes on ace rewriteman Fred McCord. Their combined effort would appear, faultlessly, in the Sunday paper. Moriarity was a master at getting grieving widows and petty criminals to tell him everything they knew. "How do you do it when you're out of town and don't even know anybody?" I once asked him. "Kid," he said, "the first thing you do is go to the fire house. Those guys know everything and they're just sitting around with nothing to do most of the time. They'll talk for hours." I have tried this technique through the years, and he was right: It's a winner.

Lots of people worked hard at the *Bulletin*, but it was never a requirement. James C. Bleloch, the *Bulletin*'s City Hall reporter, was a well-dressed gentleman who never left Room 212, the press room, in search of a story except to walk with stately precision to attend the regular meetings of City Council. He spent the rest of his time seated behind his immaculate desk, waiting for people to come to him.

Along with his counterpart from the *Inquirer*, he also badgered judges and other city officials to contribute cases of booze for the City Hall reporters' annual Christmas bash. There was usually enough left over to keep both of them from going dry for the next 12 months. When I was sent to City Hall to cover the district attorney's office and the criminal courts, I climbed up on my high horse and said these shakedowns were wrong. I was joined by another *Bulletin* reporter, Harmon Y. Gordon, and we put an end to it. The old-timers never forgave us.

Harmon Gordon was special, representing, I think, what was best about the *Bulletin*. As far as I know, he never went to college and never worked in a law office. Yet, as the *Bulletin*'s reporter covering the civil courts, he knew everything. I don't remember that he was ever beaten on a story, big or small, in the three years I worked for him.

Big newspapers probably wouldn't hire a Harmon Gordon today—not enough education, the editors would say. Where's his journalism degree? These days, big papers hire reporters with doctorates in things like Chinese studies, and the reporters who cover the courts usually have law degrees.

But we lose something when we don't have Harmon Gordons at our side. We're all college-educated now and we all make salaries that would have dazzled old *Bulletin* hands. We profited from their ways of thinking and their deep knowledge of the city and its quaint byways.

Then, too, almost all of us had served in the armed forces, and that helped. We had learned a lot there about folks who came from other backgrounds. We miss all of that now. There are hardly any working-class kids in our news-rooms and even fewer veterans. I always like to tell the story of a colleague at the *Journal* who asked me one day if marines had served in World War II. Indeed they had, I responded, and in the Revolutionary War, too. He went on to cover the Pentagon.

Nor would newspapers these days tolerate Jim Bleloch's laid-back report-ing habits. The editors at my paper keep a careful count of all the front-page stories (plus, for the Washington bureau, all the stories on the politics and policy page) written by every reporter, and reporters who don't make the count go down for the count. Big papers fire people—even, during layoff sweeps, good people. I don't remember the old *Bulletin* firing anybody.

There was stress at the *Bulletin*; almost all of us died a little when we were beaten by the *Inquirer*, a paper we all loathed, and it was almost worse when our own ace columnist, Earl Selby, beat us in our own paper. But I don't think it was the Maalox kind of stress we see at big papers today.

The *Bulletin* was a fun place to work. We went to lunch with our colleagues every day and we contributed to the Flower Fund. These days, most reporters eat take-out food at their desks or take a source to lunch at some fancy restaurant. We even take sources to breakfast.

But there was always a downside to the *Bulletin*, just as there was at most big dailies in the '50s and '60s. The pay was lousy, for everybody. Talent—almost all of it white, male and Christian—was never sufficiently rewarded. And for those who stayed through to retirement, pension benefits were ludi-crous. I can remember Tom Lewis, a rewriteman, spending hours, week after week, trying to figure out just how much income he could anticipate when he retired. He never did figure it out until it actually happened, and then it was even less than he figured. The legendary Duke Kaminski, the *Bulletin's* long-time correspondent in Harrisburg, the state capital, spent his career insulting politicians and officeholders. "Governor," he would ask, "could you survive an audit?" But when he finally retired, he found he couldn't support himself and his wife without taking a make-work job from these same politi-cians he had reviled all his life. He killed time in a cubby hole in the Capitol's basement.

Big papers are better about pay and retirement benefits now, and we have made serious efforts to reach out to women and minorities. We are all better for that. At my paper, we can shuffle our pension money around from one fund to another at Fidelity Investments, and we can call a number 24 hours a day to make our moves and to see how we're doing. By the time we retire, we can dip into a fairly nice mound of cash.

There was another big problem at the old *Bulletin*: not enough guts at the top. It wasn't just the editorials, though they gave new meaning to the word wishy-washy. It was the news pages themselves. The people who owned and ran the *Bulletin*—the McLeans and their relations—didn't want controversy. They saw their paper as an establishment institution. It wasn't an elite newspaper—that didn't happen until later when the Knight chain bought Annenberg's disgraceful *Inquirer* and turned it into a prize-winning machine. But the *Bulletin* was set in its ways. Smug. Unwilling to take risks. Philadelphia changed, but the *Bulletin* didn't. Not in time anyway.

For years it ran pieces on its "society" pages about debutante tea dances and coming-out parties. My stepfather was coming home one evening on the Chestnut Hill local when for reasons of his own he began reading one of these articles. Suddenly, smack in the middle, were these wonderful words: "This is bullshit, pure and simple"—one of the soundest editorial statements ever to appear in the *Bulletin*. For the printer, banging away on his Linotype, the story had been too much at the end of what no doubt had been a bad day. My stepfather gleefully pointed it out to everybody in his car and soon the whole train, front to back, was rocking with laughter. My stepfather treasured that story—he clipped it, of course—and I wish I had it now.

It would be unfair to say the paper never tried to step out, for sometimes it did. Harmon Gordon and I provoked outrage and anguish from the city's judiciary when we did a lengthy study that demonstrated most of the city's 21 Common Pleas Court judges didn't work very hard. Criminal-court judges, we found, averaged less than four hours a day on the bench. One judge, we reported, routinely caught a train home at 3 in the afternoon.

Worst of all, we ran little charts showing just how much work each judge had done during the period tested. Judge Hagan, for example, disposed of 224 criminal cases, while Judge MacNeille took care of five. We had little robed figures representing each of the judges. In color, too. The judges were livid, and we loved it.

We ran these results in the Sunday paper's News & Views section, a vibrant journalistic exercise that pioneered the use of color in daily newspapers.

It is extraordinarily self-indulgent for me to keep referring to my own stories, but unfortunately those are the only clippings available to me. So I would mention a series that I helped Peter Binzen write, about the state of public schools in Pennsylvania. It was a careful piece of work exposing all kinds of problems. These days, at first glance, it might be mistaken for one of those mind-numbing series papers stretch out in hopes of winning a big journalism prize. But we actually wrote that series for our readers. How terribly naive.

But other times we didn't do so well.

I remember once proposing a series of stories about how developers were eating up open spaces in what is now suburban Philadelphia at a prodigious pace, and making a mess out of some of the prettiest real estate on the East Coast. Mr. Thompson kicked it up to the executive editor, Walter Lister, always, to me at least, a remote figure. In the ten years I was at the *Bulletin* we had actual conversations no more than a dozen times. Mr. Lister called me into his office and told me it was an intriguing idea, but a reporter wouldn't be qualified to write it. We'd have to hire a city planner, a professional of some kind—an expert!—to do the job. Of course we never did.

Instead, as I recall, we ran what seemed to be an endless and perfectly inane series of articles called "The Zooming Suburbs," fatuous pieces aimed at corraling readership that had moved away from the city. It didn't work.

Another time, thanks to some eavesdropping by my wife, I learned that Governor Nelson Rockefeller of New York was planning to marry a young woman from the Main Line—as soon as she managed to shed her husband. This, I thought, was big news, because Rockefeller was getting set to run for President and his divorce from his first wife already had caused a stir. Now he was planning to break up someone else's marriage. I told Mr. Thompson what I knew and he instructed me to see if I could pin the story down. I went to New York—a rare out-of-town trip—and managed to put several knowledgeable and reputable sources on the record saying the story was true. One of them was the unfortunate husband's mother; she cried.

But it wasn't enough. Keep pushing, I was told. So I went to see the woman's Main Line family. Her stepfather met me at the door and asked me the purpose of my visit. "To find out if your stepdaughter is going to marry Governor Rockefeller," I said. "That's a good story, if true," he said, as he ushered me into the library. There he told me that my publisher was one of his best friends. In the distance, I could hear a car revving up and then the gravel flying as it sped down the driveway. Good-bye, I said to myself, for the future Mrs. Rockefeller was flying the coop. Her name, it turned out, was Happy Fitler Murphy, and she always struck me in the years that followed as a very nice lady.

I returned to my office to face, this time, the icy Mr. Lister. No dice, he said. The *Bulletin* wouldn't run the story unless either Mrs. Murphy or Governor Rockefeller confirmed it. That, of course, was never going to happen, and so the *Bulletin* killed the best unpublished story I ever wrote. I didn't expect an explanation, and of course I never got one.

So the big question still remains: Could the *Bulletin* have survived?

Not, I guess, the way it was when I was there. It needed a general housecleaning—probably one of those awful bloodlettings we see all the time today—but even more important it needed a new attitude. That could only come from the family who owned it, and I don't recollect that any of them sensed the disaster that was looming.

To move ahead, the paper required a sharp new editor, willing to take risks and run down big stories. The curious thing is that after Mr. Thompson died it got such an editor—Earl Selby. Selby was one of the toughest, most aggressive reporters I had ever seen, the author of his own popular, news-breaking column. They made him city editor, but management must have found him too abrasive, too aggressive. Eventually, almost predictably, he lost out in a power struggle and left the paper to work for *Reader's Digest*, a huge loss to the newspaper business.

If management had recognized the paper's problems and allowed Selby to change the paper's tone and direction...If Selby had been allowed to build his own staff and cover his own kinds of stories...If the paper had switched from being an evening newspaper to being a morning paper, challenging the *Inquirer* head on when it was still vulnerable...

That's a lot of ifs. Too many, probably. What grates the most, I suppose, is that the *Inquirer*, the paper we all loathed, is still publishing, and that the *Bulletin*, the paper we loved, isn't.

Chapter 9

From Labor Reporting to Editorial Writing

By Harry G. Toland

ON FEBRUARY 2, 1952—GROUNDHOG DAY—
City Editor Stanley Thompson swiveled in his
chair at the city desk and motioned me forward.
"How would you like to cover the labor beat?" he
rumbled.

I said something like, "OK, I guess." In my
Pottstown Mercury years I had covered a rubber
workers' strike at the Firestone plant there, plus
some union meetings. Given a choice of beats,
mine at that moment would not have been labor.
But for the seven years I covered it, I found it the
pick of the lot, the place to be in the 1950s.

In 1954, 34.7 percent of America's work force
was in unions, compared to 15.5 percent 40 years
later. In the eight-county Philadelphia region,
600,000 people worked in manufacturing jobs,
most of them unionized. The United Steelworkers
represented 35,000 in the area. In Philadelphia
alone, the Amalgamated Clothing Workers listed
25,000 members in men's clothing. Milk came to
the doorstep by the grace of 2,450 Teamsters
delivery drivers. The meal ticket for local coverage, though, was the 9,500-member Transport
Workers Union Local 234. They moved the buses,
subway trains and trolleys of the private
Philadelphia Transportation Company (PTC)—or
struck them to a standstill, paralyzing the region.

On the national side of the beat, the Congress
of Industrial Organizations only in 1950 had
expelled the last of 11 unions for Communist

domination and was still fighting on that front (the United Auto Workers' Walter Reuther was battling Communists and McCarthyism simultaneously). The American Federation of Labor was beginning a move against corruption that would see the expulsion of the longshoremen's union. Capping the era was the merger of the AFL and CIO in 1955, followed by their expulsion for corruption of the Teamsters, the Bakery Workers and a couple of lesser unions. And in 1957, Jimmy Hoffa rose to Teamsters power. Slack days on the beat were rare.

It produced its share of surprises, too. In the summer of 1952, I was tipped that a man named Abraham Goldberg, who had been convicted of extortion in 1948 and barred from holding union office for two years, was trying to organize workers in a Camden toy factory. The restriction was now behind him. But I learned that Goldberg was seeking to persuade the workers to join a union whose New York regional director, John Dioguardi, a.k.a. Johnny Dio, had been convicted with mobster Louis Lepke Buchalter of racketeering.

Goldberg told me the toy workers knew all about this and were unconcerned. I turned in a story for the Sunday paper. But late on the Friday before publication, the subject of my piece called me back, sounding distraught. If we ran the story, Goldberg said, he would jump off the Benjamin Franklin Bridge.

Never before had anyone threatened suicide because of a story of mine. I went to Thompson. Should we run the piece? I asked. He had not a moment's hesitation. Of course we run it. But suppose he jumps? "Well, if he does," Thompson said, a smile flickering across his face, "that'll give us a second-day story." I was relieved—and Thompson anything but surprised—when Monday did not present us with a second-day story.

* * *

The first out-of-town assignment came in November 1952. By then I had learned something of Thompson's views on labor. He had been a standout reporter/writer for the *Philadelphia Record*, generally regarded as the city's best-written newspaper. That chapter of his career ended in 1947. David Stern, its owner, had been the first publisher to recognize the CIO's American Newspaper Guild. Thinking him an easy touch, the union launched a strike that, after more than three months, ended in the paper's demise. Whatever sympathy Thompson may have had for unions was dissolved in that trauma. Yet as a professional he kept his feelings in check. Sometimes he growled about "labor skates," but never did his antipathy to the labor movement lead him to interfere with my coverage of the beat.

The death of Philip Murray, grand old man of the United Steelworkers and the CIO, took me to Pittsburgh. The body was hardly cold before jockeying started over who would replace him as CIO head. Intensifying the scramble was the scheduled CIO convention only a couple of weeks away. Before leaving, I asked the city editor what he was looking for in the coverage. "The juicy, inside stuff," was his sole direction. Oh, one might have said. But there was something about Thompson, his standards, his expectations, that summoned prodigious labors from his staff.

Not much juicy, inside stuff issued from the gathered union leaders at the Murray funeral. The choice for CIO leadership was to be between Allan Haywood, 64, its genial, white-thatched executive vice president given to leading songs at union meetings, and Walter Reuther, 45, the driven, red-headed energizer of the United Auto Workers.

The next phase, at the convention in Atlantic City a fortnight later, was different. Michael Quill, the tempestuous Transport Workers Union president, was both Haywood's floor manager and leader of a bloc of 22 small unions. It seemed important to find out what he was up to.

Steve Galpin, the *Wall Street Journal's* labor reporter, and I discovered a closet with a wall shared by the room in which the Quill group was meeting privately. Hiding in this stuffy cubicle and scribbling notes in the dark, we had no trouble picking up the unionist's piercing County Kerry brogue booming through the wall.

Thus, we could report a Quill ploy to propose an amendment to the CIO constitution forbidding its president from holding office in a constituent union—an arrow aimed at Reuther. It went nowhere, of course, and the Auto Workers' chief ended up winning election with 54 percent of the vote.

At the time, though, it seemed like just the sort of hot stuff Thompson had asked for. Maybe it was. After his fashion, he never said.

* * *

The *Bulletin* expense account, filed on yellow sheets, was an eccentric institution whose intricacies took time to master. It seemed to be a tool management used to keep salaries down. No one ever told a staffer: Cheat on your expense account. But it was expected that some, especially district reporters covering sections of the city, would routinely file for phantom expenses. One reporter bragged that he had bought his summer home on the fruits of yellow paper.

I learned a small lesson about the tab during the surprise four-day PTC strike in January 1953. Quill's Transport Workers Union, in its usual kabuki theater dance, had breathed hard about striking until the afternoon of deadline day. Then, in the Mayor's reception room with management, a tentative agreement had been initialed. It needed only ratification by the membership at a meeting that night.

Someone from Mayor Joseph Clark's office announced grandly that the strike had been averted. And the *Inquirer* played the theme in an eight-column banner in its bulldog edition: "No PTC Strike." It was Philadelphia's version of the *Chicago Tribune's* "Dewey Defeats Truman."

At the steamy meeting of 3,500 union members in the Met, people were cruising the aisles, holding aloft copies of the paper and howling, "Says who?" That spirit carried the evening, despite pleas by local and international union aides. Quill later fumed that the strike had been fomented by "drunks, punks and blowhards."

The walkout began at midnight. For four days, coverage for some of us was almost around the clock. Far more than today, people then depended on public transportation to get to work, do business, shop. Local news didn't get any bigger than a PTC strike. The paper got us rooms at the Essex Hotel next to the *Bulletin* Building at Juniper and Filbert Streets. We slept there fitfully when we could.

Going home to get clean laundry or a toothbrush was out of the question. By the fourth day my shirt was so gamy that it was repelling even me. I went to Wanamaker's, a block from work, and bought a replacement. When the strike was over, I entered its price on yellow paper.

Bob Williams, an assistant city editor sitting in for Thompson, called me up to the city desk. "I can't approve this shirt," he said, pointing to the offending voucher. I explained that the sensibilities of society at large seemed to demand it. "Yeah, but this is a permanent possession," Williams complained. "I can't clear it." I can see now that it might have set a perilous precedent, but at the time I was steamed.

Back at my desk, and mindful of days' worth of uncompensated overtime I had logged in covering the strike, I was raging about the economic injustice of the expense rejection to an unsympathetic colleague. "Put in for it as something else," he shrugged.

I was not in the habit of inventing expenses out of whole cloth, but I was mad enough to take his advice. The next week a spurious cab ride or some other fakery paid for the shirt. The city desk cleared it without a murmur.

* * *

The onset of the Christmas season was always proclaimed by the arrival in the newsroom of a PTC employee with a handcart filled with fifths of whiskey.

The bottles were distributed to all those who had anything to do with covering the transit system. Newsroom brass looked on benignly at this crass currying of favor. And the PTC was hardly alone in distributing yuletide largess. It was an accepted part of the system.

The common rejoinder to any criticism was, "Nobody buys me with a bottle of booze." Especially, one might add, if the PTC's jug was balanced by one from TWU Local 234. So a fifth of bourbon became the norm for the institutional gift, the "innocence" limit. Anything beyond that could be viewed with suspicion.

That limit was clearly breached one December after I had covered a strike of the Sley parking lots and garages. The story was routine, simply reporting the action, its effects and quotes from both sides.

But as Christmas approached, an emissary from Sley appeared at my desk with a whopping gift certificate to Jacob Reed's, the city's premier men's clothing store, and a pure silk necktie heavy enough to round one's shoulders. I bundled them up and sent them back.

Then I called Harry Sley, the company's president, to explain. Much too much, I said. But, he persisted, he did so want to convey season's greetings with a little remembrance. Surely there was something he could send? I told him I really didn't want anything, and then made a dumb mistake: I told him we had this rule of thumb of accepting nothing more expensive than a fifth of whiskey.

Within the hour, the emissary was back carrying an oblong box wrapped in Christmas paper. I took it home and unwrapped it, revealing a fifth of 12-year-old Ballantine liqueur scotch in a square, cut-crystal decanter, worth the price of at least three bottles of hooch.

"He's done it again," I said to my wife, after an explanation. "It's got to go back." Her response, with an eye on the decanter: "Don't you dare send that back. You *told* him a bottle of whiskey was OK."

Well, I rationalized to myself, technically it *is* within the limit. So I kept it and, what's more, enjoyed its rare old contents. But I resolved at that moment: no more gifts of value from anyone. The whole thing had become slippery as an eel.

* * *

If ever a newspaper loved local angles, it was the *Bulletin*. In the "city of neighborhoods," this was no doubt part of its appeal, helping it to sell more copies than any other evening paper in the Western Hemisphere. An office joke was that when World War III started, the lead on our story would be the impact on Kensington.

This passion for local interest infused all beats, all coverage. An opportunity presented itself when I was covering the first meeting of the newly merged AFL-CIO Executive Council in Miami Beach in 1956.

It was a hassled reporter's dream assignment—10 days in Florida warmth in early February with just enough news to persuade the editors that it was worth covering. Even tidbit items held interest. Reuther, for instance, stayed in a motel, hand-squeezing his own orange juice, rather than joining the federation fat cats in the headquarters hotel.

One day the U.S. Navy offered to take the union chiefs on a cruise in two submarines. And—joyous news for the *Bulletin*—the skipper of one of the subs proved to be a Philadelphia Biddle, specifically Lieutenant Commander Edward Biddle, late of Bala Cynwyd.

Someone in the newsroom, eager to exploit this nugget, plugged into my story the names and addresses of Biddle's mother and father, and the names of two of his uncles. I added a paragraph on his education and Navy career. The headline read: "Labor Brass and Phila. Biddle Dive Together in a Submarine."

* * *

The *Bulletin* prided itself on being fair and objective, carrying all sides of a dispute in news columns. The philosophy seemed to be generally applied at the paper. A conspicuous blind spot, however, was in covering unions representing *Bulletin* employees. That cut too close to the bone.

In handling news of such a union, the *Bulletin* could be overcome by timidity and fear of reprisals. That was my experience in 1955 on a story about corruption in Local 14 of the International Mailers Union, which represented mailers at the paper and elsewhere.

Leonard Sagot, secretary-treasurer of both the local and the international union, charged that Samuel Wax, the local's longtime president, had borrowed substantial sums from an employer under contract with the union, a definite no-no.

Sagot, a lawyer, spelled out to me the charges he was bringing before the international union. The Mailers were a small union, but they had the potential of striking—and picketing—important enterprises, including us, of course. After trying and failing to reach Wax, I wrote the story full, maybe as long as a column of type.

When my story was published the next day, it had been cut to five or six paragraphs under what we called a 7-head. And after the early editions it was dropped altogether. Whose call that was I never discovered. Outraged, I blew my stack to Thompson. He seemed to understand and even sympathize. Rumbling and snuffling, he signed off with this comment: "If this were the *Inquirer,* you know, not even a 7-head would have made it."

I couldn't argue with that; the "Inky" in those days was a pretty miserable paper. And it was highly unlikely that they would have gotten the story in the first place since their labor reporter was an alcoholic. But none of that made me feel any better about our handling of it.

Ultimately, when the international union suspended Wax indefinitely— and it was safe—we carried a slightly larger 7-head, about nine inches long and in all editions.

A second example was the five-week *Bulletin* delivery drivers' strike in 1958. At the start of the strike, we carried a long article which included the views of the lawyer for Teamsters Local 628 and the head of the *Inquirer's* Newspaper Guild unit, also on strike.

During the course of the strike, however, the *Bulletin* bizarrely "covered" the walkout in a series of "To Our Readers" reports, written in the executive offices. Some of these were quite long, but none carried any direct reportage of the union's position or its comment. On strike and beyond the pale, it was being stonewalled.

I thought this was a weird form of coverage, especially since the strike was producing interesting news. The paper was circulating a quarter million copies a day through "young entrepreneurs," as we called them. These newsboys and others bought bundles of papers at five cents a copy at the *Bulletin* Building, now at 30th and Market Streets, and sold them for a dime or a quarter each in the neighborhoods. The cottage industry was credited with reducing juvenile crime in Philadelphia by 45 percent in the month of June. But we didn't print a word about it at the time.

When the walkout ended, a group of us were summoned down the hall to the executive suite for a discussion of our coverage. Someone asked if we should now get the union on record. The executive answer was no.

Suppose, came the next question, the union calls up trying to air its position. "I think they will find," said publisher Robert McLean with a distant smile, "that the line is busy."

* * *

When I was asked to join the *Bulletin*'s editorial page staff on April Fool's Day, 1963, the unresolved question was: Who was fooling whom?

I agonized through three days of conversations and soul searching before deciding to take the plunge. *Bulletin* editorials were notorious for on-the-one-hand/on-the-other-hand nonstands. Did I want to be part of that collective dithering?

Years earlier, I had argued with my father about the paper's editorials. "They never say anything," I told him. His point, as I recall it, was that they were part of the *Bulletin*'s genius—never riling people too much.

That was intentional policy and the result was a sometimes ludicrous indecision. Too often, the paper wasn't so much strongly conservative as simply waffling, or ducking an issue altogether. Once, in an election campaign, an aide brought word to Richardson Dilworth that the *Bulletin* had editorially endorsed him. "How could you tell?" Dilworth cracked.

In joining the staff, I was determined to bring more resolution to the editorials, but it was uphill work. During an editorial conference early in my tenure, one indoctrinated staffer raised a hot topic, then quickly added, "Morley, we can get into this without touching on any of the controversial stuff." That seemed to be a prevailing approach.

Morley Cassidy, the page's thin, bespectacled editor, was one of the gentlest, most amiable men I ever met. A one-time public relations man for Huey Long, he told hilarious stories about his time with the Kingfish. After duty as a war correspondent, Cassidy had been the paper's only foreign correspondent. Based in Paris with his wife, Phyllis, he roamed the globe, sending back eminently readable reports.

The staff, when I came aboard, was a collection of assorted but often impressive talents.

Franklin O. Alexander, the genial, cheerful, pipe-smoking cartoonist, had been the creator of the comic strip "Hairbreadth Harry." Alex was widely known for his political cartoon character Joe Doaks—the balding, bespectacled "little guy" perennially at the mercy of politicians and tax hikes. Alexander was no Herblock; his well-crafted cartoons tended to be mild. But on some subjects, like McCarthyite attacks, he could be incisive.

Don Rose, author of eight books and writer of the whimsical "Stuff and Nonsense" column, was a one-time London brewery clerk and teacher. He was almost blind, the result of having watched a solar eclipse with unprotected eyes, I was told. He was the father of 12 and, when he died in 1964 at age 73, the grandfather of 74.

Paul J. Jones, a University of Pennsylvania Ph.D. and former Penn faculty member, had lectured at universities in South Vietnam and Thailand at the request of the State Department. A handsome man of courtly bearing, he wrote editorials and a column, "Candid Shots," and had authored two books.

John Calpin, a former City Hall news bureau chief and veteran political reporter, wrote most of the local political editorials. Not a sparkling writer, he was a walking encyclopedia of politics with a memory of granite.

Melvin K. Whiteleather, a former war correspondent and Associated Press reporter in Europe, wrote foreign affairs editorials and columns. Every other year the paper sent him to Europe to gather material. A humorous, affable pipe-smoker, Whitey fell dead during a Sunday service at the Swarthmore church both of us attended.

Frank McBride, a native of the city's Olney section, had come to the page in 1954 from the city desk. His abiding concern was fiscal responsibility in government. Inured to wartime deficit spending, I naively thought this a quaint obsession, only later to discover its validity.

Gordon Whitcraft, a West Chester Quaker who had served as a lieutenant colonel in the wartime Army Air Corps, edited the Op-Ed page. In his spare time he operated a sprawling antique store in his hometown.

Paul Trescott, Cassidy's assistant director, a native of Millville, Pennsylvania, came to the paper from the Berwick Enterprise. He had, if anything, too much facility; to meet demand, he told me once, he had churned out as many as half a dozen editorials in a day.

Presiding over the editorial page didn't come easily to Cassidy, it seemed to me. He was too agreeable.

Editorials on Vietnam, for example, had been Paul Jones' field when I arrived. Having lived there, he was understandably credited with expertise, and was a devoted partisan of South Vietnamese President Ngo Dinh Diem. After considerable research, however, I came to believe, along with a great many Americans, that Diem's regime was autocratic and corrupt, and didn't deserve U.S. backing. Thus, under Cassidy's tolerant eye, Jones could write an editorial extolling "our friend and ally Ngo Dinh Diem," to be followed by one of mine declaring that "satisfaction with our present policy is unwarranted." The reader could choose.

As much as *Bulletin* editorials were berated, two things should be said for them. Often they were well-researched and offered facts not found in news columns. And they changed over time, sometimes as the nation altered its perceptions, but also because of staff pressure. Don McLean, the Major's son, who succeeded Cassidy in 1965, helped in that direction. And when the McLeans sold the paper and Jerry Bellune became editor, the journey was completed.

But in earlier days, examples of transformation were not hard to find. Take civil rights.

James Meredith enrolled at the University of Mississippi as its first black student in September 1962, over the flinty resistance of the state's governor, Ross Barnett. A riot, quelled finally by federal troops, followed. The *Bulletin*'s received wisdom on the uproar came down to observing that Meredith and Barnett had opposing points of view. The editorial's closing words: "...the fact that the problem stems from sincerely held convictions is the thing which makes solution slow and difficult." Vintage old *Bulletin*!

But a year later, in August 1963, when Meredith graduated, we were calling Barnett's policies "racist" and adding: "That [Meredith's matriculation] cost two lives and the services of 23,000 troops is, in one sense, a national shame: but it has also been concrete evidence of national determination to enforce equal rights." Some progress there.

A month after that, when Alabama's Governor George Wallace sent state police to keep African American kids out of white schools, the paper came out flatly for immediate integration of the schools and told Wallace he should be ashamed of himself. More progress.

The most celebrated local civil rights case of the era was the effort to get Girard College in North Philadelphia to admit African American students. Stephen Girard's will, which established the school, specified that it was for "poor white male orphans." But the Board of City Trusts, a public body, administered the will. City Councilman Raymond Pace Alexander, whose district included the school, pointed out in 1953 that Girard College was recruiting thousands of miles away in order to fill vacancies with white students. Admit local blacks, he asked the Board.

Alexander's point was unarguable, I thought. In 31 years at the paper, I took part in only two demonstrations, objectivity being one of journalism's commandments. But forgetting that for a day, I marched outside Girard's wall with fellow church members.

Bulletin response initially was generally integrationist, then swerved the other way and finally came back with vigor to its original stance. The paper seemed to know what was right for Girard, but sometimes it tuned out the better angels of its nature. The swings may have reflected the mindsets of individual writers or—more likely—the power balances of the moment.

When the courts finally ruled that the school was essentially a public institution and should be open to persons of all races, the *Bulletin* applauded the outcome.

I have a dim recollection of writing an editorial on May 22, 1968, that I think still stands up. This is how it ended:

"Some persons will go to their graves convinced that iniquitous courts 'broke' the Girard will in putting aside its insistence on *white* poor male orphan children. But they forget that it came down to a choice of which way the will would be bent—that way or replacing the city trustees—and the courts, citing law and Constitution and Girard's own intent, made the choice of emphasizing the school's essentially public character.

"The decision seems wise and equitable. Girard should be a better educational establishment for being integrated—can monoracial education in a multiracial society be wholly valid? The Commonwealth's good sense in taking the case to court to get it off the streets seems all the more praiseworthy now. The college's trustees have, with admirable speed, accepted the final ruling and are moving to implement it. The acceptance can be commended to other Philadelphians."

* * *

But what about Dilworth's jibe—How could you tell? Was the old marine on target?

In 1955, he ran for mayor against Thatcher Longstreth. The paper's November 1 editorial, titled "Candidates' Records," summed up the campaign. Longstreth, the *Bulletin* observed, was young (35), "full of pep and self-confidence," but had never held public office. Dilworth, however, had "served acceptably" as City Treasurer and "made a good record" as District Attorney. This was the wind-up paragraph:

"Many young men today occupy important executive positions in great corporations. But they didn't attain directive leadership without having had some previous experience in the kind of business they run. The City of Philadelphia, an enormous corporation, needs capable leadership, and it's the business of the voters to select such leadership next Tuesday."

Was that an endorsement of Dilworth? Could you really tell? In a back-handed way, I suppose it was. Basically, though, more old *Bulletin*.

Four years later, when Dilworth sought re-election, running against Harold Stassen, the paper's choice stood forth more clearly. First, in the title of its October 20, 1959, editorial: "Four Years More of the Same." The piece noted that great progress had been made in the eight mayoral years of Joseph Clark and Richardson Dilworth.

"There have been some mistakes and there is some dissatisfaction. And remodeling the City has been costly," the editorial concluded. "Have we got what we paid for? The *Bulletin* believes that on the whole we have." An endorsement? Not to knock your socks off, but identifiable.

Three years later, when Dilworth ran for governor against William Scranton, he might have wished that the *Bulletin* had returned to its old equivocal self. Its October 31, 1962 editorial warned that Dilworth had become too close to Philadelphia's Democratic machine and might open the door wide in Harrisburg to the pols.

"The Commonwealth's best hope seems clearly to lie in the fresh approach promised by Mr. Scranton and his program," the editorial ended. The voters agreed with the *Bulletin* on that one. When Dilworth took on his final public service as president of Philadelphia's Board of Education in 1965 at age 67, the paper's commentary was almost wholly supportive, at times even emotionally warm. I wrote most of the editorials on the extraordinary *perestroika* he wrought in the school system and made no secret of my support. Under conventional rules of journalism, for reporters if not editorialists, I was probably friendlier with Dilworth than I should have been. It was difficult not to like the man. I still have some postcards he sent me from trips.

On his appointment to the school board, our editorial said, "Most Philadelphians will rejoice to see that irrepressibly candid battler, Richardson Dilworth, back in the thick of public life again. His appointment augurs well both for the school system and the cause of liveliness in municipal affairs. Practically no one would be surprised or disappointed to see him elected president of the new board."

After ending the tour on the school board, Dilworth became a part-time teacher of political science and sociology at Temple University. A short editorial, "'Professor' Dilworth," in June 1972, contained this paragraph:

"As district attorney, mayor and school board president in Philadelphia over a stormy and eventful quarter-century, Mr. Dilworth already has proven himself an able and remarkable teacher. He's taught all of us the meaning of dedicated public service, outspoken candor, high principle and courage under fire."

If the *Bulletin* had been ambiguous about Dilworth early on, then it was not hard to catch its later drift.

* * *

Over time, various leavening influences came to the staff, writers like Don Harrison and Russell Cook. Other memorable additions included:

Adrian Lee, a feisty refugee from the newsroom, who joined the page's staff in 1967. Life in the conference room, with its plate-glass overview of the 30th Street rail yards and the Art Museum, became more interesting. The fold had its conservatives, certainly, but none who argued his case as aggressively as Adrian. You felt at times that you were on the floor of Congress debating a shrewd Dixie senator. Neither of us, I think, budged from his stance; certainly he didn't move a millimeter. But it helps now and then to have long-standing positions challenged. You could argue policy and leadership with him—there was no other choice for me—while cherishing the man.

Michelle Osborn, Philadelphia's first woman editorial writer, who came aboard in 1969. The writer of a news-side column on architecture and city planning for four years, she was brought in to supply a "woman's point of view." Her chief recollection of the page at the time was one of timidity. "Some subjects were allowed, others were not," she recalls. "The environment was OK." When she left us a few years later, William McLean III, then publisher, asked her in an exit interview, "Why do you want to work?" The idea of a working woman not driven by economic necessity seemed foreign to him. It took society's curve some years to catch up to her.

Willis Harrison, a North Carolina preacher's son who came in 1967 from the editorial page of the *Toledo Blade*. When he retired after a heart attack in 1978, he was assistant editor. "The *Bulletin* page was out of sync with its times," he recalls. "The times were rough. People were yelling at each other. The editorial page persisted in being restrained and gentlemanly. It was an admirable effort, and I appreciated it as I got older. But in competition with the *Inquirer*, we were too bland." A meticulous, fatherly professional of the old school, he had a capacity for compassionate analysis and an irreverent sense of humor. Politically, he, Michelle and I were considerably left of the page's center.

Douglas Bedell, another veteran of *Bulletin* labor beat coverage, who came to the editorial page staff in 1970 after two years on the *Wall Street Journal*. He remembers a staff of seven writers who had time to call up sources and get out on the scene before writing an editorial or column. "We had the luxury of time," he recalls. He also remembers a page that was tepid, frustrating, sometimes kindly, in a period of tumult. When he left after 10 years he was the page's assistant editor.

All of these later additions to the staff brought with them a conviction that an editorial, even if it had to be qualified, should set forth a position in unambiguous prose. For the most part, I think, we had climbed out of the pit of equivocation well before the paper was sold.

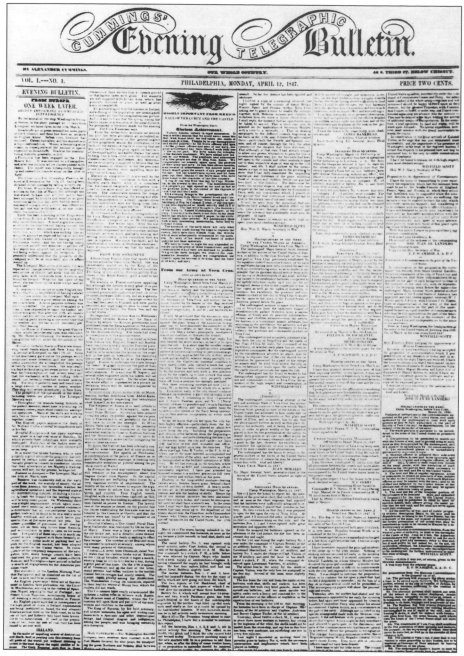

Page one of the first issue of the *Bulletin*, April 12, 1847, with the latest news from the Mexican War. Founder Alexander Cummings left the paper in 1860. After a complicated series of partnerships, the *Bulletin* was sold to William L. McLean on June 1, 1895. *Temple University Archives*

William L. McLean, Sr., who bought the *Bulletin* in 1895 when it was last of 13 dailies in circulation. In 10 years, it became number one. The McLean family owned the paper until 1980. *Temple University Archives*

The Bulletin building at Juniper and Filbert Streets, opposite the northeast corner of City Hall, undergoing a steam cleaning of its facade in June 1937. It was the home of the *Bulletin* from 1908 to 1955. *Temple University Archives*

William B. Craig, who joined the *Bulletin* in 1902, became city editor in 1906 and was managing editor from 1921 until 1947. *Temple University Archives*

Twisted wreckage of the Congressional Limited blocks the Pennsylvania Railroad tracks near Frankford Junction, September 6, 1943. The wreck killed 79 passengers and injured dozens. *Temple University Archives*

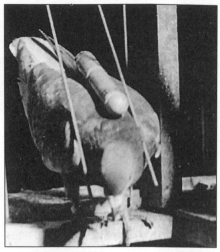

Charles J. Love, *Bulletin* pigeon expert, with one of his pedigreed homing pigeons used in the 1940s to carry photographs to the *Bulletin* at Juniper and Filbert Streets from such events as the Army-Navy Game, Athletics and Phillies baseball games and horse racing at Delaware Park.

A homing pigeon returns to the 11th floor loft at the *Bulletin*, carrying film of a news event in an aluminum cylinder on its back. Photographers transferred the 4 x 5-inch film from cameras into the cylinders inside black cloth bags to prevent exposing it until the cylinder was opened in the darkroom.

Editors at work in the *Bulletin* newsroom, May 1950. A picture editor types captions in the foreground. At left is the city desk, with rewrite men lined up at the counter behind it. At right is the national and international news desk, still called the "telegraph desk." At the head of the horseshoe-shaped desk complex, the assistant managing editor (hand on chin) is in command. *Temple University Archives*

City desk, October 9, 1951. Big stories of that day: battle of Heartbreak Ridge in progress in Korea; Democrat Joseph S. Clark leads in Philadelphia mayoral election race against GOP machine in City Hall for 67 years. *Temple University Archives*

Heart of the newsroom, October 15, 1952. City desk is at right, rewrite men at their long counter, and desks of general assignment reporters at left. *Temple University Archives*

Caroline Trotter worked in the *Bulletin*'s society department in the '20s, left for 10 years, and returned in 1937. She became society editor in 1945 and retired in 1957. During her decade elsewhere, she once was hoisted to the top of a 75-foot flagpole on Atlantic City's Steel Pier to interview Shipwreck Kelly, who sat atop the pole for seven weeks. *Temple University Archives*

Paul F. Cranston was a reporter and features editor in the 1930s, became a war correspondent, and returned to become the first Sunday editor when the *Sunday Bulletin* was launched in 1947. He resigned in March 1951 to complete a novel, which was published posthumously; he collapsed and died at Garden State racetrack in May 1951, at age 46. *Temple University Archives*

Theo Wilson, a rewrite star at the *Bulletin* in 1950-51, pictured here at her desk at the *New York Daily News*. She was one of the nation's top murder-trial reporters.

George R. Staab, irrepressible reporter, who enlivened the *Bulletin*'s newsroom from 1930 until his death in 1969.

Richard W. Slocum (left), *Bulletin* executive vice president, with President Dwight D. Eisenhower (right) at a meeting of the American Newspaper Publishers Association, of which Slocum was president in 1954. In center, Stuart M. Chambers of the *St. Louis Post-Dispatch*. *Temple University Archives*

Dedication of the new *Bulletin* building at 30th and Market Streets, June 1, 1955. It had 562,000 square feet of floor space on a six-acre plot. The *Bulletin* then had 2,500 employees and daily circulation of 720,000. *Temple University Archives*

Publisher Robert McLean, son of William L., Sr., and usually called "the Major" by *Bulletin* staff, speaks at the 30th and Market Streets dedication, 1955. *Temple University Archives*

Donald McLean (left), son of publisher Robert McLean, and his cousin, William L. McLean 3rd, raise the flag at the 1955 dedication of the 30th and Market Streets building. The child is Don's son, Robert McLean 2nd, then two years old. *Temple University Archives*

Walter Lister became managing editor in 1947 and moved up to the new title of executive editor in 1958. Despite a crippling stroke in February 1963, he came to his office, with assistance, daily until retirement in October 1964. *Temple University Archives*

Stanley G. Thompson, city editor from 1951 until his death in February 1959. He was "the Colonel" to his staff. *Temple University Archives*

Henry Yocum (left), then night city editor, and Jim Smart, then a reporter, in the wee hours in January 1956 at the city desk. Note the two-way radio that maintained contact with reporters' cars, and the multi-speaker unit monitoring police and fire radios, which Yocum designed.

Richard W. Slocum, *Bulletin* executive vice president, examines wreckage of his office after the Tidewater Granary exploded across Market Street, heavily damaging the 10-month-old Bulletin building, March 28, 1956. *Temple University Archives*

William B. Dickinson came to the *Bulletin* after covering MacArthur headquarters in the Pacific for United Press in World War II. He became managing editor in 1958, executive editor in 1964 and retired in 1973. *Temple University Archives*

Earl Selby, city editor from 1959 until 1964. Previously, he wrote a daily column for 11 years. *Temple University Archives*

On the day of a huge snowstorm in 1967, Henry Darling, *Bulletin* feature writer, skied to the Paoli railroad station and took the train to work. He was photographed just after reaching the newsroom.

Reporter Rose DeWolf, a soft hat among hard hats, covers a carpenters' strike in Valley Forge, about 1969.

Covering hearings on possible impeachment of President Nixon in May 1974 were the *Bulletin*'s Washington reporters (from left) Sandy Grady, Robert Roth, Lawrence M. O'Rourke, Joseph R. Daughen, Adrian Lee and Robert E. Taylor. *Temple University Archives*

Peter Binzen (left), metro editor, and political writers John T. Gillespie (center) and Ron Goldwyn, in the *Bulletin* newsroom on election night 1979.

B. A. Bergman (left), longtime *Bulletin* editor, with columnist Claude Lewis in 1974.

A modern newsstand at 15th and Market Streets, first of a new design introduced in 1975. *Temple University Archives*

Chapter 10

The Rarest of Rare Birds

By Peter Binzen and Harry G. Toland

JOURNALISM IN ITS ROOT AND TRUNK is serious business. It casts itself, after all, as nothing less than the objective chronicler of the planet's ongoing tragicomedy. But the branches of the tree are something else. As Alexander Woollcott once said of newspapering, it is "a trade which, all in all, is more fun than any other."

The craft—don't call it a profession—therefore draws the serious-minded as well as the free spirits, and yeasty amalgams of both. It embraces more characters per capita than any walk of life short of Broadway. Or it did, anyway, a generation and more ago.

Perhaps the rarest of rare birds at the *Bulletin* when the paper was in its prime were two polar opposites—George R. Staab, an irrepressible reporter who enlivened newsroom life for 39 years, and Stanley G. Thompson, the legendary city editor from 1951 until his death in 1959.

* * *

Theo Wilson, who won a reputation as the nation's best reporter of criminal trials during more than two decades at the *New York Daily News*, spent one year at the *Bulletin*. In her memoir, *Headline Justice*, published just before her death in 1997, the *Bulletin* reporter she remembered most fondly was George Staab. Yet Staab did not take kindly at first to her position on the *Bulletin*'s rewrite battery. Wilson described her baptism in 1951 this way:

There had never been a woman on rewrite before, and George, without addressing me directly, loudly made queries about whether there would now be lace curtains on the city room windows and whether we'd be serving tea and decorating our desks with potted plants. George had a big mouth and used terrible gutter language but I had met his kind before—blusterers on the outside, puppies on the inside—and I let it ride a couple of days. Then, one morning, as I sat down and George began some anti-female bellowing, I turned squarely around in my chair and stared at him. I looked like a little kid in those days, even though I was a mother, and I used a little kid voice for the occasion.

"George?" I said.

"Whaddya want?" he rumbled.

"Go fuck yourself." Then I smiled at him and turned back to my typewriter.

Fifteen minutes later he shambled over to my desk. "Kid, wanna go to lunch with me and some of the troops later?" We went to lunch then and nearly every day after that. Staab (I never called him George) became one of my dearest buddies. He carried me around with him like a watchfob, and he loved telling everybody how I had, as he put it, won him over.

* * *

When her husband's transfer to a job in New York forced Theo to leave the *Bulletin* in December 1951, the editors and reporters threw a huge party for her at the Pen and Pencil Club. They gave her a small Seth Thomas clock on which was engraved: "Her copy is always on time." Her account continued: After the presentation, one of the reporters took me aside and suggested I go out to the club's public bar. I went out and there was Staab, holding a drink and crying so hard his shoulders were shaking. I put my arms around him and cried, too.

* * *

When George Staab was an 11-year-old student at Horatio Hackett School in Kensington, he won first prize and a medal in an essay contest sponsored by the Women's Christian Temperance Union. The essay dwelt on the evils of drinking, and in later life he delighted in regaling friends about his prose triumph as they bellied up to hospitable bars.

Staab was an original, the closest Philadelphia came to Baltimore's H.L. Mencken. Like Mencken, he was largely self-taught. The Sage of Baltimore rejoiced in "my days as a reporter when I was young, goatish and full of an innocent delight in the world." Staab was not young when most of us knew him—he was a middle-aged 45 in 1950—but he never seemed to lose his delight in the world, innocent or otherwise, or his good humor. When a savage nor'easter wiped out the house he had built with his hands at Whale Beach on the Jersey shore, he reacted to the calamity as one might to a flat tire.

Born and reared in Philadelphia, he "resigned," as he put it, from Northeast High School before graduating and took a construction job. After that he drove a cab and delivered ice door to door, ten cents a cake. Hearing a call to newspaper work, he applied to the *North American* in 1925, unwittingly on the very day it was printing its last edition. After another tour in construction, he knocked on the *Bulletin*'s door. We're not hiring, he was told. Day after day he besieged the paper. The city editor told a staffer to get rid of the pest. But Staab persisted—even as Mencken had at the old *Baltimore Herald*—and finally was hired in 1930 at $22.50 a week.

He became a police reporter and he loved the rough-and-tumble hard-deadline work, checking in daily with police and fire stations and phoning in accounts of robberies, fires and murders. Next came the labor beat, and although it represented a promotion, he made no secret of his distaste for it. To Staab organized labor was "agonized labor," and in making the rounds of union offices his greetings were cheerfully defamatory. Shaking hands with a labor leader, he would open with a comment like: "Still at the same old trough, eh, you dues-grubbing, larcenous old bastard." Yet the relationship did not suffer. It was the nature of the man. Whatever he thought of the labor movement, he liked the people he covered. And even if reluctantly, they couldn't help reciprocating.

In 1952, Staab was shifted to general assignment. This gave him the opportunity to extend his unorthodox brand of journalism over a wider area. Hank Darling recalls his coverage of the demolition of the Pennsylvania Railroad's Broad Street Station across from City Hall. Over the station's main entrance was a statue depicting Faith, Hope and Charity. Staab's lead: "A workman yesterday took a sledgehammer and hit Faith, Hope and Charity on the head with it."

No respecter of the establishment, Staab once brashly asked Eugene Ormandy, the Philadelphia Orchestra's revered conductor, "How long have you been leading the town band?" With a penchant for loquacity, he conferred nicknames on friend and foe alike. In Staab's lexicon, City Hall was "the stone pile," and the facility housing Pennsylvania state employees was the "chock-full-of-nuts building." City Editor Thompson, with his somewhat doleful countenance, was "Our Father of Sorrows," and publisher Robert McLean "Our Father Who Art in the Corner." Staab dismissed the American Newspaper Guild, which had once sought vainly to organize the *Bulletin* newsroom, as the "little scorpions' club." His shorthand for the sedate German Society of Pennsylvania, of which he was a member, was simply "The Bund," the abbreviated name of a pro-Nazi group of the 1930s and '40s. When a Filipino exchange journalist briefly joined the staff, Staab greeted him as "our little brown brother," a term borrowed from William Howard Taft at the time of the Spanish-American War. Some colleagues winced but the visitor, warmed by the Staabian camaraderie, appeared to take no offense at all.

When Staab subjected Claude Lewis, the *Bulletin*'s first—and only—African American columnist, to an outrageous hazing, Lewis, too, accepted it in the spirit in which it was administered.

It began when Staab strolled over to Lewis' desk one day and with a great flourish slammed down a heavy cigar box. The newsroom grew silent waiting to see what its most unpredictable denizen would do next. With all eyes on him, Staab sucked hard on his yellowing plastic inhaler and ordered Lewis to open the box.

"I flipped the lid back," Lewis recalled, "and inside lay a gruesome-looking gray pistol."

Staab, pointing to the pistol and looking Lewis squarely in the eye, then announced: "That's what I'm gonna use the first time one of your brothers pokes his big black nose through my window."

Without another word, Staab collected his weapon and sauntered back to his desk.

"Staab was one of the more friendly types in the newsroom," Lewis said. "He was kidding me, but I wasn't so sure." However, his friend, Orrin C. Evans, an older black reporter, convinced Lewis that Staab meant nothing by it.

"That's his way of saying you've won his acceptance," Evans told Lewis.

In today's tense racial climate, such a shocking performance might lead to blows, if not shots in a newsroom. But times were different then. And Staab was just being Staab.

His relations with his editors were often stormy. The late Rex Polier remembered when Staab was sent to the Delaware Bay backwater to board a Philadelphia-bound ship and write a story about its trip up the river. After refreshing himself at one or more watering holes, he missed the designated vessel. "Instead," said Polier, "late at night he was observed standing alongside a dock throwing stones at a ship he thought was his. Unable to rouse the captain, Staab illegally boarded a ship in quarantine." He was arrested by a federal health agent who notified City Editor Thompson the next morning.

Toward noon the abashed reporter appeared in the newsroom to be confronted by an enraged Thompson. "You have caused this place enough trouble," Polier quoted the editor. "You can get out of here immediately and don't ever come back." As the afternoon wore on, however, Thompson, perhaps remembering past scrapes of his own, became more forgiving. In the evening when Staab returned, the two repaired to a bar behind City Hall to fraternize as if nothing had happened.

Staab had his own way of dealing with an afternoon ritual, the distribution to reporters of press releases that had to be turned into "overnights" for the next day's early editions. Slim Sawyer, an assistant city editor with sore feet from his years as a vaudeville hoofer, shuffled around dispensing these chores. Most staffers accepted them glumly. "Staab," said Jim Perry who sat near him, "would see—or maybe hear—Sawyer approaching and would quickly begin an animated and completely fake conversation on his phone headset. It was a game and it went on for years."

Late in his career, George was given armed services news to cover, an assignment he embraced as enthusiastically as he had the police beat. He won several prizes from an appreciative military and became the first civilian to receive a U.S. Navy Merit Award for outstanding reporting. He and a friend, Dr. David Shuman, co-authored a book, *Your Aching Back and What to Do About It*, which enjoyed brisk sales for a time.

Health, in fact, became an increasing problem for him. Having started smoking at age 10, he inhaled two to three packs of cigarettes a day through most of his adult life. The price he paid was, first, asthma and then emphysema. From that and circulatory blockage he died in 1969 at age 64, leaving the newsroom a considerably duller place.

* * *

Stanley Thompson, a native Kentuckian, was the son of a Methodist preacher and, to him, newspaper work was akin to holy orders, the only meaningful way to spend time. A reporter who managed to wangle a three-day weekend would be greeted on his return by Thompson: "Well, did you enjoy your extended leave?"

Like many great editors, Thompson had been a star reporter and writer. In 1950, he covered the perjury trial of Alger Hiss in New York. A week before the guilty verdict was handed down, he wrote a monumental summation of the testimony filling 25 columns of type—18,000 words—in the *Sunday Bulletin*. "All that can be said safely," he wrote in an author's postscript, "is that the big issues have been covered and that there has been a scrupulous effort to be impartial." He was right on both counts. Beyond that, his epic was masterfully organized and an enjoyable read.

He was a pioneer, too—certainly at the *Bulletin*—of the chronological lead which brings the reader immediately into the story's action, catching up on the background later.

Somehow he was able to convey his passion for accuracy and good writing despite having the articulation skills of a hedgehog. Jim Perry remembers a conference with the city editor before being dispatched to cover the 1959 trial of Philadelphia's Democratic leader, Congressman William J. Green, and six others charged with conspiring to defraud the government in the construction of a Signal Corps depot in upstate Pennsylvania.

"Thompson—we called him 'Mr. Thompson'—loved criminal trials, and he wanted the *Bulletin* to get this one right," Perry recalls. "He called me aside one day and began mumbling into his vest about how important this assignment would be. Then he began talking about [the Hiss] trial he had covered. He went on and on, rumbling into his vest, occasionally peeking up to see if I was listening. It finally occurred to me that he was trying to tell me how to cover the Green trial. It was indirect and circumlocutory, but it worked."

On his return after the 12-week trial in Lewisburg at which Green and the others were acquitted, Perry was summoned to the city editor's office. "I think he said I had done a pretty good job. It was the only time in the ten years I worked for the *Bulletin* that anyone went out of his way to say a kind word about what I was doing."

If Thompson was grudging with praise, he was also careful to conceal his disappointment when one of his stars left the paper, as Jim Owen did. Early in the 1950s, he seemed destined for an executive post at the *Bulletin*. Instead, after a year or so, he decided to quit journalism and enroll in law school in

Denver where his father was a prominent attorney. On his final shift in the newsroom, Owen kept plugging away on rewrite, the dupes of his stories piling ever higher on his spike. The city editor gave him the silent treatment. Finally, just at quitting time, Thompson crooked his finger and motioned for Owen to approach the city desk. The departing reporter thought that at last his boss would wish him well. All he grumbled to Owen was: "Don't forget to turn in your locker key."

As the Owen incident made clear, Stanley G. Thompson expected almost monk-like commitment to newspapering. And from most of us, he got it. Like George Staab, he was a certified character, but his ways were not those of the wayward reporter.

A staffer arriving late for work would be admonished: "Not everyone can be a genius, but everyone can be punctual." He considered all sports a waste of time. When Don Larsen of the New York Yankees pitched a perfect game in the 1956 World Series, the city editor alone displayed indifference in a cheering newsroom. "Isn't that what he's paid to do?" Thompson growled.

When he could stand some public foolishness no longer, he would write a letter to the editor over his patented alias, J. Darlington McKeester. The letter would be published and the readership would be duped. But such deception was commonplace back then.

While he was all business on the job, Thompson would loosen up at staff parties. After a couple of drinks he might break into the Methodist hymns of his youth. Often obliquely, he conveyed his affection for his staff. Polier remembered how he would occasionally hand reporter Jim Magee two dollars and ask him to light a candle in his name at a church near the *Bulletin*'s office. By this time, Thompson was an Episcopal vestryman, but the church he selected was Roman Catholic. The mystified Magee later discovered what was behind the ploy.

"From time to time," said Polier, "Stanley had to let someone go who was not measuring up. Rather than dump him on the street, he would call up various communications executives and recommend the reporter for some kind of job. Often they agreed to a tryout. But during the trial period Stanley endured agonies worrying that the reporter might not make it. His solution was to have Catholic Magee light a candle in the name of Stanley Thompson, Methodist turned Episcopalian."

Any staffer landing in the hospital could confidently expect to find the city editor at his bedside at least once.

Probably on orders from the executive suite, Thompson was tight with raises. "He had a highly original way of disposing of appeals for a raise," Adrian Lee remembered. "He would bury his chin in his chest until he was addressing not the supplicant but the second button on his vest—he wore a black suit with a gold watch chain year-in, year-out. And from his hiding place in his vest would come explosive snortings—'What do you want a raise for? You'll just get drunk Saturday night.' We would come away shaken, not so much about the raise but about the pain we had apparently inflicted...he seemed more anguished than we were."

"Trying another tack," Lee continued, "a reporter would say, we have a new addition to the family. That, Thompson had anticipated and prepared for. His head would come up, and he would suddenly become expansive. 'Well now, congratulations.' And he would reach into his desk and bring out a silver dollar. My wife and I still have the first one he gave me, plus five others."

If he was chary with raises, however, he was open-handed with the *Bulletin's* alternative to overtime pay, time off. Time due, of course, had to be documented by the reporter and the chits were kept by Thompson in an "overtime book," brought out and dusted off from time to time.

Although he sometimes appeared to frown on college education, Thompson was a graduate of the University of Louisville. After World War I Army service in France, including the battle of Belleau Wood, he began newspapering on the *Louisville Times* and rose to be its city editor. In five-year hitches, he worked for the Associated Press in Detroit, New York and Berlin, for the *New York Post* as rewriteman and foreign desk editor and for the old *Philadelphia Record* where he was day city editor when it expired in 1947 during the bitter Newspaper Guild strike. Before coming to the *Bulletin*, he worked briefly for the ardently reactionary National Association of Manufacturers, perhaps as a reflex to the *Record* strike.

He made no secret of his political conservatism. Anyone in the newsroom was likely to hear his mumbled veneration of President William McKinley. Lee, invited with his family to visit the Thompson holdings in Kellers Church, discovered an immense lithographic portrait of the 25th President, four feet by five and a half, in the living room. "He followed my eye approvingly to the grim visage over the mantle," Lee reminisces. "Yes, he said, with an air of confirming that what I had probably heard was true, he did indeed have the biggest picture of McKinley in creation."

Among the city editor's strengths were some notable flaws. Like so many of his generation, he held African Americans in low esteem. Even so, Thompson, the professional, seemed able to rise above his prejudices. Assigned by the *Philadelphia Record* to root out the causes of the 1943 Detroit race riots, for example, he sent back a balanced report of overcrowded, restricted housing and a shortage of recreation facilities for blacks, coupled with large wartime pay increases. And he added: "Before citizens of other communities—especially industrial areas such as Philadelphia—criticize Detroiters too harshly, they might do well to ask themselves what they...and their cities have done in advance to prevent just the sort of thing which happened here."

More than anything, though, people who worked under Thompson remember him as a teacher. Early in his editorship he came across a young reporter frozen with writer's block on a story about City Hall statuary. Thompson sat down at the reporter's typewriter and pounded out a lead: "The statues around City Hall are in absolutely filthy condition and a public disgrace as anyone can see..." He told the reporter to carry on in that vein. "How long should I write it?" the young man asked. "Keep on writing as long as it's interesting," said the city editor.

One of the writers of this piece recalls another memorable instruction. Shortly after being hired, the reporter was assigned to write Korean War casualty news. The wire service list gave him the name of a casualty's father, but not his street address. Working under the usual deadline crush, the reporter found the name, middle initial and all, in the phone book and ran it without calling the people. Or he might have called and got no answer. Next day the man phoned to protest. Wrong person. Thompson asked the reporter how he had goofed. Shamefaced, he said he had assumed that, with the identical name, it was the right family, right address. "Never assume anything," the city editor intoned, words still branded on the reporter's brain pan. The next day the *Bulletin* printed a correction, a newsroom stigma on the offender only a shade lighter than a jail sentence.

* * *

Late in February 1959, Thompson had just begun a two-week vacation at his father-in-law's Florida home when he was found dead in his bed, an open book on his chest. He was 61.

Chapter 11

Hotdogging Through a Storm Sewer—And Other Stories

By Henry R. Darling

ON THE AFTERNOON OF SEPTEMBER 18, 1953, three young girls were playing near a bush in Philadelphia's Fairmount Park, a 4,000-acre expanse of greenery extending northwest from the center of the city.

The girls, 12 to 14 years old, stopped their play when, they said later, they saw a vision of the Virgin Mary either in or over the bush. Frightened, they ran home holding each others' hands. The next evening the girls returned to the bush with two friends and all five reported seeing the same vision.

The area is on the edge of the park, near 51st Street and Parkside Avenue in West Philadelphia. Word of what the girls had experienced gradually spread through the neighborhood. People began coming from all over the city, and then outside the city. Many said they, too, could see the Virgin Mary standing near the bush.

About six weeks later, the crowds had grown so large and reports of the vision so numerous the city's newspapers could no longer ignore them. The *Bulletin* sent me to get the story.

"Why me?" I thought.

I was fairly new in the city room. My news-writing experience to date had been limited to obits, 50th wedding anniversaries and a few innocuous features.

I had written about a loon chase by Philadelphia Zoo keepers in the lake at Willow Grove Park and a window-washer who said he liked old Philadelphia buildings because they have wide windowsills. I'd covered the Mummers' Parade the year before, but that was a heartily disliked rite of passage that all new *Bulletin* reporters had to endure.

I'm not sure who gave me the assignment. It was Sunday and I was working the 4 PM to midnight shift. Stanley Thompson was the city editor, but I think he probably told Izzy Lichstein, the night city editor, something like: "Send that new guy out there when he comes in."

The "new guy" wasn't even sure how to get to 51st and Parkside. I lived in the Jersey suburbs at that time and was just learning my way around the city. I checked the big, pull-down city street map that hung in the corridor outside the Photographic Department, then took the "El" out to 52nd and Market Streets and started walking north.

No need to worry. I just followed the crowds.

There had been rumors Saturday night that the Virgin Mary would reappear the next night. Fairmount Park officials told me more than 50,000 people visited the area between noon and midnight. At one time, they said, there were more than 20,000 gathered around the bush.

I arrived around 5 PM and for the next six or seven hours I talked to everybody who looked like they might have a story. The desk had given me no definite instructions, no specific questions to ask. I talked to young and old, well-dressed men and women, some bums and panhandlers, police and park guards, shopkeepers and residents in the area.

A young woman told me: "I saw her but she was not as distinct as she has been." A man leaving the scene said: "There was certainly an outline of a figure in the trees behind the bush, but it was just the way the branches looked against the sky."

An elderly woman left the park weeping audibly and crying: "She didn't come, she didn't come." I overheard bits of conversation from others. "Not enough faith." "Too many disbelievers." "Perhaps we should have stayed longer." Once or twice I heard someone mumble something about "mass psychology."

Several times I asked about the five girls who first said they had seen the vision. Some people told me they knew they lived nearby, but they were not sure just where. Nor did they know their names.

There were many Gypsies wandering about, their colorful dresses and scarfs brightening the night. Two policemen, seated in a patrol car on the edge of the crowd, told me that at 3 o'clock that morning, Ephren J. Stevens, 48, known as the King of the Gypsies, collapsed and died on the ground near the bush.

I remember studying the bush carefully. Was there something there? Was there a shadowy face among the twigs and withered leaves of the bush? If there was, I could not see it. Years later, the paper sent me to cover a convention of hypnotists with instructions that I should volunteer to be hypnotized. It didn't work. The hypnotists told me it was because I was concentrating on the story I would have to write. Could that have been why, that night in Fairmount Park, I could only see twigs and leaves and a blank sheet of paper in a typewriter?

Around midnight, I went back to the office and wrote my story.

It wasn't as difficult as I thought it was going to be. As usual, I had taken copious notes—page after page of blurred (it had rained lightly at one point during the evening), scribbled pencilings, some of it illegible. It didn't matter. As usual, I spread the notes out beside the typewriter and barely ever looked at them. Once I got the thing rolling, it just sort of glided along by itself.

Here is some of what I wrote:

Many persons brought rosaries, miraculous medals and flowers directly from Mass to place them at the foot of the bush, an old overgrown privet hedge now bare of leaves except for the topmost branches.

To many gathered around it, it was not a bush, it was a shrine.

It looked like a shrine. For weeks now, vigil candles have burned continuously under the bush and its branches are loaded down with handkerchiefs, scarfs, crucifixes, holy pictures and religious articles.

Last night, the ground in a 200-foot circle around the bush was a mass of flowers—cut flowers, potted plants and corsages. Tucked in around the bouquets were hundreds of candles ranging from small tapers to big seven-day vigil lights. Incense sprinkled on the flames made the air around the bush heavy with fragrance. Other articles on the ground and suspended from the limbs of the bush included dresses, shoes (many of the orthopedic type), crutches and canes, handbags, necklaces and bracelets, a pink bathtowel and a huge orchid.

Many of the visitors left money on the ground. Park guards and police, who kept a watchful but unobtrusive patrol around the area, collected the money in a cardboard box. They told me it would be held in escrow for some future appropriate use. They said a total of $2,200.78 had been collected since the crowds first started coming.

While none of the people I questioned seemed to know the names of the girls who claimed to have seen the vision, most agreed that they were pupils at a nearby Catholic parochial school.

I suppose I should have—and certainly today I would have—checked with the school or the Philadelphia Archdiocese. I didn't, and I don't remember anyone at the *Bulletin* suggesting I do so. The last line in my story read:

"The Catholic Church has given no recognition to the reported manifestations and the Archdiocese has made no statement of any sort about them."

Twenty years later, in April 1973, the paper assigned reporter Rowland T. Moriarity to find the five girls and do a story about them. He did. Two were still living in the Philadelphia area; the others were in Florida and upstate Pennsylvania. Then in their early 30's, they all remembered seeing the vision and were still convinced it was authentic. They asked that only their maiden names be used and no addresses be given. Moriarity respected their requests. How would the media have handled this story today? Would they have preserved the girls' anonymity on ethical grounds? Would they have treated the story respectfully as we did nearly half a century ago? I don't think so. The competition would have been too great. *Hard Copy* or *Entertainment Tonight* would have fallen all over themselves getting the details. The *National Enquirer* would have paid witnesses to say the Virgin was pregnant. It would have been a media circus. And souvenir hunters would have torn apart the bush, twig by twig.

Surprisingly, the bush still lives. The Fairmount Park Commission built a small open-sided pavilion near the bush using some of the $5,000 collected at the site. Picnickers use it although they don't know why it's there. An old privet hedge grows a few feet away in about the same location as the original.

I have special reason for remembering the Vision in the Park story. The *Bulletin* gave me a $100 bonus for it. In those days, that was tantamount to winning the state lottery.

* * *

I started with the *Bulletin* in the fall of 1945, after serving four years with the U.S. Navy during World War II. (As a junior officer, I was at Yalta when Roosevelt, Churchill and Stalin met for the last time. I even caught a glimpse of the great men, but never had the opportunity to write about them.)

Before joining the *Bulletin*, I had worked for International News Service and then with United Press. They later merged to become UPI—United Press International. It was while working for these news agencies that I learned to use a teletype machine. Teletype machines produced a tape with little holes in it that translated into words when run through a transmitter. Since the tape moved through the transmitter at a rate of 60 words per minute, the operator had to type at least that fast. If he failed to do so, the transmitter would rip up the little holes and all the wire service clients would be receiving messages that read "EEEEEEEEEYYYYYYYTTT." That's when I became fairly fast on the teletype.

And this talent got me my job at the *Bulletin*. Two weeks after leaving the service, I was hired as a teletypist to work in the *Bulletin*'s Radio News and Flashcast departments. Flashcast was a device that used teletype tapes to send news reports from the *Bulletin* building to signs at Broad and Walnut Streets, Broad Street and Erie Avenue, 69th and Market Streets, and over the entrance to the *Bulletin* building. Words were produced in lighted letters that moved across the signs, similar to miniature versions now used for advertising in many stores.

In this age of television, it is difficult to believe those primitive newscasts would have hundreds of people standing on the curbs in all kinds of weather watching Richie Ashburn's progress around the bases spelled out in slow-moving letters.

* * *

After a few years, I was moved out of the Radio/Flashcast operation and into the city room. That's when the fun began. I got to know some colorful characters. There was Bix Reichner, a police reporter who was also a song writer. Somehow Bix managed to cover holdups and murders in Philadelphia from music publishers' offices in New York. There was Harold Hadley, a flamboyant newspaperman of national repute and friend of such journalistic celebrities as Damon Runyon and Gene Fowler. Besides being an excellent newsman, Hadley was a coffee addict and one day, dissatisfied with the cup delivered to him from Sam's sandwich shop on the first floor of the *Bulletin* building, he heaved its contents out the window to the street below. When a member of the Philadelphia mounted police walked into the city room a few minutes later with his cap and shoulders dripping coffee, Hadley had to think fast. Somehow he talked his way out of that one.

Like many of his colleagues, Hadley bet on the horses. He and Andy Hamilton, a police reporter, would spend hours studying the racing charts and trying to pick winners. One rainy day when the track was muddy, a bystander recorded the following exchange:

Hadley: "They're changing the shoes on our horse, you know."
Hamilton: "Yeah? What are they doin', putting galoshes on him?"

Sure, there were shenanigans in the city room, but prodigious labors were also performed there. When I arrived at the paper, staffers were still talking about Tom Lewis' remarkable feat in covering the crash of the dirigible Hindenburg at Lakehurst, New Jersey, on May 6, 1937. Working through the night, Tom, who was an eyewitness, turned out enough copy on the disaster to fill a book in time for the *Bulletin's* Bulldog, its early morning edition. Among other superb examples of newspaper work, I still have memories of Ray Brecht, his desk piled high with envelopes of clippings from the *Bulletin* library, pounding out background material for a fast-breaking news story. Brecht was a master at sorting through his own notes and library clips and writing clear, concise copy in the face of rapidly approaching deadlines.

As for me, over 30 years and more, I enjoyed some great assignments on a wide variety of subjects. The *Bulletin* sent me to Japan with the Philadelphia Orchestra, to London for a story on the foundry that cast the Liberty Bell and to the North Pole to cover the cruise of the *SS Manhattan*, a 10,000-ton tanker converted to an icebreaker. (The *Manhattan* was supposed to clear the way for Humble Oil Company tankers to transport oil from Prudhoe Bay on Alaska's North Slope to the lower 48 states via the famed Northwest Passage. But Humble's icebreaker made it to Prudhoe Bay only after a Canadian icebreaker freed it from the formidable ice of McClure Strait. A pipeline proved to be more effective in moving Alaskan oil.)

None of my stories changed the course of human events, but I think some of them revealed the ingenuity of the human animal. And the idiosyncrasies of other animals, too.

I wrote about the company that invented a powder that takes the stickiness out of lollipops, the Academy of Natural Sciences' bugs that had bugs, the milkman who delivered 7 1/2 million quarts of milk in 51 years, the parking meter that gave back nickels, the problems of a zoo curator trying to count prairie dogs, a gorilla that liked rock 'n' roll, a town in New Jersey called Hog Waller and a camel afflicted with fallen humps.

I wrote about a 200-pound bull mastiff that drank beer, a rabbit that flew a cardboard space ship, an engineering professor who discovered the Liberty Bell rings—well, rang—in the key of E, an Englishman named Algernon Greaves who brought a piece of Westminster Abbey to Philadelphia, a peacock that took up winter residence at the zoo in a telephone booth, a Swarthmore professor who had his socks chewed up by red ants.

I wrote about how to hypnotize a chicken, what happened when Leopold Stokowski let Harpo Marx conduct the Philadelphia Orchestra, the Pennsylvania Railroad conductor who sprinkled his riders with little martini glasses (the fallout from his ticket punch), two brothers who found a way to park 300 cars in the space of a city backyard (run them through the junk car compactor) and a belly dancer named Azeeza who danced for the American Civil Liberties Union (to prove to Philadelphia police her dancing was not objectionable).

I also wrote a correction on a story I did. It was a Thanksgiving Day story in 1966, and it said there were no longer any live turkeys sold in Philadelphia. The next day most of the city's kosher butchers called demanding a correction. They got it. The lead: "The cry of the turkey still sounds loud and clear in Philadelphia."

I had violated one of the cardinal sins in newswriting. Don't assume anything. Actually it was my second violation. The first occurred in May 1957.

The paper sent me to South Philadelphia to cover the opening of the new Walt Whitman Bridge. Big event. Cars lined up ten abreast, each driver waiting to be the first across. For an interview, I picked out a car with a nice young couple in the front seat, two kids in the back seat. The man said his name was, let's say, Jack Smith. The woman said her name was Joan, or some such. My story said, "Mr. and Mrs. Jack Smith and their children...etc."

The next day I got a call from John Doe. He said, "That may have been Jack Smith in the front seat, but it wasn't his wife with him. That was my wife and I've been wondering where she had been the last few days."

I lucked out on that one. No correction. I think all parties involved were willing to keep a discreet silence.

On January 12, 1971, I wrote a story about the first black to be listed in the Philadelphia Social Register. His name was Meredith Shannon Jones, Jr., and he married Susan R. Hoffman, of St. Davids.

In the spring of 1963, the *Bulletin* sent me on a bus trip from Panama City to Mexico City to mark the opening of the new Inter-American Highway. It was a great trip. The bus went up mountains, through gorges, over muddy gravel roads and around scary curves. I wrote my stories on the way with my old Royal portable typewriter on my lap, and every time we went around a sharp left turn, the carriage return would zing over to the right.

Each time we entered a new country, the bus would stop and we would be greeted by top-ranking officials. In Nicaragua, we were met by President Somoza.

"Aha, the *Bulletin*," he said when I was introduced. "In Philadelphia, Nearly Everybody Reads The *Bulletin*."

* * *

At the old *Bulletin*, editors ruled supreme. They cut, crossed out, pasted over, eliminated and added whatever they saw fit. The writer might grumble, but he seldom won an argument. And invariably, the editor's handiwork produced a better product. I know. *Bulletin* editors saved my neck on numerous occasions by correcting stupid or thoughtless errors in copy.

Some editors had their own unique interpretations of certain words and phrases and insisted that writers adhere to them in copy. Al Roberts didn't like to read about rescue workers evacuating people in floods. "Only horses evacuate," he would say. Frank McBride would get unhappy when someone wrote about the Schuylkill River. "It's redundant," he would tell us. "Kill means river."

None of us had any doubt that whatever the *Bulletin* was doing, it was doing the right thing. We all had great respect for the paper and so did our readers. Usually the words, "I'm from the *Bulletin*," were sufficient to gain the cooperation of the people to whom we talked.

One of the few times I was ever asked to show my press card was after a holdup at the old Fox Theater on Market Street. Among the eyewitnesses was a boy about 12 years old.

"I'm from the *Bulletin*," I told him. "Tell me what you saw."

"Show me your press card," he countered.

There was another time when I had to show my press card. Again it was a holdup. This time at a small hotel on the northwest corner of 12th and Market Streets across from the Reading Terminal. In fact, I think it was called the Terminal Hotel.

Since it was only a couple of blocks from the *Bulletin*, I got there shortly after the police. They were questioning the clerk about the holdup man.

"What kinda clothes was he wearin'?" asked one of the cops.

"He had on a black raincoat, a brown fedora, a white shirt, a red tie..."

I was wearing a black raincoat, a brown fedora, a white shirt, a red tie...One of the other cops was eyeing me.

This time, no one had to ask me for my press card. I was waving it in the cop's face before he could say anything.

Later that night, they picked up a suspect and took him to detective headquarters in City Hall. Again he was being questioned when I arrived. But the detectives weren't doing so good. The suspect kept falling asleep. Holdups must be tiring, I thought.

One of the detectives reached over and squeezed him between the legs. Maybe that's police brutality. But it worked. He woke up.

* * *

In the 1950s and '60s, newspapers concerned themselves with the daily doings of politicians, government leaders, businessmen, scientists, criminals and others who had direct impact on our lives. We covered township meetings, court trials, PTA affairs and city hall operations in detail. Wearisome stuff, perhaps, but the information was there for anyone who was interested or needed it. Maybe many of today's scandals in high places wouldn't have occurred if we had paid more attention to the nitty-gritty aspects of the news.

Today we all know who Princess Di is, we follow the yo-yo weight variations of Oprah Winfrey, we can tell the highest-paid baseball players and, thanks to the *National Enquirer*, we all know about the pregnant man. But how many of us can rattle off the names of our state or U.S. senators and congressmen?

The media—press, television and radio—have abdicated their primary responsibility. They have substituted entertainment for information.

Having said all this, I will have to admit that much of what I wrote for the *Bulletin* could be described as entertainment—at least, I hope it could.

In May 1965, reporter and editor Burton Chardak and I rode horseback from the covered bridge in Valley Forge to the steps—halfway up the steps— of the state capitol in Harrisburg. We followed the old Horseshoe Trail which meanders across the eastern half of Pennsylvania, up mountains, through valleys, across farm fields and streams. We saw beautiful countryside. We also saw junk cars and trash dumped along the trail.

What did it all prove?

"Well, maybe not much," our story said. "We proved you can't work in an office all day, then ride 120 miles on a horse without feeling it."

In 1964, Reginald Beauchamp, assistant to the president of the *Bulletin* and the paper's indefatigable promotion director, and I paddled a canoe around the city of Philadelphia—almost.

We had a two-mile portage north of the city between the headwaters of Tookany Creek in Glenside and the headwaters of Sandy Run Creek in Flourtown. The Tookany, better known as the Tacony Creek, flows eastward into Frankford Creek and then into the Delaware River at the Northeast Sewage Treatment Plant near Castor Avenue. Sandy Run flows westward into the Wissahickon Creek which enters the Schuylkill near the City Avenue Bridge. The Schuylkill joins the Delaware just below the Philadelphia Naval Base at the south end of the city.

The most exciting part of the trip was hotdogging through a storm-sewer sluiceway that carries Frankford Creek about a mile under city streets. We did not have to paddle. The fast-flowing current swept us along in darkness until we bounced over a two-foot drop into daylight.

The most scenic part of the trip was paddling along the tree-lined Wissahickon, enjoying the natural beauty of the stream. I could have enjoyed it more if Beauchamp had not insisted on standing up in the canoe, ostensibly to watch for rocks, more likely out of a spirit of derring do.

The ugliest part was navigating the oily, trash-laden stretch of the Schuylkill between Fairmount Dam and the Delaware. We survived the trip better than our rented metal canoe. It was a battered, gummy mess when we returned it.

* * *

When the *Bulletin* was located at Juniper and Filbert Streets, its ninth-floor newsroom overlooked the gargoyles and other baroque features of City Hall's upper reaches. We could see weeds, tomato plants and small saplings growing in the roof gutters. At one time a peregrine falcon inhabited one of the higher cornices, and his diving attacks on the City Hall pigeons entertained reporters and editors alike.

One day one of the editors, probably the *Bulletin*'s beloved Stanley Thompson, happened to glance down to the plaza in front of the north entrance to City Hall. A water-ice vendor's cart was parked near the entrance and the cart was surrounded, several people deep, with customers. Thinking it unusual that one lone vendor of water-ice "snowballs" should be attracting such lively business, the editor sent a reporter down to investigate.

The reporter arrived on the scene about the same time as the police. Along with vanilla, strawberry and chocolate, the guy was selling martini snowballs.

After the *Bulletin* moved to 30th and Market Streets in 1955, some of us missed the convenience of the old Center City location. The new building had a Flashcast sign on the front that, along with the news, occasionally carried a house ad. One day it got stuck and for several hours, to our glee, read: "In Philadelphia Nearly...."

The public was invited to visit the new building. Tour groups were led through the various departments by trained tour guides. It was not unusual for a rewriteman to be working on a deadline piece, concentrating on notes and typewriter, when he would suddenly become aware that a bunch of kids from one of the area's schools was looking over his shoulder.

The tours covered the entire building from the newsroom on the fourth floor through photographic, composing, production, engraving, advertising, classified, stereotype foundry, mailroom and press room. The building had the longest line of presses in the world. There was an observation gallery on which visitors could stand and look down at the rapidly moving "web" of newsprint rolling through the huge presses.

One day a seventh grader started leaning over the gallery railing and the tour guide warned him to stay back or he might fall into the presses. A passerby overheard the boy say: "That's OK. I always wanted to be in the newspaper."

* * *

I worked nightside for several years after the *Bulletin* moved to the new building. I enjoyed it. Commuting was less of a hassle, the final Four-Star edition came out about 5 PM and the six or eight of us who worked the 6 PM to 2 AM shift had no deadlines to worry about. The presses were no longer running—during the day their deep rumble could be heard throughout the block-long *Bulletin* Building—and generally things were quiet.

But not at 8:05 PM on March 28, 1956. That was the night the Tidewater Grain Company, directly across Market Street from the *Bulletin*, blew up. Grain dust, it seems, is highly explosive. The blast produced a shock wave that was felt 35 miles away, killed three workers in the granary and severely damaged the paper's new building, opened just 10 months before.

I was sitting at my desk in the newsroom and I could swear the big old Remington typewriter in front of me bounced a foot into the air. Even though the newsroom was on the opposite side of the building from the explosion, we all saw a brilliant flash light up the sky over the Pennsylvania Railroad train yard to the north of us. We were sure a freight train had fallen off the high line and crashed into our building. The elevated high line crossed over a two-story section of the *Bulletin* building, separating the administrative and news departments from the mechanical.

John Gerfin, night city editor, had us check out some of the departments around us. Fourth-floor offices on the south side, overlooking what was left of the Tidewater structure, were in shambles. All the windows were broken, ceiling tiles and filing cabinets littered the floor, and choking dust and smoke were everywhere. There were about 100 people in the building at the time. Fortunately only two, a telephone operator and an employee in the engraving department, were injured, cut by flying glass.

Exterior and interior walls were cracked throughout the building, and there were large bulges in the roof. Because the ventilating system in the press room was knocked out, the engravers found themselves working in thick, acrid smoke. But the next day's editions of the *Bulletin* came out on time. They contained more than four pages of photographs of the disaster.

An indication of the loyalty *Bulletin* people felt for the paper was apparent in the large number of employees—reporters, editors, photographers and others—who showed up minutes after the blast. No one called them in; many had already put in a full day. But the thought of being anywhere else than 30th and Market Streets under the circumstances had never occurred to them.

Chapter 12

A Personal Odyssey

By Joseph R. Daughen

WHEN RALPH ELLISON PUBLISHED *INVISIBLE MAN* in 1952, there were almost 400,000 blacks in Philadelphia. They made up about 19 percent of the city's population. It was a population that had been growing steadily throughout this century, both in the city and, to a lesser extent, in the region. Back in 1900, blacks were about five percent of the city's total, but every 10-year census showed that share increasing, from 5.5 percent in 1910 to 13.1 percent in 1940.

But like the central character in Ellison's seminal novel, Philadelphia's blacks largely were invisible as individuals in the city's newspapers, both in the newsrooms and the news pages.

"I am an invisible man," Ellison's protagonist says. "No, I am not a spook like those who haunted Edgar Allan Poe; nor am I one of your Hollywood-movie ectoplasms. I am a man of substance, of flesh and bone, fiber and liquids—and I might even be said to possess a mind. I am invisible, understand, simply because people refuse to see me."

The refusal to see blacks as individuals was a fact of newspaper life in 1956, when I became a reporter. My first job was working the police beat for the *Philadelphia Daily News*, but it didn't take very long to learn that all three newspapers in the city had the same view when it came to news about blacks. The view, essentially, was forget it. Frank Toughill conveyed that viewpoint to me rather bluntly after I had collected the details of a murder that occurred south of Pennsylvania

Hospital near Lombard Street. A bemused homicide detective named Sam Hammes told me about the fight that broke out over a bottle of wine, leading to the fatal stabbing.

"Why do you want to know all this shit?" Hammes said. When I told him I wanted to put it in the newspaper, he smiled and walked away.

"Is it black?" Toughill asked me when I called the city desk.

"Yes," I replied.

"Fuck it," Toughill said, and hung up the phone.

Toughill was an assistant city editor at the *Daily News* and a somewhat legendary figure. When I met him, he was a rotund man in his early 50s with straight gray hair and suspicious eyes peering out from behind horn-rimmed glasses, a cigarette seemingly always in hand or in his mouth. I didn't really see all of this at first, though. What I saw was a hard-bitten guy who had smuggled the innards of a telephone into a New Jersey courtroom and then had beaten an army of competitors by speaking into the palm of his hand the news that Bruno Hauptmann had been given the death penalty for kidnapping the Lindbergh baby. Toughill had a friend—he always had a friend—who had hooked a line up to a telephone wire that ran under a ledge outside a courtroom window.

Coming into the courtroom, Toughill sat next to the window, spliced his bootleg contraption to the wire that branched off the telephone line, and sat waiting for the verdict. The operation, he told me, had been approved and paid for by Walter Lister, who was then the city editor of the *New York Post*. Toughill at the time was a reporter for the *Philadelphia Record*, which owned the *Post*. Lister was the executive editor of the *Bulletin* when I arrived there, but I never had the opportunity to talk to him about Toughill.

Toughill was reunited with Lister in 1959, when he was hired by City Editor Stanley Thompson to be a sort of roving correspondent for the *Bulletin* in South Jersey. Shortly before that, at a Philadelphia Press Association awards dinner after Toughill had left the *Daily News* as a result of one of the purges that marked the transfer of the paper from contractor Matthew McCloskey to Walter Annenberg, I found myself listening to Toughill and James V. Magee exchange war stories. It was in the old Ben Franklin Hotel, and fetching drinks for the two of them was a small price to pay for admission.

It was here that Toughill and Magee explained to me the philosophy of the city's newspapers concerning black residents. News was something out of the ordinary, they said, and black crime was ordinary. That's why news of a homicide involving blacks was greeted with the word "hush" by the *Bulletin*'s city desk, Magee said. Except for a judge or two, no blacks played a visible role in the life of the city and as far as social events went, the attitude was, "Let the *Tribune* (Philadelphia's paper for the black community) cover them."

I had long since figured this out for myself; but it was undeniably fun for me to drink and gossip with my former boss, whom I still feared, and Magee, whom I believed was a top reporter for the best paper in town. Magee would win a Pulitzer Prize for reporting in a half-dozen years, along with reporter

Albert Gaudiosi and photographer Fred Meyer, for a series exposing the pay-off of police officers by South Philadelphia gamblers. Their chief source for the series—and this is no secret—was Police Captain Frank L. Rizzo, who would go on to become police commissioner and then mayor of the city. And Gaudiosi would become his campaign manager.

But that was in the future that night in the late 1950s when I stood drinking with Toughill and Magee. The Press Association party was an awards ceremony and the talk naturally turned to prizes. Toughill had won the Headliners Club Award years earlier for exclusive stories about a murder-for-hire ring that used arsenic as a weapon and was responsible for a truly awesome number of bodies, fixed by the police at 50. Winning the Headliners Club Award carried with it as a bonus a trip to Atlantic City and a stay at the old Traymore Hotel. And Toughill said he often returned to the Traymore in years when he wasn't a winner. He and Magee were friends, he said, and sometimes he'd take Magee along and they'd share a room.

Then Magee took up the story, and it was clear the two of them had gone through this routine before. A few years ago, Magee said, they were staying at the Traymore and had celebrated perhaps a little too much. But they made it back to their room, though neither of them had a clear recollection of it.

"I got up in the morning with a headache," Magee recalled. "Frank was still asleep and he wouldn't wake up. I needed to get some coffee. So I got up and shaved and got cleaned up. I got dressed and got my teeth out of the glass in the bathroom and went down to the dining room. I ordered coffee and some breakfast, but something just wasn't right. My mouth felt funny. I just drank the coffee and went back to the room. Frank was up, sitting in a chair in his underwear and holding his teeth in his hand. As soon as the door closed, he jumped up and said, `You son of a bitch, you've got my teeth in your mouth.'"

Toughill, listening to Magee, kept nodding and chuckling.

Toughill made it to the *Bulletin* before I did, but he had a track record dating back more than 35 years, and that record included a lot of big stories. I never asked him for advice, but it seemed evident that the best way to get the *Bulletin*'s attention was to come up with good stories. One opportunity presented itself early in 1960, when the city was transfixed by the murder and rape of a 16-year-old girl named Maryann Mitchell, who was abducted while waiting for a bus to take her home to Manayunk. Her body was dumped in a ditch in Whitemarsh Township, just outside the city, on December 28, 1959, and on January 4, 1960, police arrested a man named Elmo Smith for the murder.

While Philadelphia police made the arrest, Montgomery County had jurisdiction since the body had been found there. The district attorney of Montgomery County was a genial Republican named Bernard "Bennie" Di Joseph, and he immediately took control of the case, including the dispensing or withholding of information about it. What caused me concern was that the *Bulletin* not only had a great stable of reporters to work the Elmo Smith story, it had a secret weapon named Pinkerton. Pinkerton had been hired as a reporter a few months earlier, after his retirement as a Montgomery County detective on Di Joseph's staff. Because of his relationship with Di Joseph, Pinkerton was in a position to run away with the story.

After Smith was arrested, he was taken to the Montgomery County Courthouse in Norristown to be questioned by Detective Chief Charles "Chick" Moody, Pinkerton's former boss. A couple of Philadelphia homicide detectives participated. The questioning went on long into the night, but the only Philadelphia reporters hanging around were me and Al Gaudiosi, who was covering for the *Inquirer*. The *Bulletin* wasn't there, a clear signal to us that Pinkerton had arranged for his old bosses to tip him off when something happened.

Gaudiosi and I left at about 3 AM with nothing to show for our time there. Smith's hearing was set for the following day at the Whitemarsh Township Building on Ridge Pike. I had scouted the building out and found there was only one public telephone, so I arranged to have Dave Racher, a reporter even younger than I was, arrive there at 7 AM, two hours before the hearing, to take over the telephone. I got there at 7:30, and not long after that the place started to fill up. Pinkerton came in, dressed in a nice plaid suit and a smug smile, which made me nervous. What would the *Bulletin* have in its first edition? After talking to Bill Blitman, the city editor, I walked to an area resembling a lobby to smoke a cigarette, and just then Captain David Brown and Lieutenant Andrew Waters of the Philadelphia Homicide Squad walked in the door. We talked for about five minutes and they almost casually told me that Smith had given a complete, signed confession containing details only the murderer could have known.

I dashed to the phone with a major scoop. E.Z. Dimitman, Walter Annenberg's right-hand man, was walking through the newsroom when Blitman announced that Smith had confessed and we had the details. The *Daily News* Eight-Star edition was just beginning to roll when Dimitman yelled, "Stop the presses!" The front page and page three were replated to accommodate a screaming headline and a story that ran about six inches.

In August 1960, Smith's trial began in Gettysburg, where it had been moved because the case had received so much publicity. Joseph F. Lowry was the *Bulletin*'s reporter and he told me what had happened inside the paper the day of Elmo Smith's hearing.

The hearing was delayed, Lowry said, and the city desk was starting to get edgy. Lowry had been assigned as the rewriteman to take notes from Pinkerton, but the postscript came and went with no word from the reporter. Finally, Lowry's phone rang and it was Pinkerton. The hearing would be getting underway shortly, Pinkerton said, but meanwhile he had something the paper might be interested in.

"What's that?" Lowry asked.

"Well," said Pinkerton, "it is rumored that Elmo Smith may have confessed to the murder of Maryann Mitchell."

"Rumored?" asked Lowry. "Rumored? Come on, Pinkerton, who the hell's spreading the rumor?"

"The district attorney," said Pinkerton.

Pinkerton's divided loyalty was a stark reminder that while reporters should go to great lengths to protect a source, they must never forget that a source is a source is a source. A source supplies information for the newspaper. The information is of no value if it just rattles around in the reporter's head. And a reporter rarely, if ever, should give a source the power to decide when it is appropriate to print information. The Pinkerton case would not be the last example that I would encounter of a reporter catering to a source to the detriment of the *Bulletin*.

Earl Selby hired me in September 1963, but he refused to pay me a penny more than I was making at the *Daily News*, which probably was about $7,500 or $8,000. Selby was the city editor who pulled off the amazing feat of succeeding Stanley Thompson, keeping the quality of the newsroom at the same level, and ultimately persuading almost everyone that he wasn't such a bad fellow after all. As a columnist, Selby had embarrassed reporters by breaking stories in areas they were responsible for covering. The most embarrassed were those who worked for the *Bulletin* and had to face Thompson or his assistants after Selby had beaten them. Selby could be remote, but when he put his arm around a reporter's shoulder, bent his crew-cut blond head close and said, "This is a terrific story I'm assigning you to work on," it was difficult not to get swept up by his enthusiasm, even if the story wasn't all that interesting.

The *Bulletin* had a system of rotating reporters into its Harrisburg bureau on a two-year cycle, and that was my first real assignment. When the General Assembly was in session, which was most of the year, I would take the train to Harrisburg on Monday morning, rent a room at the Penn-Harris Hotel, and walk across the street and up the hill to the newsroom in the Capitol building. In a normal week I wouldn't get home until Wednesday or Thursday evening.

Duke Kaminski was the *Bulletin*'s Harrisburg bureau chief, and he never tired of complaining to the city desk about the quality of the people that were being sent to him. Kaminski had only a few rules for his temporary helpers, and he enforced them with vigor. The visitor was there to cover the House. He was not to go near the Senate or the Governor's office, which belonged to Kaminski. But Kaminski covered those two institutions with a thoroughness that I have never seen equaled.

Early in 1964, Governor William W. Scranton held a budget briefing for reporters to outline his spending and revenue-raising plans for the coming fiscal year. It was a nicely done evening affair, complete with steak dinner that the reporters ate without ever questioning who was paying for the food. The briefing was handled professionally, with charts and graphs showing income and spending, and the governor, his budget secretary and other aides were ready to answer questions.

"You know, Governor, the Surgeon General's report on cigarettes is going to be coming out next week and it's probably going to say that smoking causes cancer, that it kills you," said Kaminski, between puffs on his own cigarette. "Have you factored that into your revenue estimates? What happens to the receipts from the cigarette tax when the Surgeon General tells everybody to quit smoking?"

There was an embarrassed silence. Scranton looked at his aides, and they mostly looked at the floor. One glared at Kaminski. Then the budget secretary, Marty Brackbill, said that, yes, the cigarette tax had been discussed and it had been concluded that if the government report was unfavorable to the tobacco industry, it still would have little effect on tax revenue.

Kaminski was forever asking embarrassing questions, no matter which party was in power. As he demonstrated at Scranton's briefing, he knew at least as much about the budget process as the responsible government officials.

In mid-1964, Managing Editor William B. Dickinson called me into his office to give me a special assignment. It was the first time this had happened, and I was a little nervous, even though Sam Boyle was present. Sam had succeeded Earl Selby as city editor, and over the years Sam proved to be a true friend and valuable advisor to me. Dickinson was a courtly, handsome man, unfailingly polite, with sound judgment. He had been a distinguished wire service reporter and he retained the ability to write, or to edit, copy so that it was clear, concise and unambiguous. What he wanted me to do, in addition to my Harrisburg duties, was to undertake a reporting job on a section of the city's life that had been woefully undercovered. The city and the nation were changing, Dickinson said, and people like Martin Luther King, Jr., were going to make that change speed up. The *Bulletin* had an obligation, he said, to tell its readers what life was like for blacks in the area. Only Dickinson used the word "Negroes." Take as much time as you need, six months, if necessary, and bring me back the story of "The Negro in Philadelphia," said Dickinson.

It took all of six months for me to do it, and it probably was the most rewarding assignment I've ever had. I traveled all over the city, into good neighborhoods and bad, interviewing more than 200 persons, reading books and reports by the government and foundations, and learning more than I would have thought possible. I also learned something about the people I worked for.

The project, when it finally was completed, was the size of a small book, 280 typewritten pages, more than 70,000 words. It attempted to cover the major concerns of life. Housing. Education. Employment. Crime. Prejudice. Health.

To deal with these subjects, I visited executives who exercised power over hiring, lending money, government policy. One of the first was Reeves Wetherill, a senior officer of John Wanamaker's, the department store chain that was the largest advertiser the *Bulletin* had. Strawbridge & Clothier, another locally owned department store chain, spent almost as much and, over the years, fared better than Wanamaker's. Strawbridge's ultimately became the *Bulletin*'s biggest advertiser and it stayed with the paper until the end.

Wetherill came from a wealthy old Philadelphia family and he reported directly to store president Richard C. Bond. He greeted me warmly. He said he admired the *Bulletin* for attempting to write a comprehensive story about the city's black community, although he, too, said "Negro." But when I asked him for a breakdown of Wanamaker employees by race and status, he got angry, which was very uncharacteristic of Wetherill. He told me he thought it was none of my business, then he picked up the telephone and called Bond. He told Bond what questions I was asking, listened for a few moments, and hung up.

"Who the hell are you to ask me how many Negroes work here?" Wetherill said to me. "Do you have any idea of the program we've put in to recruit Negroes?"

"No," I answered. "Tell me about it."

"I'll tell you what instead," he replied. "Go back to your paper and find out how many you have. I'll compare our record to yours anytime. Who do you think you are to come in here with such questions? Do you have any idea of how much money we pay out to the *Bulletin*? We pay your salary. That's something you'd better remember, because your bosses know how important Wanamaker's is to your paper."

With that, he ended the interview. When I talked to the personnel officer of Philadelphia National Bank, the *Bulletin*'s bank, I got a similar response. Gimbel's refused to talk to me at all. But after I got over the embarrassment of being thrown out of Wanamaker's, I realized Wetherill's position on the store's hiring policies vis-à-vis the *Bulletin*'s might have had some merit. In that football field-sized newsroom, I had seen only two black reporters, Malcolm Poindexter and Orrin Evans. And Poindexter had quit to go to work for a television station.

Nevertheless, Bill Dickinson recognized that America was in the process of changing and, like the professional he was, he committed some of his resources—six months of a reporter's time and 14 full news pages—to examining a heretofore overlooked element of Philadelphia. We never discussed the obvious irony of having a white reporter write about the city's black population.

Another subject that we didn't discuss was the pressure that I heedlessly brought to bear on the paper by going around and offending advertisers like Wanamaker's and Gimbel's. Sam Boyle let me know that Richard Bond was on the telephone to Robert Taylor, the paper's publisher, probably before Wetherill threw me out of his office. Boyle also told me that complaints had come in from "other people," whom he didn't identify, but it didn't tax my brain to realize he was talking about Gimbel's and PNB.

Dickinson never said a word to me about these complaints. He never told me to back off. To the contrary, he encouraged me to keep doing what I was doing. About a week after I had finished writing "The Negro in Philadelphia," telegraph editor Bill Townshend told me I was in trouble because I had on several occasions referred to Negroes as blacks. You can't call Negroes blacks, Townshend said, because they'll resent it. I informed Townshend that I used the word blacks because that's what most of the young Negroes called themselves. He was not convinced.

When Sam Boyle told me a week later that the publisher wanted to see me, I was not convinced either. Townshend was right. I was in trouble, either because of the use of blacks or for some other reason. But when I got to Taylor's office, I saw Dickinson there, and a photographer. It was the first time I was in that office, and I felt disoriented. The photographer's flash went off, then Dickinson and Taylor smiled and, together, held out a beautiful new portable typewriter to me. On the inside lid of the case was an engraved plate which read, "To Joseph R. Daughen with Respect and Admiration." I knew then that this was the place I wanted to be and these were the men I wanted to work for and with.

Dickinson had instituted a rotation system in which young reporters would be assigned to a year's tour in the paper's Washington bureau. I knew of the program but didn't think it was in the cards for me because, relatively speaking, I was the new kid in town. It had begun shortly after I was hired, when Lawrence M. O'Rourke was sent to Washington for 1964. O'Rourke went into an uncertain situation, because the previous year had seen some turmoil in the bureau. John G. McCullough had been the second man in Washington, working for Robert Roth, the bureau chief, and he had been replaced by Anthony Day, who was a promising young reporter in Philadelphia but who had virtually no experience covering politics. McCullough was unhappy at being called back to Philadelphia, but he ended up showing the city how politics should be covered before going on to become editor of the editorial page. Tony Day, son of *Baltimore Sun* editor Price Day, proved to be a first-rate Washington reporter who agonized over his copy and earned a reputation for almost never being inaccurate.

In any event, O'Rourke enjoyed his year and didn't want to come back, a continuing hazard with a Washington rotation program. He was succeeded by Hugh Flaherty, a tall Irishman who preceded me in Harrisburg. Flaherty returned to Philadelphia in 1966 and, after Raymond P. Shafer, a Republican, was elected governor in November, Flaherty quit to go to work for him.

Dickinson picked me to go to Washington in 1966 to succeed Flaherty, although I'm convinced he did so at the urging of Sam Boyle. Washington is the destination of choice for most reporters interested in government, but this was a stressful time for me and my wife, Joan. Both of us had grown up in Philadelphia and had our families there. We had bought a house in Glenside, in Montgomery County, about a year earlier and now we had to find someone to rent it. Our daughter, Joan Patrice, would not be two until March 1966, and now there would be no familiar baby sitters. But we found a tenant, and on January 2, 1966, North American Van Lines showed up, and we were off to Washington and an apartment in Alexandria, six miles from the White House, that Tony Day had helped me find. It was near dinnertime on January 3rd, and we were in the early stages of trying to settle in to the apartment, after spending the first night in a Holiday Inn nearby, when the doorbell rang. It was Lynne Day, Tony's wife. She had driven from her home in Rockville, Maryland, to deliver to us a huge meal of spaghetti and meatballs which somehow she had managed to keep warm. She also had china and utensils for us to use. While I knew and liked Tony, I barely knew Lynne, who met Tony when she was a *Bulletin* reporter. And Joan had never met either. Nevertheless, Lynne had driven more than 25 miles on the Beltway to get to us and now had to turn around and go back to take care of her family.

The *Bulletin's* Washington bureau was in a suite of rooms on the 12th floor of the National Press Building at 14th and F Streets, just one flight down from the National Press Club. Bob Roth was the bureau chief, but he was much more than that. He understood government and he understood politics, and he recognized the differences between the two. What's more, he was willing to teach what he knew to young reporters who wanted to learn, and I counted myself among his students. He spent some time at Amherst and even though he never graduated, he was one of the best-educated persons I have met. He started every morning off by doing the *New York Times* crossword puzzle, using one of his favored black felt pens. On the days he was due to write a column, it would be done usually before 8 AM. Roth's primary job was covering the White House, which he had done since Franklin Roosevelt was president.

With a third reporter in the bureau, Tony Day was freed up to write about the State and Defense Departments and pick out other targets. My job was to cover Congress, particularly the members from Pennsylvania, New Jersey and Delaware. And I got to write a weekly column. All three of us were involved in political coverage, and I became the paper's Southern expert. Tony Day arranged for me to take his place in something called the Sperling Group. This was a collection of reporters organized by Godfrey Sperling, the *Christian Science Monitor* correspondent. The group met once a week or so for lunch with a newsmaker, generally under confusing ground rules. One week, off-the-record meant just that—no information could be printed (there were no electronic reporters in the group). The next week, it might be a variation of that. But it was useful. Where else could I have managed so quickly to sit next to Bobby Kennedy at lunch? Or William Fulbright, George Romney, Eugene McCarthy and a series of other prominent officials?

Among the reporters in the group was a tall, patrician correspondent for *Newsweek* who sought me out and introduced himself. His name was George Packard and I found him to be a likeable, well-informed man. Packard had been an assistant to Edwin O. Reischauer, the U.S. Ambassador to Japan, and his knowledge of that country and international affairs generally dwarfed mine. He was not as strong on domestic politics or policy, but he was eager to learn. If I had to choose a word to describe Packard at this point, eager would be the word. And earnest. After one of our lunches in January 1967, Packard asked me to sit down with him on a sofa in the lobby of the Statler Hilton Hotel, where our group had gathered that day.

"Joe," Packard said, "I want to tell you something, but you've got to keep it to yourself for now, okay?"

"Sure, George," I answered.

"Listen," he said earnestly, "I'm going to work for the *Bulletin*."

"That's terrific," I said, "but why does it have to be a secret? Everybody's going to see your name in the paper anyway." "Yes, but it's not going to happen right away," Packard said. "I'm not starting until next September."

I was startled by that. I'd never heard of such a length of time between an employment agreement and a starting date. I knew that George had gone to Princeton, as had members of the McLean family. But Packard insisted to me that Bill Dickinson was the one who had agreed to hire him without intercession by anyone named McLean. Bob Roth, who was perhaps Dickinson's best friend on the paper, knew all about it, of course. He, too, thought the long lead time was unusual. However, he told me to be prepared for the unusual where Packard was concerned.

"This young man is being put on the escalator and he's going right to the top," Roth said.

That fact didn't affect me one way or the other. I considered Packard a friend and colleague, not a close one, but a comfortable one. Later, it developed that Packard's emergence did cause Tony Day some pain. Tony had an excellent reputation in Washington and he clearly had hoped one day to have the top editing job at the *Bulletin*, just as his father did in Baltimore. But Dickinson, who had been looking for a successor for several years without finding one to his liking, obviously had decided that Tony Day, like Assistant Managing Editors B. Dale Davis and Malcolm Deans, and Paul Grimes, whom he spirited away from the *New York Times*, was not the one.

Tony had extensive contacts in Washington and even before Packard started at the *Bulletin*, *Newsweek* tried to recruit Tony. "They want to make it a straight trade," Tony told me. "They get me and the *Bulletin* gets Packard." There was no doubt that Tony believed *Newsweek* would be getting the better deal. But he received a more intriguing offer from the *Los Angeles Times*. Relocate to the West Coast and become editor of the editorial page for the *Times* with a large raise and foreign travel every year. Tony consulted Bob Roth and both later said that Roth had told him it was a job he couldn't turn down. And he didn't.

As the junior member of the bureau, these maneuverings didn't have much impact on me. My job didn't change. Because of my involvement in "The Negro in Philadelphia," I functioned for a time as the paper's civil rights reporter. When Alabama's segregationist governor, George C. Wallace, invited reporters to spend a week in his state, the *Bulletin* sent me. The paper also allowed me to roam from Georgia to Florida to Alabama to Mississippi to Louisiana, sending back reports on the progress of the civil rights movement. The South during the mid-'60s was a crossroads of sorts, and reporters were always bumping into each other.

On the Wallace trip, my seatmate was a man my age named Jim Batten, then a reporter for the *Charlotte Observer*. He was sent to Washington at the same time I was, and we traveled together on political reporting trips through the South. In October 1969, I was in my room at the New York Sheraton, which I was using as a base to cover John Lindsay's successful mayoral reelection race, when I had a telephone conversation with Batten, who was then on his way to the *Detroit Free Press* as an assistant city editor.

"We've bought the *Philadelphia Inquirer* and *Daily News*," Batten said in his soft Southern voice. "Gosh, I'm sorry, but I guess we can't work together anymore."

Another memorable moment for me occurred during that mayoral race. Lindsay had lost the Republican nomination to state Senator John Marchi, and the Democratic nominee was Councilman Mario Procaccino, leaving Lindsay to run on the Liberal Party ticket. Lindsay was losing the battle for conservative voters to Marchi, but he was having great success with black voters, a major component of the Democratic Party constituency. If this success wasn't reversed, Procaccino was doomed. But Procaccino, a rotund man with a Gay '90s mustache, couldn't seem to make any progress with the blacks.

In desperation, the Democrat's campaign scheduled an early-evening rally on 125th Street in Harlem. A surprisingly large crowd turned out, so large that Procaccino's people suspected Lindsay had something to do with it. Their suspicions probably were correct. When Procaccino began to talk, the boos erupted and signs denouncing him and praising Lindsay were raised. The boos were so loud Procaccino was having difficulty being heard.

"Let me talk," he yelled. "Give me a chance. Please listen to me. Boo after I'm done if you don't like what I say. You got to give me a chance. I've been discriminated against like you because I'm Italian. I'm with you. Listen to me. MY HEART IS AS BLACK AS YOURS."

The booing died instantly, overtaken by a stunned silence. Procaccino fidgeted on the platform of the truck, apparently sensing that he had just done something horribly wrong. Then, from the front of the crowd, came a titter. It grew to laughter and before long most of the people in the audience were laughing.

Although I had returned to Philadelphia in June 1967, I continued to be assigned to do national political stories. The political conventions were, for a time, fun to cover, and the *Bulletin* spent a lot of money on them. In 1968, the paper sent at least a dozen of us to report on the Republicans, who met in Miami Beach, and the Democrats, who became involved in a political riot in Chicago. Sam Boyle was in charge of the convention bureau, attending to the physical set-up and to many aspects of the coverage. He arrived in the convention city first, usually with one or two others who were acceptable eating and drinking companions. And he arrived with a pocketful of cash. I found out how important that cash was when I was chosen to run the paper's coverage of the 1972 Democratic Convention in Miami Beach. The setting up of facilities for thousands of news reporters in a headquarters hotel (the Fontainebleu, in this case) and in an arena or convention center is a massive undertaking, not unlike the logistics required to provide an army with the means to conduct a war. Sam Boyle knew how to do this, and he made liberal use of the paper's cash to get the curtains up, the furniture delivered, and the wire machines and telephones installed.

The 1972 Democratic Convention set-up proceeded at a different pace for the *Bulletin*, which now identified George Packard as the editor on its masthead. I arrived without any bribe money and for two days felt like the man on a streetcorner in a driving rain futilely trying to wave down a taxicab. Packard, working as Dickinson's assistant, had produced a lengthy critique of the paper, and it was largely unfavorable. But he was running things now, and he didn't think we needed so much convention coverage. The bureau was cut back to three persons, and the expense money was cut back even further. Without bribes, we got our bureau put together, but it was late and it was rudimentary. Never did I appreciate a Sam Boyle-run convention bureau more.

In any event, after leaving Washington in mid-1967, I found myself traveling there or to some other out-of-town assignment very frequently. One of my first assignments was to return to Washington and cover the weeks-long investigation and ultimate censure of Senator Thomas Dodd, a Connecticut Democrat, for misconduct.

Virtually all of the following year was consumed by politics. George Wallace formed his American Independent Party, persuaded General Curtis LeMay to be his running mate, and began his third-party campaign for the presidency. I knew Wallace and knew more about him than any other *Bulletin* reporter, so I was responsible for covering him. But I also got to spend about 10 days each with Richard M. Nixon and Hubert H. Humphrey.

When Wallace ran his wife, Lurleen, for Governor of Alabama in 1966, I was there for the *Bulletin*. Looking back, it seems incredible that the newspaper was willing to spend as much as it did to send me to cover races in Alabama, Florida and Georgia. On one trip, I arrived at Hartsfield International Airport in Atlanta to catch a plane to Birmingham. In the airport, I bumped into Robert E. Lee Baker, a genial reporter for the *Washington Post* who was traveling through the South recruiting prospects for his paper's intern program. We checked in and obtained adjoining seats in the first-class section. Back then, *Bulletin* reporters always traveled first-class, slept in first-class hotels and ate in first-class restaurants. Leaving the ticket counter, we met Ben Franklin, a *New York Times* reporter. Franklin was headed to Birmingham, too, but he sheepishly told us he couldn't sit with us. The *Times* wouldn't pay for first-class tickets.

An opportunity to work on a nonpolitical story came along in 1970, after the Penn Central Railroad went bankrupt on June 21. It was the largest bankruptcy in the country's history and, since the company was headquartered in Philadelphia, it was major news for the *Bulletin*. I was assigned to work with Peter Binzen, a tall, lean, self-effacing man who sometimes affected a Lincolnesque beard. Binzen was a Yale graduate with an intimidating reputation. He had been a Nieman Fellow and he had written a book, *Whitetown, USA*. He developed the education beat for the paper, but after he went on to other things, no one ever matched his performance in that area. Binzen had written for national magazines, and he would go on to become metropolitan editor and then author of a business column. But in June 1970, he became my partner on the Penn Central story.

It was a difficult story because the stakes were so high and the egos so swollen that most of the principal players initially refused to talk to us or to other reporters. But we had some modest successes, more than holding our own against the *New York Times* and the *Wall Street Journal* and absolutely murdering the *Inquirer*. A couple of directors gave us information, as did a key government official.

But the top three officers wouldn't talk. Board Chairman Stuart Saunders, who lived in Ardmore, refused. I guess he was angry because of a story we ran about his taking a limousine to work, rather than the railroad. Alfred Perlman, the president, lived in New York, and his attitude toward us was the same as it was toward the Penn Central's board. That attitude, one director told us, was, "Fuck you, see my lawyers." And David Bevan, the chief financial officer, who also lived on the Main Line, would not return phone calls.

It didn't take long for Binzen and me to realize the Penn Central story had the makings of a book, and Little, Brown senior editor Harry Sions agreed and gave us a contract. It was the fact that there was going to be a book that induced Saunders to finally agree to sit down with us. Perlman and Bevan, however, wouldn't budge.

But then Wright Patman, a Democratic curmudgeon from Texas who was Chairman of the House Banking Committee, began looking into the operations of Penphil, a private investment club run by Bevan. The club's investments closely paralleled investments made by Penn Central, and those investment decisions were made in both cases by Bevan. Generally, Penphil would buy a stock and then the railroad would jump in heavily, pushing the stock's price up.

Before Patman's findings were made public, Sam Boyle called me into his office. David Bevan was willing to start talking to the *Bulletin*, said Boyle. Joe Livingston had gone to Bill Dickinson and offered to set things up. Livingston was better known as J.A. Livingston, the paper's financial editor and the author of a nationally syndicated column. Livingston won the Pulitzer Prize for international reporting in 1964, and he was widely viewed as the *Bulletin*'s most valuable asset. Now he was approaching 65, and he planned to spend a year teaching at Temple University and so wouldn't have the time to devote to developing stories based on information supplied by David Bevan. But he would help his paper by arranging for someone else to interview him.

I was the natural choice. At this point, I was spending more time on the Penn Central story than Binzen was. I respected Livingston and knew him slightly. And so, with the approval of Dickinson and Boyle, Livingston convened a luncheon meeting at a private club situated, appropriately enough, atop the Suburban Station building. I arrived by myself and found Livingston and his assistant, William Marimow, waiting. Marimow went on to win two Pulitzer Prizes for the *Philadelphia Inquirer* and subsequently became the paper's metropolitan editor. Bevan was inside at a table, sitting with his brother, Thomas, a lawyer, and his own lawyer, Edward German.

A certain camaraderie seemed to exist between Livingston and Bevan's group, and I found that curious. I said very little and Marimow said nothing. Then German began to talk business.

"You know, we want to do this right," German said, looking at Livingston but speaking to me. "We want the true story to come out. David Bevan is a true hero who single-handedly tried to save that company even though those two monkeys tried to screw him. Saunders and Perlman kept him off the board. And now Wright Patman's going to start demagoging. Joe, you remember when you were advising us not to talk to the papers until we saw which way this was going? Well, we know which way this is going now and we want to get our side out."

That got my attention. What the hell had I walked into? Here I had been calling Bevan for weeks and weeks and Joe Livingston was advising him not to talk to me or the *Bulletin*, the paper that paid his salary? As soon as the lunch was over, I hustled back to the paper and gave a complete report to Boyle. Sam must have gone through eight cigarettes while I told him the story. When I finished, he told me, "Keep this under your hat for a while," and walked across the newsroom to Dickinson's office. I did tell Binzen about it.

Predictably, at two meetings with Bevan, the first in Livingston's Rittenhouse Square home, the former chief financial officer of the railroad was interested in putting his spin on things. He pooh-poohed the importance of the investment club whose existence he hid from the railroad's board. He urged me not to place any credence in what Wright Patman was doing. I was interested in what Bevan had to say because he hadn't talked to anyone else and potentially, he could have provided a good story or two for the *Bulletin*. Obviously, it would also be helpful to me and Binzen in preparing the book. But what Patman had to say was more important. Bevan, the congressional inquiry found, was in a serious conflict-of-interest position, using railroad money to run up the value of stocks that he had purchased earlier for his own portfolio.

After a series of stories, some of which reflected unfavorably on Bevan, Sam Boyle told me that Bevan and his lawyer, German, were coming in to complain to the publisher. He wanted me to sit in while they met with Robert Taylor and Bill Dickinson. As the meeting began, Bevan started recalling his days as a Provident Bank executive in the late 1930s, and he asked Taylor if he didn't remember that Bevan helped arrange loans for the *Bulletin* from the bank. Taylor said that he did remember and I thought, "Oh, shit."

Then German started accusing me of violating an agreement to let Joe Livingston have final say over what stories went into the paper. I said I had never entered into such an agreement; I worked for the city desk, not the business section. German said I was trying to screw Bevan by getting material from him for the Penn Central book. "You knew all about the book before we even met for lunch," I told him, and said if he wanted to talk anymore about the book, we would have to do it elsewhere. German then demanded to know if Taylor was going to permit me to continue to violate the agreement by putting stories in the paper that didn't have Livingston's approval.

"My understanding from the start was that Joe Daughen was going to write the stories, not Joe Livingston," Taylor said, and I felt like cheering. "Is that your understanding, Bill?"

"That's right," Dickinson said, and the meeting ended.

After finishing up his stint at Temple University, Joe Livingston resigned from the *Bulletin*, where he had started as business editor in 1948. He took his column and Marimow to the *Inquirer*.

I never asked Dickinson or Taylor the reason for Livingston's resignation, but he was an extraordinarily proud man who would not have been at all pleased that the editor and publisher of his newspaper had seen fit to support a reporter in a dispute with people who clearly were his friends. As for me, if I had had a couple of spare typewriters, I know who I would have given them to. They, too, would have had engraved plates stating, "With Respect and Admiration."

Chapter 13

Selby Scared Me to Death

By John F. Morrison

CALL ME LUCKY. When I started with the *Bulletin*, newspapers competed with one another but not with radio or television. There was no such thing as 24-hour radio news, and TV news was still a bawling infant with little impact on the lives of people or their knowledge of the world.

A storied area of American journalism—the era when the newspapers had all the news to themselves—was ending. But we didn't know it was ending, and I'm glad we didn't. We wanted it to go on and on.

In "The Front Page," Ben Hecht and Charles MacArthur wrote about Chicago papers in the 1930s, but their play caught the spirit of Philadelphia papers in the 1950s and early '60s.

Or so it seemed to me when I joined the *Bulletin*'s city staff, then headed by the remarkable Earl Selby in 1959. Selby, who had just been named city editor on the death of Stanley Thompson, was a Chicago native and he practiced slam-bang journalism like Hildy Johnson.

To tell the truth, it was with considerable trepidation that I entered that cavernous newsroom to go to work for him. I was a new kid with nothing behind me but a reluctantly granted high school diploma, a stint with a U.S. Air Force newspaper in Cheyenne, Wyoming, a few years of small weeklies plus one year helping to cover the suburbs for the *Bulletin*.

Before being named city editor, Selby had written a column six days a week, and it was probably the *Bulletin*'s most-read feature. He had great sources in City Hall, the police department and elsewhere. You really had to read his column to know what was what in Philadelphia. It was on the strength of his brilliant column that Executive Editor Walter Lister picked him to succeed Stanley Thompson.

Shortly before he died, Thompson had experimented with a loudspeaker system to communicate with his staff. The newsroom was huge and he was soft-spoken. Over the speaker he would address individual staff members as "Mr." or "Mrs.," or "Miss." I would hear him say: "Mr. Morrison, talk to Mr. Storm, please." The calm, sonorous voice of the city editor seemed to emanate from somewhere overhead like a ghostly presence. I would don my headset and take a story from Bill Storm, one of half a dozen police reporters who roamed the city daily.

On taking over as city editor, Selby disconnected the loudspeaker system. He was less concerned with decorum than getting the news fast. He didn't care what people wore, smoked or said to one another as long as they did the job his way.

And his way was the only way. I still have a picture in my mind of one of our best rewritemen standing uncomfortably by his typewriter while Selby sat in the man's seat pounding furiously on the keys to show how his story should have been written.

One day he brought a piece of my own copy to my desk, put a fatherly arm around my shoulder and said, "This is just ordinary writing." He suggested a better way, and I had to agree it was a better way. He wanted me to soar above the ordinary, and I vowed then and there that I would soar. He never had to say that to me again. I was a quick study.

I discovered that even what looked like a routine handout or boring assignment could be brought to life with a little extra effort, and that became my forte—making something out of very little, making something worthy of page one that might have been relegated to back-page limbo in less caring hands.

As a columnist, Selby had been a loner and he was unpopular with much of the staff. That was because he had never hesitated to cut stories out from under beat reporters who had been trying vainly to get them.

I didn't realize until later with what shock and chagrin Selby's elevation to city editor had been greeted by much of the staff.

Although I never really got to know Stanley Thompson, I had the impression that he was loved by the staff. No one loved Selby, a fact over which I'm sure he lost very little sleep.

I worked for him for five years and I never knew what he thought of me. But I know what I thought of him. I thought he was a great city editor, and I still feel that way. I think a city editor should be what Selby was, a person furiously dedicated to getting the news and prepared to smash anybody who gets in his way.

He was also the best reporter on the staff, a role he never really relinquished, even after becoming an editor. The Pulitzer Prize the *Bulletin* won during his regime was really Selby's Prize, and he didn't even get a piece of it.

Of course, Selby scared me to death. I had never met anybody like him before, and never would again.

I think he appreciated my writing gifts, but he didn't think I was an aggressive enough reporter. One day, I was trying without success to get the public information office at the Willow Grove Naval Air Station to cough up a story about some fraud arrest. Under constant badgering by Selby, I made phone call after phone call to the PIO office, whose minions kept putting me off.

Deadlines were slipping by and Selby was getting increasingly annoyed. He finally picked up the phone himself and literally wrenched the story out of those people by brute force.

I was, of course, duly humiliated. My boss had gotten the story that I couldn't get.

When things had calmed down, he took me into his office and gave me a lecture on aggressive reporting, the climax of which came when he fixed me with an angry stare and snarled out something like: "Anybody who keeps news from me, *I hate 'em!* I hate 'em!"

That's the way he wanted me to feel, but I was never able to muster that kind of passion for the news. And so I fear I never did meet Selby's standards for aggressive reporting. He had his favorites, several of the paper's toughest reporters. I was not among them.

Selby was a bit of a mad man, without a doubt. I remember once he was editing copy on the city desk, working with his usual intensity and absorption, when his wastebasket caught fire. He reached over, turned the basket upside down, and went right back to editing, leaving the smoldering mess for someone else to clean up.

On another occasion, I was using the facilities in the men's room, when I happened to notice a stack of copy on the floor behind the door of one of the commodes and a ghostly hand turning the pages. It was Selby. He wasn't going to allow the intrusion of nature to interrupt his work.

* * *

My great hero as a newspaper writer was rewriteman Fred McCord. I made a careful study of Fred McCord. I went to Fred McCord University, you might say, and I don't think he ever knew he had such a devoted student.

I wanted to be able to write a news story like the ones Fred McCord turned out early every morning after unloading John Gaffney, the midnight-to-eight police reporter. I thought some of McCord's crime stories were classics. They should have been preserved and used in journalism courses.

The *Bulletin* had a reputation for being stodgy and dull, but it was undeserved. We had excellent reporters and writers, and a fine bank of rewritemen, with McCord as the linchpin, to handle breaking news on deadline.

He was on the receiving end of one of my most satisfying reporting jobs. A character we had dubbed the "Gentleman Bandit" kept invading the best homes in the suburbs, always waking his victims for a polite chat before taking their valuables.

I was jarred out of bed early one morning and told to get to a victim's house on the double.

When I got there, Jimmy Smythe, the Lower Merion detective sergeant whom I had known for years, greeted me angrily at the door. He was about to turn me away, when the woman of the house invited me in.

She graciously laid out the entire story for me and I had my scoop. There were no other reporters around. I bolted for the nearest phone, a pay phone by the side of the road, as it turned out, and got McCord on rewrite. The story made the first edition, beautifully written, of course.

When McCord said to me, "Good job, good detail," I was tripping among the stars.

I discovered something that day, something I have verified several times since, concerning the tenacity of the human spirit. As I said, I never measured up to Earl Selby's standards of aggressive reporting, but when faced with the absolute necessity of getting a story, which I faced that morning, some inner pool of invincible strength that I'm sure dwells in everyone, became accessible to me. With that power, I could have gone through walls. Jimmy Smythe was taking his life in his hands trying to get between me and the story of the Gentleman Bandit. I might have killed the poor bastard.

Usually, in those years, I was on the other end of the phone, as a rewriteman myself, and McCord taught me another important lesson—how to take a story from a reporter. It's a lost art now, of course, but in those days that's how news was handled. Reporters phoned in their stories to rewritemen, who were trained to write brilliant prose at impossible speeds to make deadlines.

McCord was always very gentle with reporters, who could be keyed up to the point of incoherence if the story was dramatic and difficult enough.

He had a soothing effect on even the most hyper correspondent. He asked questions calmly and quietly, drawing out the details he needed, making the reporter feel that everything was fine, he was doing a great job, all was well.

Adolph Katz was also an excellent writer under pressure, but he was maddening to give a story to over the phone. He would badger reporters, interrupting them with constant annoying questions. He imparted his own nervousness to the reporter, and it's a wonder they both didn't have breakdowns before they were finished.

I used to wonder why Adolph still got so nervous after all the years he had been doing his job, but I know now that without some tension, you can't work at peak efficiency. It's probably true in any job that a person cares about, but it's especially true in the newspaper business, I think, because you never know what's coming next and every story is unique and requires a unique treatment.

Part of the tension comes from the irrational fear that maybe you won't be able to bring it off this time. Even though it never happened to you and your rational mind knows it won't, there's something inside the bravest soul that worries that, yes, this time it won't be there. This time you'll freeze at the keys.

It never happened to me, but the fear still nags a little, and I think it's good that it does. It keeps you sharp. It keeps you from apathy and overconfidence. I'm sure McCord felt the same tension, but he was able to keep it under control, as I was later in the same role.

* * *

I entered the world of daily journalism in the relative quiet between two of this century's greatest social cataclysms. The hysteria of McCarthyism had run its course, and the civil rights rebellion was on the horizon.

In this period the *Bulletin* had a way of creating instant experts. If you covered one subject more than once, you were likely to find yourself viewed as the newsroom authority on that subject and covering it over and over again.

I became the paper's expert on Martin Luther King, Jr.

I first covered a speech by King at one of the suburban high schools in the early '60s. I was the only reporter there.

I spoke to him afterward and found him extremely defensive and difficult to deal with. He spoke so rapidly it was impossible to take notes fast enough to keep up with him. He obviously was distrustful of the white press, and I didn't like him very much.

The *Bulletin* probably buried that story, too. I don't remember.

What a contrast when a couple of years later he had become "news" on an international scale. I was among a great clamor of reporters crowding around him in the Bright Hope Baptist Church, where he intended to preach a sermon, and I was able to blurt out only one question. I don't even remember what it was.

The last time I saw King was in the Bellevue-Stratford Hotel. He was touring the big cities, making his pitch for his vision of a color-blind America. He was really news then and I figured the only way to get an exclusive interview with him was to get to the hotel early, before he even woke up.

The police had set up headquarters in a room just down the hall from King's suite, and I hung out with the cops for a while.

At one point, King emerged from his room to pick up a newspaper left at his door. He was wearing some colorful pajamas. I don't remember the color, but the next time I called the office, I told them about the pajamas. It made a little box to go with the main story. That's how newsworthy King had become. The color of his pajamas was news.

I was the only reporter in the hotel at that hour, and I was sure I would get my exclusive interview.

Finally, King came out of his room with his entourage and I fell in step with him, firing my questions. His manner was totally different from what it had been that night in the suburban high school. He was extremely gracious and kind. He spoke slowly so I could get his words down accurately.

I rode down the elevator with him, still asking questions and getting great answers.

Then I bolted for the phone. The first deadline was looming. I gave my notes to Jerry Dietz and we made the deadline.

But imagine my horror when I picked up a copy of the paper later in the day and saw that in quoting King, Jerry had written "...King told reporters."

I had gotten my exclusive interview and Jerry had made it sound like King was talking at some kind of press conference.

I swallowed my anger, blaming myself for perhaps not making it clear to Jerry that I was alone with King when he made those remarks.

That was one of the flaws of the reporter-rewrite system. Miscommunications were not uncommon. It's much better for reporters to write their own stories and now, with the pressure to make deadlines no longer as great, this is the way it's usually done.

I always enjoyed covering King's speeches. The whole world knows about his "I Have a Dream" speech in Washington, but I was far more impressed by the talks he gave in the dusty old theaters and churches of Philadelphia to audiences made up almost exclusively of black men and women. They hung on every word and talked back to him as blacks often do to their preachers. These were mostly people of poor or modest means and they looked upon King as a savior, as someone who could deliver them from their plight as members of America's scorned underclass.

He always gave the same speech in those days, and it was necessary to pick out different parts of it to lead with so each story would sound fresh.

His style of speaking was that of the black preacher, building slowly to a crescendo as the audience urged him on, until he reached those final words with which he ended every speech: "Free at last, free at last. Thank God Almighty, I am free at last!"

And the audience would be on its feet by then, shouting and weeping, and I always had goosebumps and a lump in my throat.

He was only flat once. I covered a speech he gave at Bryn Mawr College after receiving some kind of honorary degree. He stood at the lectern in cap and gown and talked to this dead audience of rich college girls and their snooty teachers, who gave him nothing back except a little polite applause at the end, and they must have wondered what all the excitement was about this boring colored person.

Sitting next to me at that event was an *Inquirer* reporter who took no notes. I was scribbling away, of course, and I kept thinking that this guy must have a photographic mind. He was just sitting there listening when he was supposed to be covering the speech.

After the speech was over, he turned to me and said, "Let's get together and we can go over your notes."

I slipped out of there as fast as I could and I don't remember if the *Inquirer* even had a story. But that was not uncommon behavior by *Inquirer* reporters in the days when Walter Annenberg owned the paper.

* * *

After a couple of years of bouncing back and forth between the nightside and early morning rewrite, I was sent permanently to the niteside. And there I remained for the rest of my 23-year, 7-month *Bulletin* career. In fact, I still work at night, now on the city desk for the *Philadelphia Daily News*.

When I arrived on the *Bulletin* nightside, Bill Lohan, one of the most underrated newspapermen I have ever encountered, was the night city editor. Bill had an excellent news sense, perhaps a trifle too eccentric for the *Bulletin*, and he was full of good Irish humor and fun. He commanded the absolute loyalty of his staff.

That staff included Tony Day, Fred Hauptfuhrer, Maurice Lewis, Dave Newhall and John Hamilton Gordy. Dan McKenna came in a little later.

It was a remarkable crew. We worked very hard, sometimes not finishing until 2 or 3 in the morning, at which time some of us would repair to Chinatown for a late bowl of won ton and an egg roll, or to the bowling alley in the 30th Street train station across the street.

Most of us were carefree bachelors and having a great time. We were working for one of the biggest and best newspapers in the country. We never knew when we got to work whether we would be chasing down a house-end on some miserable victim of tragedy, or sitting in the august precincts of the Union League listening to some right-winger talking about government policy.

And when we got back to the office to write our stories, we would be expected to interrupt our writing without complaint to take stories from police reporters, far-away correspondents, or obits from undertakers like Levine's and Oliver Blair.

We had to write fast if we wanted to finish up before the dawn, and we had to write well or face the absolutely unacceptable prospect of being rewritten by the dayside. It was the best experience a young newspaperman could have gotten, and I am grateful for it to this day.

Bill Lohan was soon replaced as night city editor by Bill Grover, who came over from the *Inquirer* during some labor dispute. Bill was an excellent newspaperman who taught me how to be a supervisor. It was a skill I wouldn't need for another decade or so, but I never forgot the lesson.

Bill was low-keyed and soft-spoken and retained his calm demeanor even under the pressures of organizing the coverage of a major story. He never hurried, never raised his voice. He was Earl Selby's exact opposite.

Bill was a man of precise and unvarying habits. He went to the cafeteria for dinner every night at 5 PM. And he disliked eating alone. It became the job of the 4 o'clock man, which I was at the time, to eat with Bill.

To this day, I don't know why Bill needed company. He never initiated a conversation and would happily have sat in stony silence through an entire meal unless his companion started a discussion.

I was always relieved when his old friend Bill Ingram, an Associated Press photographer, or some other crony would join us. Then the talk could become lively and interesting. But when it was just he and I sitting there, I had to begin every conversation.

I became so desperate on occasion that I would draw up and memorize a list of topics before dinner to have them handy for conversation starters. Even then his replies would be perfunctory, and my list of topics would quickly be used up.

Although I loved and respected Bill as a newspaperman and as a fine human being, I was greatly relieved when I was moved to the 6 PM shift and the chore of dining with the boss fell to another staff member.

The night staff shifted and changed. Tony Day went to the Washington bureau and eventually became editor of the editorial page of the *Los Angeles Times*. He and I married roommates.

Tony was one of the best newspapermen I ever met. And I always thought his was the best possible preparation for such a career: His father, Price Day, was a Pulitzer Prize winner for the *Baltimore Sun*, so the genes were right, and Tony had studied the classics at Harvard.

Yes, Latin and Greek. I always think of him when I hear young people talk about majoring in journalism at some state college. "Go to Harvard and study Sophocles and read Caesar's Commentaries in the original," I cry. But they don't listen to me.

Dan McKenna went off to become Senator Arlen Specter's administrative assistant. Fred Hauptfuhrer moved to London to continue his journalism career. Dave Newhall became Senator Richard Schweiker's aide, and John Hamilton Gordy went to Scott Paper in public relations.

Their replacements came and went—many good young men and even a couple of women—but I stayed. Five years before the *Bulletin* closed, I was named night city editor.

I replaced a curious character named Lew King, who had his own very original ideas about how to run a staff. He liked to drink and he would often send out for six-packs of beer for the staff when the work was done.

Lew was a former minor league baseball player, New York newspaperman, pal of Jimmy Breslin, and was the traditional American tough guy with a heart of gold. He was easy to get along with as long as you didn't cross him. I never did, but others made the mistake.

One of his nightly tasks was to leave a note for the dayside explaining what his staff had done and what, if anything, needed to be followed up. He ended every note with "To the bar."

Lew was a real pro who commanded the fierce loyalty of his staff, but he was something of a throwback. He had little patience with those who didn't measure up to his idea of what a newspaper person should be, and he had standards that might have been more acceptable in the hard-boiled '20s than in the more effete '70s.

He didn't care for very many of the dayside editors, and they didn't know what to make of him.

They finally asked him to resign, and he finished out his career in the Sports department of *Newsday* on Long Island, New York, where he died—too young.

I had no interest in being night city editor or any editor at all, for that matter, but I learned a long time ago that it's not a good idea to turn down an assignment, especially if it means a promotion. It sets people's teeth on edge.

And so I took the job. I found myself blessed with what I considered the finest pound-for-pound newspaper staff in the world, and they made me a star every night.

All I had to do was pass out assignments and sit back and wait for the stories to come in. I or my assistant, Bill Forsythe, would give the stories a quick read, because that's all most of them needed, and send them through.

I became a legend. Totally undeserved.

My best writers, the three Mikes—Schaffer, Ruane and Coakley—and Tom Infield, went on to careers at the *Inquirer.*

As the end neared, the energetic and imaginative Craig Ammerman tried to pump a little more juice into the paper when he became editor. If he had had the time, the backing of management, and money, he might have matched Gene Roberts as an exciting, innovative editor and, who knows, maybe saved the paper.

But the *Bulletin's* arteries had hardened. It was tottering. It was doomed.

Ammerman asked me to write the paper's obit. It appeared on the last day of publication, January 29, 1982.

A great Philadelphia institution was no more. But what the hell, the paper had lived 135 years. What more do you want?

Chapter 14

BERGIE

By Hans Knight

I HAVE ALWAYS BEEN SOMEWHAT ADDICTED to understatement, and I suppose it is too late to fight it now. So the only way I can describe my entry into the *Philadelphia Bulletin* is that I did so in the manner of Dorothy bouncing and floating to the Emerald City, along the Yellow Brick Road.

To this day, three and a half decades later, I pity all who never knew the joy coursing through my every inch when I picked up the phone in Harrisburg and heard the magical words: "OK, kid, you're hired." The voice was mellow with a trace of toughness. It sounded like Edward G. Robinson in a post-gangster role. It belonged to Bernard Aaron Bergman. Later on, I would call him "Bergie," as nearly everybody did at his insistence. But at that shining moment, as he ushered me into the fiefdom of the *Sunday Bulletin Magazine* with a genial wave of his short arm, I saw him as the great and powerful Oz. Were he around right now instead of prodding a lazy writer somewhere in the ink-spattered sky, he'd surely scribble in the margin, "Who he? Explain." He probably would add, "How much he make?"

Bergie had developed this penchant for precision over two years as the managing editor of the *New Yorker* under the legendary Harold Ross, a fact which he ever so casually dropped about 30 seconds into our first tête à tête, pausing just long enough to savor my gasp of unfeigned admiration.

In the midst of my euphoria, I remembered suddenly that I had no money. Maybe a couple of dollars in change, no more. I had spent my first night in the City of Brotherly Love in a small, gray room at the YMCA on Arch Street. I'd proudly saved up $400 and, in a fit of insanity, spread out the greenbacks on the night table. Upon my return from a shower in the hallway bathroom, the money was gone. Hardly surprising, considering I'd left my door unlocked.

Fortunately, I had written a piece about the half-forgotten patients at the state mental hospital at Byberry, and Bergie had bought it. He wrote me a check for $50. "This should keep you going for a while," he said. "But do me a favor—write me a short piece about the robbery. Make it funny." He was a wizard all right, I thought.

Bergie, who was born on July 8, 1894, in Chillicothe, Ohio, was no youngster when we met in 1961. He was built close to the earth, like a small Russian bear. His thick, brown hair displayed just a few strands of gray. He moved with a rolling gait. Thick glasses did not obscure the bright, probing intelligence, the skeptical flashes of humor in his dark eyes. At 66, he seemed ten years younger.

He had founded the *Sunday Magazine* maybe a month before I joined it. In at the creation, I recall thinking, how wonderful. The *Bulletin*, I knew, was not journalism's Everest. But it was at least Kilimanjaro to this dogged climber. It was big-time. After so many seasons in the minors, I had finally made the major league. And, I bragged to myself, I had come a longer way, perhaps, than most.

There never was a moment, within my memory, that I wanted to be anything but a newspaperman. It started with puppy love. I was seven and living in Mödling, a small, paradisiacal town in the Vienna Woods. Schubert once composed music there; Beethoven, too.

One day, Fräulein Sola, our teacher, assigned us to write a letter to someone. I addressed mine to the school principal. Herr Professor Doktor Wild was a tall, stern-faced man who walked the corridors like a scowling Wotan. My letter described the ups and downs of my short life—scoring a goal on the soccer pitch, seeing a dachshund run over by a coach, loving the fragrance of schnitzels and hating the scent of boiled carp. I asked him why he never smiled, and suggested it must be because he saw so many kids all day long while his own life must be nearly over. He sent me a nice note back. It said he liked my letter, the way it was written, and that I should keep it up. After that, I told everybody who would listen that I was going to be a famous author and make lots of money, and build great hospitals for injured dogs. Or sail to Africa in a U-boat and meet Tarzan.

There were some snags. I had no sooner passed my 14th birthday than the Nazis took over the country. The sylvan beauty of the town was no antidote to the brown poison. Almost overnight, many once-friendly neighbors turned into heiling bullies, beating up Jews while smiling cops looked on, setting fire to the ancient synagogue as the fire brigade carefully doused the adjoining houses. I was mad as hell, mainly because, having had two Jewish grandparents, dead before I was born, I was not only kicked out of school but, far worse, was drummed out of our ice hockey club. I sneaked into the skating rink one night for a last, fond look. One of my former pals had broken into my locker and was happily flaunting my knee pads. Soon after the Nazis took over my father's tiny radio store, so we holed up in my aunt's crowded walk-up flat in nearby Vienna.

The yellow brick road that led to the *Philadelphia Bulletin* was at that juncture nowhere in sight. Yet some incipient literary germ must have been nudging my brain, because one late afternoon I climbed up the narrow spiral staircase to the top of St. Stephen's Cathedral in the heart of Vienna. There was a visitors' book on an ancient stone shelf up there. After making sure nobody was watching, I scribbled in it. "These are damned hard times. Heil." It was my first journalistic offering to the world, a brazen act of defiance.

It seems peculiar, looking back now, but I was not afraid in Vienna. I roamed the streets at night, pretending I was invisible. Sometimes I'd march right along with the frequent torchlight parades as the Hitler Youth guys sang "Tomorrow the World" and other Nazi hit tunes. I also saw gangs of Brownshirts bursting into coffee houses to round up people they thought were Jews. It was not until my father and my aunt started talking about friends who had committed suicide and friends who had been released after a spell in Dachau concentration camp and looked like wild-eyed ghosts, that the seriousness of the situation dawned on me. I began to think that if I ever survived all that, I might write about it someday. (Much later, on the *Bulletin*, I did so from time to time.)

One by one, kids who were classified as non-Aryan left the City of Dreams for safer places around the world. And so, one late night, I sailed across the choppy English Channel on the Dutch steamer Volendam with my sister Liz, age 10, and a bunch of other children. It was very cold aboard and a lot of us got seasick. Some of the smaller kids cried for the parents they'd left behind, but to me it was a grand adventure. I was sure we'd all be together again. As it turned out, I was wrong, but that is another story.

England was a haven. No more Nazis, no more subtle, gnawing fear, no more Fuehrer placards glowering in the streets. Just quiet, smiling people, friendly but incurious.

I wound up working in a textile mill in Halifax, Yorkshire. I loved the people, who were rough and ready but whose dreams were different from mine. I picked up English very fast. I reveled in the sound of it. One day, I went to see a film called *This Man is News*, starring a thin, British actor named Barry K. Barnes. He played a dashing reporter who chased enemy spies in dark alleys, tapped out great stories and invariably strolled off into the foggy night with a pretty girl on his arm. And, of course, he always wore a trench coat, its belt carelessly knotted. I watched, transfixed. There were two sequels to the movie and I saw them, too. My path was clear. Every sweaty, dull day in the mill I polished the vision of working for a newspaper someday. With a bloody trench coat. I was Walter Mitty long before he sprang from Thurber's pen.

The war was finally over. I suddenly got lucky. I landed an interpreter's job with the U.S. War Department at the Nuremberg War Crimes Trials. I worked there two years, then, in 1948, came to America. Another year in a factory, this time making toothpaste in New Jersey. And then, miraculously, I was hired by the *New York Times*—as a copy boy, to be sure, but it was like inhaling the breath of the gods.

Five weeks into carrying coffee, sorting papers and filling paste pots, another miracle occurred. I sat up one night and typed out an editorial about the Nuremberg Trials. I put in on the editor's desk early next morning. Three days later it appeared in the *Times*. They paid me 15 bucks, half a week's salary. I felt mightier than King Kong.

Nothing was to come close to that thrill until I entered the *Bulletin*. Earlier papers I'd worked for, after the *Times* stint, were romantic flirtations. The *Bulletin* held out the promise of consummation.

The affair had a somewhat rocky start. Just before I bade farewell to the *Times* I had asked Herb Mitgang, a brilliant writer and a nice guy, if he had any advice to give me. He said, "Think big."

So, maybe a month after joining the *Bulletin's Sunday Magazine*, I wrote Bergie a long memo, suggesting he send me to Communist East Berlin. After all, I argued, I spoke German and might win a Pulitzer Prize. It was almost a week before Bergie called me into his cubby-hole. "Bad idea, kid," he snapped. "You're thinking big. This is Philadelphia—think small."

I withdrew, cut to the quick. But the next morning, Bergie walked over to my desk. "I changed my mind," he dead-panned. "You're going to East Berlin. East Berlin, Pennsylvania."

"But," I wailed, "nothing happens there."

"Right," said Bergie. "That's your story."

So I went to that rustic little town and did a "mood" piece. A photographer went along. His name was Eddie Adams. Years after he quit the *Bulletin*, he won a Pulitzer. I'm glad one of us did.

Bergie, I soon discovered, tried to run the *Sunday Magazine* like a bargain basement *New Yorker*. He kept a huge ideas file in his office. But most of his ideas he carried in his head and all of them had to do with painting precise word pictures of people—how they lived, how they talked, what they ate for breakfast. If I wrote somebody started off the day with eggs, Bergie was sure to query, "How many? Fried, poached? Bacon?" He believed that it was the little idiosyncrasies that illuminated a person's character. I think he was right, but he could drive you crazy. Once I did get the better of him, though. I'd turned in a short profile of a local dancer and Bergie penciled nine questions in the first three paragraphs. I answered them all. Bergie came over, frowning. "Your lead is all cluttered up." I said I'd simply done as I was told. "Oh, hell," he chuckled. "You shouldn't believe everything I say."

I was to remember that advice, somewhat painfully, on a few occasions. There was, for instance, a world-famous fashion photographer in New York. Bergie, anxious to get some of his pictures into the *Sunday Magazine*, assigned me to do a piece on the man. The photographer agreed to be interviewed with one proviso—that the piece be confined to his work without touching on his personal life. Bergie told me that this would be okay. When I finished the article, Bergie asked me to find out whether the photographer had been on an island vacation with a certain beauteous model. "Call his secretary, she'll tell you." I should have refused but I chickened out. I told the secretary she needn't answer my question. Of course, she didn't. But she told the photographer and he sent me a withering letter accusing me of bad faith. Bergie brushed it off: "Kid, you're not writing for the *Montana Bugle*." Eventually, the story ran in the back of the book, sans sexual innuendo, and also bereft of the photographer's fashion photos. It was not Bergie's finest hour, nor mine.

Another time, we did a piece on a fascinating woman who had Philadelphia roots but had settled in Nigeria where she was running for parliament. She was charming and told a wonderful tale. "One favor," she said. "Please don't mention my age." I gallantly promised I wouldn't. Bergie said, fine with him. Then he dug around in the clips and inserted her age in the article. "She won't mind," he told me. But she did. Her letter, more in sorrow than anger, reminded me that I had broken my word. I still feel rotten about it.

Compared with current journalistic practices, with the line between hard-nosed reporting and character assassination often blurred, such ethical slips seem trivial. But they happened in the early Sixties and they shouldn't have happened on the *Bulletin*. Not in my righteous land of Oz.

I should perhaps feel guilty about citing some of Bergie's flaws, akin to speaking ill of the dead, but I don't. For, to me, Bergie lives. He was the most dedicated editor I ever knew. The *Sunday Magazine* was his baby and he loved it like a doting father who had sired an offspring late in life.

On many papers, a magazine is regarded as backwater. "Oh, you mean the Sunday supplement—it's in that far corner, the end of the newsroom." There was a sense of this on the *Bulletin*. "Real" reporters tend to look upon the features sections as the paper's soft underbelly, a rather useless consumer of money and space. This view is no longer as pervasive as it used to be. Some of the best investigative stuff appears in Sunday magazines these days. And it was editors like Bergie who paved the way.

At the dawn of the Sixties, while the *Bulletin* was struggling to convince itself that "Negroes" could be newsworthy outside the confines of entertainment, Bergie initiated in-depth pieces about A. Leon Higginbotham, Jr., a fast-rising young federal judge, who helped lay the juridical foundations of the burgeoning civil rights movement; and the Reverend Leon Sullivan, who founded the Opportunities Industrialization Center, a self-help training program for unskilled blacks. OIC began as a shoestring operation in an abandoned city jail. In time, it spread across the nation and to many parts of the world. During and after the Columbia Avenue riots, it was Sullivan who urged angry, frustrated blacks to ditch the slogan, "Burn, Baby, Burn," and adopt "Build, Brother, Build."

Both Higginbotham and Sullivan went on to command tons of newsprint over the years. But the *Sunday Magazine* was among the first to introduce them to the white public. No small achievement for a paper that hired no black reporters until the stately, rumble-voiced Orrin Evans finally broke the barrier.

It was around that time that Bergie suddenly discovered teenagers. In an unguarded moment, I confided to him that I had once done a series of taped Q. and A. interviews for the *Harrisburg Patriot-News*. "Great," said Bergie, "do some with young people. Let's find out what they're thinking." So, every couple of weeks, I was anointed to delve into the minds of our future leaders. They were represented by groups of six, selected by their high school teachers. They were nice, white kids with an occasional black suburban youth thrown in. Mainly, they were for greater freedom to do their own thing, but none advocated premarital sex. We wouldn't have dared to print it if they had.

Yet giving teens a platform to spout their often-refreshing views was another first for the paper. I recall despairing of our young only twice: once, when a male honor student, asked what he knew about Adolf Hitler, thought it over for a while, then said casually, "Oh, you mean that Six-Million bit?" The other time was when I asked a lovely young girl how she felt about the war in Vietnam and she suddenly looked ugly and said, "We should just go in there and flatten them, you know, teach 'em a lesson. I'm tired of this cat-and-mouse game."

Bergie and I squabbled a lot. That I took no stuff from him required no special courage on my part. I found out quite early that he had fired a writer before me. When I asked Bergie over lunch what happened to the guy, he said, "I fired him. Didn't like the way he agreed with me all the time."

He could be rough but he never carried a grudge. Defending myself against what I felt (probably wrongly) to be an unjust rebuke about coming in late, I gesticulated with my cigarette lighter. It flew out of my hand and grazed his chest.

I stammered an apology. Bergie just glared and walked away. I thought I'd better clean out my desk and compose some résumés.

Next day, Bergie ambled over. "Got a couple of tickets for the concert. Want to come?"

We heard the Philadelphia Orchestra together many a night. That is, I did most of the hearing. Right after the opening piece, Bergie would take a deep, raspy breath and slump in his seat. "Give me a nudge if I snore," he'd whisper. "Love sleeping with music."

Most of the time I worked with him, Bergie exuded unflagging energy. Yet he was not a healthy man. I never heard him complain, but I always had unmistakable clues as to what was ailing him. If he had me do a piece on a prominent orthopedist, I knew his hip hurt. If he sent me to interview a gastroenterologist, he was worried about his intestines. I knew he had a toothache as soon as he said, "I hear there's a dentist in town who just got a national award; let's talk to him for a story."

In the beginning, the *Sunday Magazine* received pitiably few letters from readers, but this didn't faze Bergie. "Let's do some ourselves," he said. "Gotta do something to prime the pump." Once again, my idealistic feathers were ruffled but as time went by, it became masochistic fun to denounce my own stuff. But since Bergie insisted on balance, I also wrote letters redolent with flattery. Anyway, the system worked, and soon our readers came forth with a steady stream of comments of their own.

In a flash of inspiration, and much to my cosmopolitan chagrin, Bergie had coined the *Magazine*'s slogan: "If it ain't local, forget it." Under his regime, no story without a Philadelphia angle ever appeared in the *Magazine*. It gave its pages a homey flavor, but I thought it imposed on us a provincialism unworthy of a major newspaper. It dimmed my visions of grandeur. Good thing. Bergie's instincts were dead right.

His instincts worked equally well in the case of Fred Pillsbury. Fred was my first companion in crime. He was a tweedy, towering New Englander who came to Philadelphia from the *Boston Globe*. A Nieman Fellow, Pillsbury was a quietly humorous intellectual with a highly developed social conscience. He commanded a vast knowledge of the world around him and the forces that made it tilt every which way. He wanted to write significant pieces. Bergie let him do a couple of weighty interviews with university professors. "Fred's a good writer," he confided one day. "But I don't know what he's talking about half the time. He's over the readers' heads. This ain't the *New York Times*."

So he assigned him to do a series of light pieces. "You're going to be Our Man," he told him. "Do things people would love to do if they could. Make 'em funny."

And so, each week, Fred produced a new adventure. Our Man Goes Up in a Balloon; Our Man Goes Down in a Submarine; Our Man Gets Executed in Puccini Opera; Our Man Paints His Boat. I still remember Pillsbury's dry punchline: "Having a little paint left over in a pail, I went to see Whistler's mother. She was fine."

Bergie loved the series. So did our readers. Pillsbury did not. He'd jam his hands into his pockets and, head bowed, pace up and down the office. Bergie called me over. "What's the matter with Fred? He scares me. What's he thinking?"

I knew, but I didn't have the heart to tell Bergie.

Fred didn't have the heart either. Down deep, we both liked Bergie. We liked his restless, quirky mind. And we admired his insatiable curiosity about people in all walks.

(Years later, though, my adoration of the old wizard took a temporary plunge. In 1975, some rebels among us, myself included, sought to bring the Newspaper Guild into the *Bulletin*. The drive was sparked by a two-fisted, warm-hearted Irishman named Joe Lowry, who felt his son, a *Bulletin* reporter, had been unfairly demoted by the paper. In the end, after a long and bitter fight, the union movement lost by a single vote. It was cast by an ailing and tenacious man who had left his hospital bed and rolled into the voting room in a wheel-chair. The *Bulletin* had been good to him. It had given him a new lease on life, to my great benefit. Still, deep down, I wished Bergie hadn't done it.)

Bergie could be irascible and irritating as hell, but his barbs rarely went deep and they were never personal. They were lances tilted at his own impossible dream—that of turning us into the kind of writers who would make the *Sunday Magazine* the envy of his fellow wizards.

Meanwhile, I secretly envied Pillsbury's fling with first-person participatory journalism. Luckily, he took a long vacation once and I was able to fill in for him. I joined the Philadelphia Judo Club at the Y to do a piece on the gentle art of self-defense. After a few lessons, I let a husky brown-belt propel me to the mat with a shoulder throw. Bergie looked at the photos and frowned. "Not dramatic enough," he said. "Would you mind giving it another try?" I bravely obliged. This time, I was flung skyward by a black-belt. I landed softly on the mat. No problem. I felt so good, I challenged another guy to exchanging a few tosses. He weighed 200 pounds and crashed on top of me. My shoulder snapped. When I showed up for work with my arm in a sling, Bergie gave me a funny look. "Like the pictures," he said. "Sorry you got hurt. Think you can type with one hand?"

In a previous life, Bergie had served as an Air Force officer in World War II. Physically tough, he displayed little sympathy with my pain. But he repaid me in another way. One of his famous friends was Andrew Wyeth. When Wyeth completed a painting entitled "Her Room," Bergie wanted the fine watercolor for a *Magazine* cover. Wyeth agreed. When the issue came out, Wyeth dropped by the office to pick up some copies. By coincidence, my daughter Kathy was visiting me. Bergie not only introduced her to the great man but asked him to sign a cover for her. Kathy was thrilled. To this day, "Her Room" hangs in her room.

When he turned 70, Bergie left the *Sunday Magazine* and became the paper's book editor. But he didn't forget his old friends. "Say, kid," he asked me one morning, "how about doing some book reviews for me?"

I said, "Sure but how much do you pay?" Ten bucks, he said. "Bergie," I said, kiddingly, "for ten bucks I wouldn't give you my autograph."

"How do you mean?" he said, genuinely shocked. "You can keep the book."

* * *

I am glad I found my Yellow Brick Road and followed it to the end. So what if the *Bulletin* wasn't quite the Emerald City and the Wizard turned out to be no more than a mortal behind that curtain? Beyond the vines that bore the sour grapes, the paper opened up for me a wondrous world.

Much of it is a distant blur now, but some things are burnt in my memory. I once did a story about the Philadelphia Orchestra and the musicians let me crouch down among them at rehearsal, and the sound still rings in my ear like a rush of warm blood. I talked about Mozart and Prokofiev with Ormandy and Muti, and ice hockey with the great Gordie Howe. I had lunch with Linus Pauling, and I traded jokes (in the original German, no less) with Mike Nichols at Sardi's. I rode all over Manhattan in a cab with a smooth killer named Edgar Smith after his release from death row, and I sat up all night with a father and mother as they awaited an army chaplain who would confirm their son had been killed in Vietnam.

I interviewed an aged Melvyn Douglas who talked about Greta Garbo, and also about Richard Nixon who had savaged Helen Gahagan Douglas. She then lay ailing in a darkened bedroom.

I met the wistful Imogene Coca and the exuberant Mary Martin. In one single week, my cheek was brushed by the luscious lips of Zsa Zsa Gabor and Sophia Loren, and I got paid for that kind of work.

And one day, I asked Jacques Yves Cousteau if he was ever afraid, and he said, "But of course. A man would be a fool not to be afraid with all this water on top of one," and I asked Moshe Dayan the same question, and he thought for a while, then said calmly, "No. Not really," and both men had told the truth.

Once, too, I went to England and talked with Barbara Cartland, the queen of romance, who plied me with honey cakes she'd made in her draughty mansion and discussed the difference between sex and true love while her small dog chewed on my shoes. I then flew to Heidelberg, Germany, where I met Albert Speer, the former Nazi minister of armaments, who had forfeited his soul to Hitler the way Faust had done with Mephistopheles. One late afternoon, I visited Andre Watts. He was a gawky kid of 15 then, and he sat down at the piano and played Debussy's "Sunken Cathedral" for me, and the small living room seemed to expand into infinity.

I heard Gore Vidal do his hilarious imitation of William F. Buckley, and I tried vainly to match puns with Isaac Stern.

I watched Joey Giardello, the middle-weight champ, knock some sparring partners silly in the ring. He invited me to his house and I came close to tears as I watched him handle his retarded son like a fragile doll. Heck, I even met Martin Luther King's father, who said little, and I phoned Jimmy Stewart, who really talked like Jimmy Stewart.

To some, all this is no big deal. For me, it was close to everything. A dream made real by a crumpled press card.

The *Bulletin* convinced me that I wasn't in Kansas anymore. Or in Vienna, or on a wind-tossed boat in the English Channel sailing away from home. Not knowing what I'd ever be.

And that was no small thing.

On the paper, I even got to wear my trench coat, once in a while. It never did much for the writing, but it was great for the image and it kept out the rain.

Chapter 15

Why I Was Allowed to Cover Golda Meier

By Rose DeWolf

I CAME TO THE *BULLETIN* IN 1969, an interesting time for the paper and for females in general. The modern women's movement was just getting underway.

The previous year, a group of women from New York City picketed the Miss America Pageant in Atlantic City, objecting to the bimbo-in-a-bathing-suit image of women then being presented there. (Typically, finalists would be asked such mind-stretching questions as: "If two men showed up at the same time to take you on a date, what would you do?")

To get the attention of the media editors, then almost exclusively a male fraternity, the women said they would protest by burning their bras. The fire marshal of Atlantic City pointed out that the famous Boardwalk was made of wood and no fires were allowed on it. No problem. The women tossed a couple bras, still in the packages they were purchased in, into a trash can to make their point, and went on with the protest.

But for several years thereafter, just about any woman interviewed for any reason would be asked: "Did you burn your bra or do you plan to?"

The *Bulletin* was no exception to this rule. But the *Bulletin* was unlike many other papers of the time in that it employed several females to cover news—not merely society and social notes—and women worked on both day and night shifts.

When I was hired by the Camden, New Jersey, *Courier-Post* in the early '60s, I was the first-ever female hired there to work a night shift full-time.

There were women correspondents who covered local town meetings and got paid by the inch; there were a few women on the full-time day staff, very few. And that was at a paper where the executive editor was female. I'd like to be able to say she got the job because she was smart and able—and indeed she was both—but more likely she got it because her father owned the paper and her brother was the publisher.

Anyway, the night-shift guys at the *Courier-Post* were delighted to see me because they thought that meant that I'd make coffee every night and they would no longer have to take turns. I told them nicely, I'd be happy to take my turn. And so it was.

I'd applied for a job at the *Philadelphia Daily News* before going to the *Courier-Post*. The managing editor there was a man famed for requiring reporters to get the hair color plus the bust and hip measurements of any female mentioned in a story for any reason. (The guys often dealt with this by making the data up.) This editor told me that he wasn't hiring a woman at that time, because the *Daily News* "already had one."

I went to the *Inquirer* from the *Courier-Post* in the mid-'60s and was one of three females in the newsroom.

Society was changing and more and more women would eventually work at all the papers where once they were so rare. But the *Bulletin*, I have to say, was ahead of the curve. Some of the women thought they were hired because they worked cheap...maybe so. The *Bulletin* was not famed for excessive salaries.

Most of my colleagues at the *Bulletin*, male and female, were terrific, welcoming people. There were a few who were determined to dislike me...even before meeting me. I suspect (though no one ever said so) that it was because I was a female, a liberal, and worst of all, had become well-known at the *Inquirer*. They did their best to try to short-circuit my career at the *Bulletin*. Sometimes I'd turn in a story—and it would mysteriously disappear.

Luckily for me, most of the people in charge treated me a lot better.

I came to the *Bulletin* from the *Inquirer* where my last job was a news columnist. After a year at the *Bulletin* (and after the new owners of the *Inquirer* tried to get me to return there), I got a column at the *Bulletin*. And I soon discovered how much society's views of women had changed.

At the *Inquirer*, whenever a tough, hard-driving political column ran, the male columnist got all the mail, no matter which of us wrote it. And when a light-hearted column ran, readers just naturally assumed it was by me. But at the *Bulletin*, I got the mail for what I wrote, no matter what its tenor. Progress.

The *Bulletin* had male readers who would add—after telling me that they enjoyed something I had written—"my wife read it to me." I'm sure they felt they would be diminished in the eyes of the world if they admitted reading a female writer *first-hand*. But at least they were willing to admit knowing of my existence. Progress.

The *Bulletin* had a policy of printing a little joke on the front page every day. "Today's Chuckle" it was called. (There was no chuckle on the very last day of the *Bulletin's* publication, January 29, 1982. Neither staff nor readers were in any mood to laugh.) Anyway, the women on the staff noticed that the "Chuckle" was frequently at the expense of women. The joke would be about a wife who spent all her husband's money on such and such. We formally protested. Managing Editor Dale Davis decreed that such jokes would be banished. But lo, the very next day, in the early editions, there was a dumb joke about a wife who dented the fender of the family car. We descended en masse on Davis' office and for the remaining editions that day, the joke was about the husband denting the fender of the car. More progress.

The women at the paper were determined to do some consciousness-raising in the newsroom. We screamed when a headline appeared that said: "Housewife Also a Neurosurgeon." (In her spare time, no doubt.)

Most of the men got the message without much pain. When I first came to the *Bulletin,* City Editor Sam Boyle sent me to cover Israeli Prime Minister Golda Meier. I was thrilled to be sent to cover a head of state, until I realized that Sam thought it was okay for a female to cover a female head of state, though had Golda been George, he would have assigned one of the guys. Yet it wasn't long before Sam was giving me political tips for the column. He simply accepted me and other women as pros.

However, although the *Bulletin* was ahead of other papers on the subject of women—it wasn't perfect. We had mixed success at best in our consciousness-raising. When black reporters formed a committee to discuss their careers at the paper, they were able to negotiate some meaningful changes. But when the women reporters committee—which, I admit, was nowhere near as cohesive as that of the black reporters—met with the editors, we got more patronizing speeches than real change.

Still, change happened. Marci Shatzman, who wrote a *Bulletin* column focusing on feminist issues, told me this story: There was an opening on the police beat and Lin Dalton applied for it. The then-deputy city editor turned her down, saying he "wouldn't want his daughter down there [at police headquarters]." Marci heard about it and told the editor: "This isn't a father-daughter thing, it's an employer-employee thing and you are opening this paper to a lawsuit." He thought it over, Marci said, and decided she was right. Lin got the police beat.

The *Bulletin* sent Marci to women's conferences, which was truly rare at the time. In the '70s, covering women was no longer weddings and social notes. It was a tough beat. The feminists got angry if Marci didn't toe the party line...and complained if her column appeared on the same page as the comics (even though our three—count them, three—comics pages were the most read pages in the paper). The traditionalists were angry that Marci didn't think every female belonged in the maternity ward or the kitchen.

One of the male editors told Marci flatly: "Women don't belong in this business." Marci didn't bother to argue. She just said: "Get used to it."

After I was named a columnist, I had almost total freedom in what I wrote at the *Bulletin,* more freedom than I'd had at the *Inquirer,* where opinions that varied from ones strongly held by the publisher would be deep-sixed.

I decided to test the limits of my literary freedom early on. One of the first columns I wrote for the *Bulletin* took the side of the farmworkers in California who were trying to win recognition of their union by asking Americans to boycott grapes. The assistant to the publisher at the *Inquirer* killed a proposed column on the subject because, so he told me, he thought it would offend the supermarkets which were major advertisers. (I didn't think it would matter much to the markets if customers bought apples instead of grapes, but as the famed press critic A.J. Liebling once wrote: Freedom of the Press belongs to the guy who owns the press...and I didn't own the *Inquirer*.)

The *Bulletin* ran the farmworker column without blinking. I was told that Mr. McLean didn't like it, but the publisher didn't interfere. That was very *Bulletin*.

This is not to say that no one ever interfered. Editors (not the publisher) killed three columns in my 12 years at the *Bulletin*, each for a different reason.

The first was about a sportswriter for the *Daily News* who was paid to appear in an underwear ad. I thought that was hilarious. I could remember the time when people never so much as mentioned they wore underwear. I used to have a neighbor who (in the pre-dryer era) hung undies out on the line discreetly covered by a sheet. And here was this very well-known writer swearing that he wore "Health-Knit because it didn't bind, itch or ride up."

I don't know why that one didn't run. Maybe because it was about a writer for a rival paper, or maybe the *Bulletin* still didn't discuss underwear. Either was a reasonable possibility. Maybe it was both. The *Bulletin* didn't mention stories that appeared in the other papers. If we didn't have it first, it didn't happen. And the *Bulletin* didn't mention...well...unmentionables.

When I was sent to cover the first press conference in Philadelphia by the famed sex research team of William Masters and Virginia Johnson, I had to write a story that did not use any of the well-known names for body parts or sexual intercourse. Talk about a challenge.

Another column that didn't run was a negative story about a member of the Philadelphia Flyers hockey team. He bought a washer from somebody and never paid for it. The man who'd been stiffed was pursuing him in court. Had I been a hockey fan, I might have realized that the column was scheduled to run on the eve of the game that was to decide which team won the Stanley Cup. An editor who was a hockey fan killed the column—he didn't want to upset the deadbeat player.

And finally, there was a funny (I thought) column about how corporate CEOs were hired. The managing editor nixed that claiming that people wouldn't accept that subject from a woman. How to run the country, okay, women did have the vote, after all—but not how to run a corporation.

Not all of the major changes that took place at the *Bulletin* in my dozen years there had to do with race or gender. There was also a tightening up of what I always thought was an amazingly leisurely pace. The *Bulletin* had a huge staff; I don't know how many, but it surely outnumbered the *Inquirer* and the *Daily News* put together.

When I was working for the city desk at the *Inquirer*, it was expected that the minute you completed one assignment, you'd call in to dump your notes on a rewrite person and go on to another assignment or back to continue whatever you were on. There wasn't much time to relax.

The day I started at the *Bulletin*, the popular president of Swarthmore College died suddenly and I was sent to the campus to interview students. I gathered the information, called it in to rewrite, and then asked the deputy city editor what I was to do next. "Don't you have any shopping to do?" he asked. I thought he was kidding. Nope.

But that definitely changed. No doubt the financial pressures that eventually caused the *Bulletin* to fold induced the editors to become less forgiving of casual work habits. Dorothy was a sad case in point.

Dorothy was an earnest soul who took great pride in what she wrote. Alas, too much so. She would become so distraught when a story she'd prepared with great care would get chopped to a couple of paragraphs by an unfeeling editor that she'd first go into the ladies room and cry. And then she'd go home.

Sam Boyle, whose gruff manner covered for a heart of gold, would send me to the ladies room to make sure Dorothy was all right. However, when a new regime came to power, Managing Editor Phil Evans told Dorothy that she could no longer just go home as she wished. The next time you go off in tears, you needn't come back, he said. (At least I was told that was what he said. I never asked him.) Dorothy became distraught and went off in tears. And I never saw her again. Possibly she decided it was time to retire.

Chapter 16

I Battled Frank Rizzo Through My Column

By Claude Lewis

IN 1967, WHEN I LEFT KYW-TV to return to the newspaper business, only one African American journalist sat among the sea of white faces in the newsroom of the *Evening Bulletin*.

That face belonged to a tall, courtly reporter with unusually long fingers and a full head of silver hair that he combed straight back and parted precisely in the middle.

A general assignment reporter, Orrin C. Evans at 64 was older than most of the staff. He was valued more for his contacts than for his writing skills. He knew just about every mover-and-shaker in Pennsylvania and was on a first-name basis with politicians, judges, most of the clergy, the mayor and the governor. Moreover, he had personal phone numbers for many of the nation's most influential and admired blacks, ranging from the Reverend Dr. Martin Luther King, Jr., to Jackie Robinson and Roy Wilkins, Executive Director of the National Association for the Advancement of Colored People.

Evans warmly welcomed me on my arrival at the *Bulletin* and immediately took me under his wing.

"Follow me," he said, flashing a mischievous smile. We left the fourth-floor newsroom and walked the short distance across Market Street to Pete Richard's Bar and Restaurant, a convenient watering hole which every evening played host to dozens of *Bulletin* reporters and editors and a noisy but friendly throng of postal workers from the main branch, just down the street.

"Look," Evans said, hoisting his first manhattan of the afternoon, "the *Bulletin* is the largest newspaper in Pennsylvania and it's interested in talented reporters. You have a good reputation. Keep it alive and you'll do well here. Anything I can do to help, just let me know. Most of the staff are real decent people. Don't let the others get you down."

I listened attentively while sipping a J&B scotch on the rocks. By the time we left Pete Richard's, it was 2 PM. I had been well-schooled on the *Bulletin*, its history and its major players.

Orrin was friendly even with those he told me harbored resentment that a few blacks were beginning to move onto their turf.

He gave me the low-down on the most talented people on the staff, including several rewritemen he said were capable of making or breaking me at the paper.

"Treat them with respect," he warned, "and they'll save your ass. Mistreat them and they'll make you pay dearly."

He paused at that point to let his message sink in, then resumed:

"Listen, I know things are changing. But don't forget you're dealing with whites and they hold the power. Don't ever lose sight of that. Yes, it's a free press, but it's Mr. McLean's press," he said with an insight based on experience.

"Don't fall into the trap of trying to prove how black you are. Everybody can look at you and see that. Just be the best damned reporter you can be and they'll eventually forget about your color."

It didn't take long to meet those "others" Evans had warned me about. To put it in polite terms, they were a conservative lot. They never mentioned race in my presence, but it was never far from their minds.

One of them, Bayard Brunt, a chesty rewriteman in his late forties, barked into the telephone the first time I called in to the rewrite desk:

"Who? Who the hell is this?" he demanded in a voice that might have rattled the windows of the newsroom.

"Claude Lewis, the new reporter," I said, unable to hide my nervousness.

"Oh," he said, lowering his voice. "What bullshit are you going to *bore* me with this time?"

I gave him the details of a fire at Pier 38. He asked a few questions and hung up the phone, but his obvious displeasure at being obliged to take notes from me shook my confidence.

Evans had warned me I would be tested, and Brunt's harsh treatment was a good example of what I would have to endure. Others on the staff searched for soft spots in my reporting to convince themselves that Bill Dickinson, a shy but highly respected executive editor, had hired me largely because of my color.

It didn't matter that my background included a 10-year stint at *Newsweek* magazine, a summer at the *New York Post*, a year at the old *Herald Tribune*, and three years as a television reporter for NBC and Westinghouse Broadcasting, or that I had authored biographies of Congressman Adam Clayton Powell, Jr. and Muhammad Ali. I still had to earn my way.

Among some older *Bulletin* staffers, racist feelings were just below the surface. They assuaged their resentment by passing insults concerning Evans and me behind our backs. We were referred to as "stove pipes," a derisive term I had never heard before. Even whites who were supportive sometimes failed to recognize the extent to which racial prejudice permeated certain corners of the newsroom. I believe that the same sorry situation existed at that time in many other cities and newsrooms. At the *Bulletin*, the discrimination was carried off with such finesse and subtlety that only the most sensitive whites recognized it for what it was.

Perhaps because of their own mistreatment, some of the women on the staff would occasionally tell us what was being said behind our backs. Gradually, however, as I demonstrated competence, I won acceptance even from the hard core. Whatever their personal feelings about blacks joining the staff, they welcomed efficiency. I soon discovered that Bayard Brunt barked at everybody, not just me. And several white staffers kept the lid on things by supporting the early black journalists—Sandra Dawson Long, Fletcher J. Clarke, Joe Davidson, Elmer Smith, Angie Terrell, Bart Tatum, Harry Kendell and Claire Smith (who today is a respected writer at the *New York Times*). In the years that followed, several other African American reporters joined the *Bulletin* staff.

The irony, for the new arrivals, was that most of them were better educated than many of the old-timers at the paper.

My testing period ended abruptly one day when Fred Zepp, who was as fast as any rewriteman I had ever met, took my call. Zepp was a gentleman and he was patient. He understood that I was new and helped me over the rough spots.

We produced several stories together and many of them made the front page. Ray Brecht, another decent and able journalist, also assisted me. When I read some of the stories he wrote from the notes I phoned in, my confidence grew.

Before long, I had settled into the routine and began covering a rich variety of stories. Then City Editor Sam Boyle, drawing hard on a cigarette, called me into his office and asked if I would help with our coverage of the State House in Harrisburg. It was an assignment I didn't want; I had been to Harrisburg. But when I mentioned Sam's proposal to Orrin Evans, his eyes moistened with a kind of fatherly pride.

"They must think highly of you," he said, "if they've asked you to work in an out-of-town bureau."

I still recall the sadness that swept over me at that moment. Evans was 65 years old by then and had missed his opportunity to cover many of the best assignments that came along during the years he was prohibited by racial discrimination from working on white dailies. Both his energy and skills were beginning to erode and without expressing it, it was clear to me that he had invested many of his professional aspirations in me.

Like so many others on the staff, he enjoyed a drink, now and then, but was always a dignified man who never embarrassed himself. Evans had been a star in the black press, but his experience was limited to covering racial news, the obvious mainstay of every black newspaper in America. Still, his accomplishments were extraordinary and he set a high standard for the blacks who followed him into the business.

My new assignment meant I would have to stay in Harrisburg, the state capital, for most of the week. When the legislators took time off, or left for vacation or holiday, I would work out of the Philadelphia office.

Despite Evans' optimism and pride in my opportunity, it was with reluctance that I accepted the assignment. Once in Harrisburg, though, I quickly learned my way around and wrote several stories that made a splash throughout the state. One of them involved Herb Fineman, a bright legislator who stupidly compromised his career, and wound up behind bars.

Duke Kaminski, the legendary State House bureau chief, turned out to be a much-loved curmudgeon. He applauded my efforts but even Duke was not enough to keep me in one of the world's dullest towns. When Sam Boyle asked me to return for a second year, I declined the offer but worried that he might hold it against me. He never did. Sam remained a good friend and mentor of mine until his death several years after he left the paper.

I've always believed Sam died as much from a broken heart as from the cancer that ravaged his body. In its fierce competition with the *Inquirer*, the *Bulletin* began to slip badly. For years, Sam had worked tirelessly to maintain the *Bulletin*'s status as one of the best evening newspapers in the country. He had hoped to be a candidate for the executive editor's job when Bill Dickinson retired. He never received that opportunity and it hurt him deeply.

The *Inquirer*'s brilliant editor, Gene Roberts, was supplied with what appeared to us to be a nearly bottomless reservoir of cash by the Knight (later the Knight-Ridder) chain that owned the paper. He wisely hired some of the best reporters and editors available. It was through Roberts' vision and leadership that the *Inquirer* became one of the nation's best newspapers. The *Bulletin*, one of the few family-owned big-city papers left in America, lacked the funds to match the spending of its feisty rival. But the battle continued.

* * *

When Executive Editor Bill Dickinson reached the mandatory retirement age of 70, he was succeeded by George Packard, a gangling man of patrician birth and almost boyish enthusiasm. A Princeton graduate with a Ph.D. from Harvard, Packard had served as an assistant to Edwin O. Reischauer, the U.S. Ambassador to Japan. Before joining the *Bulletin* and working briefly in the Washington bureau and as Dickinson's deputy, his only professional journalistic experience had been as diplomatic correspondent for *Newsweek*.

In taking over the editorship, Packard stepped into a minefield. Many of the paper's veteran reporters and deskmen wanted no part of an "outsider" with high-and-mighty ideas of how to publish their newspaper. After all, they had been running things their way for decades. They resisted Packard's changes and in some cases actually managed to get his decisions rescinded.

But Packard stiffened his jaw and went ahead changing personnel, assignments and news judgments. He sought to make the paper less parochial, and I figured prominently in his planning. For three months I shuttled back and forth between Philadelphia and Raleigh, North Carolina, covering the Joanne Little murder trial. Little was an ebony-skinned woman who, after being jailed on burglary charges, escaped by stabbing the sheriff to death with an ice-pick she had removed from his desk drawer after making a late-night phone call.

The next morning, Clarence Alligood's body was found slumped on Little's bunk, his pants down around his ankles. A trace of dried semen was plainly evident on his left thigh. Following her apprehension weeks after she had fled the jail, Little alleged that late at night, after the rest of the jailers had left, Alligood had repeatedly forced her to have sex with him in her cell. She immediately became the darling of a vocal feminist movement and her trial quickly became a cause celebre that attracted international attention.

One of the prosecutors, a cynical but soft-spoken Southerner, agreed to have lunch with me one day while the trial was in progress. I think I took advantage of his good nature. He told me he was going to lose the case and it was likely that Joanne Little would go free. He never said his comments were off the record but to be perfectly honest, I think that was implied.

However, I wrote the story. And I believed the prosecutor's premature acknowledgment that he might well lose the case had an impact on the trial. My front-page story in the *Bulletin* was picked up around the country. Numerous radio, television and news outlets sought the prosecutor. He was properly outraged, greatly embarrassed and hostile toward reporters after that. But to his credit, he never denied making the statement to me, nor did he claim to have spoken off the record. Of course, his assessment of the trial that I quoted proved accurate. Joanne Little was acquitted.

With civil rights stories dominating the front pages in the '60s and '70s, metropolitan newspapers greatly increased their hiring of promising black reporters. In this way, they hoped to gain access to the most vocal and angry black spokesmen, some of whom—H. Rap Brown, Stokely Carmichael (who subsequently changed his name to Kwane Ture) and Huey Newton come quickly to mind—refused to talk to white reporters. Many of the newcomers to journalism had little or no experience working in the media, and this caused understandable resentment in some quarters. But when the lockout of blacks in the media was suddenly ended, print and broadcast competition for talent caused the number of blacks in the news business to steadily rise.

Thanks to the feminist movement, women, too, began making inroads. They gained fresh opportunities at many large newspapers, and the *Bulletin* was no exception. The complexion and gender of the predominantly white male industry thus changed swiftly and dramatically.

One of the brightest women hired by the *Bulletin* was Kitsi Burkhart, who now teaches at Princeton. She and I teamed up to write a three-part series on social issues which won first prize in the Keystone Award contest. It might have been a first—a black male and a white female working together to capture a top journalism prize.

Like other reporters, Kitsi and I often donned our telephone headsets and talked during slow periods in the newsroom. We knew better than to meet at the water cooler or at one another's desk, so we devised this little arrangement to communicate without offending anyone.

But it seems we did offend Len Murphy, an assistant city editor. After figuring out what we were doing, he walked across the newsroom one day and turned on me.

"You know what I want to see?" he said aloud. "I want to see you talking to a *Negro* girl."

I felt my face flush. Unnerved, I shot back: "You know what *I* want to see? I want to see you *hire* a Negro girl."

Murphy's face reddened as he walked away.

Yet I grew to like him because he was a man of unusual candor and directness. After that incident, we became friends and remained so through the years.

In competing with the *Inquirer*, the *Bulletin* stepped up its out-of-town assignments, and I traveled widely. I covered riots in the South and school busing wars in Boston. I interviewed the Black Panther Party's self-exiled Minister of Information, Eldridge Cleaver, in Algeria and flew to Japan with Eugene Ormandy and the Philadelphia Orchestra. The *Bulletin* sent me to China, Cuba, Israel, East Africa, France and a host of other countries that this native of Harlem never dreamed of visiting. Sometimes I felt as though I was living out of a suitcase.

In 1968, I joined other *Bulletin* reporters covering the tumultuous Democratic National Convention in Chicago, and that's an assignment I'll never forget. I was covering the melee between Mayor Richard Daley's steel-helmeted police and Vietnam war protesters when several cops went after me with their nightsticks, beating me so badly that I was hospitalized for three days. Other reporters and photographers were roughed up, but I suspect the men in blue took special pleasure in ripping the press credentials from this black reporter's neck and tossing my blood-soaked notes in the gutter.

* * *

Almost out of the blue, it seemed, Packard asked me to write a regular column for the paper. It was a bold move that sent a message to the cynics on the staff and to Gene Roberts that the *Bulletin* was not going to walk away from a fight.

Packard's reputation, along with mine, was clearly on the line the moment he asked me to do the column. The possibility of failure didn't seem to enter his mind. He was a man of unusual faith. He didn't ask me to *try* to write a column, he asked me to write one. He didn't even ask if I thought I could handle the deadline pressure.

Without the slightest hesitation, I answered in the affirmative. When he stepped away from my desk however, I could almost hear my knees shaking from excitability.

I remember my first thought after Packard left me: This can't be real. But any doubt I might have had about the sincerity of his offer was removed when he phoned me from his office across the newsroom about a half-hour later.

"I'm going to make the announcement in tomorrow's editions that your column will begin next week," he said. "We're going to publicize it heavily. I know you'll show me your best."

One week later, I became the first black columnist in a big-circulation daily in Philadelphia newspaper history. My life would never be the same.

My first effort was about the unofficial renaming of Benjamin Franklin High School in Philadelphia to "Malcolm X High." The students insisted that even without the approval of the Philadelphia School Board, they would rename the school themselves. The Principal, Leon Bass, one of the finest and most effective principals in the Philadelphia public school system, went along with his students. For several years, the school carried on as Malcolm X High.

I'll admit that I rewrote that first column 17 times over many hours. And when I finally turned it in, it still was not as good as I wanted it to be. I was convinced I had to hit the ground running. Let's just say I hit the ground.

When Philadelphia readers opened the paper that Monday morning and saw my face above a column called "Like It Is," my telephone began ringing early in the morning and didn't stop for long throughout the entire day and half the night.

In a few short weeks, the column took off. Packard called me into his office one afternoon, extended his hand and said with a formality that made me nervous: "We're on our way. Stay with it." Then he added something that nearly floored me:

"Making the decision to have you write the column was the best decision I've made since I became executive editor. I want you to think about doing two a week and after you establish your rhythm, move on to three times a week."

Now I felt secure. He was running the paper and if I had convinced *him* I could do the job, not much else mattered—except the public.

I was no longer a reporter writing a weekly column. I was a full-time columnist, writing three opinions a week.

I remember a call from the late Bob Maynard, a friend and respected black journalist who was then a member of the editorial board of the *Washington Post*. By virtue of his charm, and ability, he had become extremely influential in the business, and ultimately began a journalism education workshop to train minority reporters. He later became publisher and owner of the *Oakland Tribune* in California.

"Tell me the truth, Bob. What do you think?" I said.

"Well, I don't know if I'd want to have to be *cute* three times a week," he said with laughter in his voice.

"You'll be fine," he added before hanging up the phone. "I just wanted to wish you well."

My mind went to my old friend and mentor, Orrin Evans, who died in 1971 while I was out of town on assignment. Later, however, I sat in sadness at a standing-room-only memorial service Orrin's family and many friends held at a Unitarian Fellowship Meeting in his honor. Even though he died more than 25 years ago, very few days pass without Orrin coming into my thoughts. A column I wrote concerning his passing brought a written response to his widow from President Richard M. Nixon.

"I finally received a communication from a President and it had to be *Nixon,*" Florence Evans lamented.

My column was both popular and controversial. When I wrote about Philadelphia's emerging drug problem, Police Commissioner Frank L. Rizzo took personal offense. Rizzo, who later became mayor, insisted there was no drug problem in his city. He suggested I return to New York from whence I came.

I took his advice and returned to New York City, but I didn't make the trip alone. I went with a Philadelphia drug dealer, who allowed me to ride there with him to pick up his stash. We left by train and returned by bus, just in case someone was watching. I wrote a series called "The Deadly Trap of Drug Addiction." It caused a great stir throughout Philadelphia, which until that time had not faced up to its growing drug crisis.

The series won two things for me: Rizzo's disdain, and the highest award of the Philadelphia County Medical Society.

I battled Rizzo through the column on several other subjects including prisons, his irresponsible habit of challenging thugs to shoot-outs in the street, and his generally egregious and excessive behavior.

He was particularly angered by a column I wrote on June 30, 1969. It began this way:

"Police Commissioner Frank Rizzo doesn't know it, but somebody in this city does a fine impersonation of him.

"A little over four weeks ago the telephone rang in the office of Water Commissioner Samuel Baxter, and a voice said:

"'Hello Commissioner? This is Frank Rizzo. How ya doin'? I just thought you might like to know that one of your guys belongs to a citizens group that's callin' for community control for the police. They're causin' a lot of problems in the 14th district, Commissioner.

"'His name? I got it right here. Lemme see...Floyd H. Platton. A guy with a beard, Commissioner. Yeah, that's him. You want to talk to him about his activities? Gee, thanks a lot, Commissioner. I sure do appreciate it.'

"The caller hung up leaving Baxter, who has known Frank Rizzo for years, with the distinct impression that it was the head of the Philadelphia Police Department who called. It couldn't have been Frank Rizzo, though, because he told me last night he never called the water commissioner about Platton.

"Maybe Baxter, who has a national reputation for competence, was just confused," I wrote with tongue in cheek.

Shortly after the Rizzo impersonator called, Platton was relieved of all his responsibilities in the water department. He wasn't fired, but put out to pasture when he collected his full salary while spending his days reading magazines and newspapers without any meaningful responsibilities.

Platton filed suit against the city and reached an out-of-court settlement after he had been reinstated.

The column embarrassed Rizzo, sending him through the roof. He never admitted making the phone call.

The police commissioner was not the only public official I went after. I castigated Judge Vincent A. Carroll after he called for the return of whipping posts to publicly humiliate young toughs in Philadelphia. Carroll told me in an interview that he had a good understanding of blacks because he was able to talk candidly to his household help.

I simply quoted him and chided him that these youths had *already* experienced enough humiliation. For many of them, that was their precise problem.

Several other pieces I wrote attacked the self-righteous, self-appointed black "leaders" of the Al Sharpton variety. They drew flak from some in the minority community, but that didn't bother me as I was determined to use my column to battle those who were causing problems in Philadelphia, regardless of their color or position.

All the while, the vultures at the *Bulletin* continued their fight to destroy George Packard. Some of them worked harder at trying to get him out than they did to make sure the *Bulletin* remained afloat in its competitive fight with the *Inquirer*.

The smart money said that both papers couldn't survive in Philadelphia. A lot of things began to fall apart at the *Bulletin*, and it was with an enormous sadness that I learned Packard was preparing to leave.

Doing battle with the front office while trying to move the paper forward with several of the old-time reporters snapping at his heels was simply too much. The front office of the *Bulletin* decided he wanted to make too many "radical" changes too quickly. Not everybody in the front office understood what both Packard and the *Inquirer's* Gene Roberts knew instinctively: the battle was about survival.

With little support from the top, Packard finally quit the paper. He ran for the U.S. Senate, losing in the Republican primary. Later he became dean of the Johns Hopkins School of Advanced International Studies in Washington, D.C., a position he held with distinction for many years.

B. Dale Davis, a features editor who had arrived many years earlier from the *Detroit Free Press*, succeeded Packard as executive editor. He ran the paper carefully and worked hard not to disturb the front office. Dale had a talent for surviving and managed to keep the paper on a path that pleased its owners. He and I had a fine relationship, but I remained sorry that Packard was pushed out.

One day, about eight months after Packard's departure, my phone rang and a secretary asked me to hold on for Gene Roberts at the *Inquirer*.

"Claude, I want to have a meetin' with you," Roberts said in his dry, North Carolina drawl. "Think you might consider writin' a column for *us*?"

Roberts was a man of infinite patience for some things, and paused to allow me to gather my thoughts. He interrupted them by adding, "I'm prepared to make it worth your while. Think about it and give me a ring."

We met on a Sunday in the apartment of one of his reporters. Roberts, who was in his shirtsleeves, slipped off his shoes and positioned himself carefully on the back of a sofa with his socks on the cushions.

He made his offer while keeping an eye on an Eagles football game.

The Eagles won the game and I found myself accepting his very generous offer. His expression never changed. We shook hands and I left for home.

Midweek, I stopped at the *Inquirer*, shook hands with a very receptive staff, and told them I'd join them in a month.

When I told Dale Davis of my decision to leave, he acted as though it didn't matter one bit.

But the next morning, he was in my office trying to convince me that my moving over to the *Inquirer* would be a great mistake.

"Working for the *Inquirer* is like working for an insurance company," he said. "The *Bulletin* is a family. It's a cold place over on Callowhill Street. Besides, we're in this fight to stay. It's your decision, of course, but I want you to think about it. And I want you to remember, you'd be leaving a staff that really appreciates your contributions to the paper. If you leave, that will be a signal for a lot of others to leave. We can't afford a bleeding here."

Then puffing on his pipe, he walked out of my office. He had promoted me some time earlier to the position of associate editor of the paper. Now I faced a dilemma that was made far worse when 33 reporters and editors arrived individually in my office to ask me to stay on. Included were some of the very people who had been so resistant when I joined the staff.

I caved in to them, but what about Roberts? I took the easiest way out. I sat down and wrote him a letter describing the pressure put on me by Davis and many others on the staff.

To my surprise, Roberts was very understanding. He obviously appreciated loyalty.

"Well," he said slowly on the telephone, "just remember the door's not slammed shut. If you have a change of heart, give me a ring. I appreciate your lettin' me know." When I hung up the phone, I felt lousy.

Davis was joyful when I told him I had turned Roberts down. He asked what the offer had been. When I told him, he blanched.

"Do we have to meet that full offer, buddy?" he asked.

For once, I used my head and said yes. Davis found the money and I stayed on with the *Bulletin*.

While minorities were enjoying new opportunities in journalism in Philadelphia, so were dozens of others at papers around the nation. They piled into newsrooms at such a steady pace that by August 1995, more than 3,000 minority reporters, editors and broadcasters arrived at the Center City Marriott in Philadelphia to attend the 20th annual convention of the National Association of Black Journalists.

Despite enormous progress, however, almost half the daily newspapers in America still have no minorities on their news staffs. And were it not for the dramatic civil rights breakthrough in the '60s, there would be far fewer minority reporters today.

B. Dale Davis was replaced as executive editor of the *Bulletin* by a bright young man named Craig Ammerman, who had not yet celebrated his 35th birthday. He had been an editor at the *New York Post*. Davis didn't leave the *Bulletin*, he simply moved over to the corporate side where he puffed comfortably on his pipe as the oil company that had purchased the paper lost its way.

Ammerman was a very likable man and an inspired leader. He made a heroic effort to salvage the paper, but by the time he arrived it was already too late. The *Bulletin*'s tombstone was inscribed with the date: January 29, 1982.

For several weeks, along with others, I assisted Ammerman in finding jobs for dozens of former staffers who had not been picked up by other newspapers.

I had been offered a highly paid position at the *New York Times*, but the job involved overseeing its newsroom budget. Since I had no experience in that area on the periphery of journalism, I decided to end the discussions after three meetings with A.M. Rosenthal, the *Times'* executive editor.

The time had come for everybody to vacate the premises of the *Bulletin*. I was the last member of the news staff to leave the building. It was ironic that on my way out of the newsroom I ran into Dale Davis who had convinced me much earlier, when I first gave serious thought to joining the *Inquirer*, that "there will *always* be a *Bulletin*."

We snapped out the lights, then shared a long and final nostalgic look at the dark cavern that had for so long served as the pulsating *Bulletin* newsroom. In my mind's eye, I could see all those reporters and editors—the black and the white—that I had grown to love and respect during my 15 years at the paper, still at their tasks, busily turning out the final edition of a once-great and cherished newspaper.

Dale and I turned away from the long rows of empty desks and rode together in silence as the elevator made its way down to the first floor. Except for a lone guard, the lobby was bare. We walked on reluctant feet through the glass doors and out into the softly falling rain.

Then, each of us hurting grievously, we shook hands, turned from one another and headed our separate ways toward home.